George Tyrrell and the Catholic Tradition

George Tyrrell and the Catholic Tradition

Ellen Leonard, c.s.j.

Foreword by Alec Vidler
Introduction by Gregory G. Baum

Darton, Longman and Todd
London

Paulist Press
New York/Ramsey

First published in Great Britain in 1982
by Darton, Longman and Todd Ltd
89 Lillie Road, London SW6 1UD

Published in the United States by
Paulist Press, 545 Island Road, Ramsey, N.J. 07446

ISBN 0 232 51558 1 (DLT)
ISBN 0–8091–2424–6 (Paulist)

British Library Cataloguing in Publication Data

Leonard, Ellen
  George Tyrrell and the Catholic tradition.
  1. Theology, Catholic
  I. Title
  230.'2   BX1751.2

  ISBN 0–232–51558–1

Library of Congress Catalog Card Number: 81–83480

Phototypeset by Input Typesetting Ltd, London SW19 8DR
Printed in Great Britain by the Anchor Press Ltd
and bound by Wm Brendon and Son Ltd
both of Tiptree, Essex

To my parents, Mary and Hugh, who first
introduced me to
the Catholic Tradition

Contents

Acknowledgements

I wish to thank all those who have contributed to the production of this book. I am grateful to my colleagues in the Faculty of Theology, University of St Michael's College, Toronto, for their interest and support. I am particularly grateful to our late dean, Elliot B. Allen, c.s.b., who inspired me in my pursuit of theology, to Professor Daniel Donovan who first introduced me to George Tyrrell and who guided the early stages of this work, and to Professor Gregory Baum who encouraged me and wrote the Introduction. I also wish to thank Dr Alec Vidler for his interest and for his Foreword. I am profoundly grateful to the Sisters of St Joseph of Toronto, especially to the sisters with whom I live, for their understanding and support.

I acknowledge and thank those who allowed me to work with unpublished materials and to quote from these: Miss Elizabeth Poyser, archivist of the archdiocese of Westminster; Dr Arthur W. Adams, dean of divinity at Magdalen College, Oxford, and keeper of the Katherine Clutton Papers; the librarians of the British Library, the University of Cambridge Library, and St Andrews University Library. Thanks to Mr Steven Corey, special collections librarian at the Gleeson Library of the University of San Francisco, for permission to reproduce the photo of George Tyrrell. I am grateful to the librarians of the University of St Michael's College, especially Bernard Black, c.s.b. and Mrs Margaret McGrath, for their assistance.

Special thanks to the Roman Catholic Modernism Working Group of the American Academy of Religion, and especially to Professor David Schultenover, s.j., for his permission to refer to his work on the Roman Archives of the Society of Jesus.

Thanks to Sister Margaret Avery for her careful reading of the final galleys and proofs and to Mrs Margaret Clarke for her secretarial assistance.

To these and to many other friends who have generously encouraged and supported me I am deeply grateful.

Abbreviations

CC	*Christianity at the Cross-Roads*
CF	*The Church and the Future*
EFI	*Essays on Faith and Immortality*
ER	*External Religion: Its Use and Abuse*
FM 1	*Faith of the Millions.* First Series
FM 2	*Faith of the Millions.* Second Series
GC	*The Gospel and the Church*
HD	*History of Dogma*
HS	*Hard Sayings*
LC	*Lex Credendi*
Life 1	*Autobiography of George Tyrrell 1861–1884*
Life 2	*Life of George Tyrrell from 1884 to 1909*
LO	*Lex Orandi*
MAL	*A Much-Abused Letter*
Med	*Medievalism*
NV	*Nova et Vetera*
OW	*Oil and Wine*
SC	*Through Scylla and Charybdis*
TI	*Theological Investigations*
TM	*The Month*
vH&T	*von Hügel and Tyrrell*
WC	*What Is Christianity?*

Foreword

Ever since I first heard of Father Tyrrell – over sixty years ago – he has fascinated me as a person, and there is no religious writer from whom I have derived more stimulus and enlightenment. I have returned to his books more often than to those of any other of my favourite authors. For a long time I seldom found anyone who shared my enthusiasm, but since Vatican II I have been delighted, though not surprised, to learn that he has been discovered by a multitude of readers and, in particular, that many academic students have found in various aspects of his teaching rewarding subjects for research.

For there is indeed in Tyrrell's books a wealth of ideas, expressed with exquisite literary skill, that invite exploration. He himself did not live long enough to work them out as fully as we may wish that he had been able to do. But perhaps it is well as it is: he was one of those prophetic thinkers whose teaching is inevitably fragmentary and inchoate, and in his case this was especially so since he was hampered by tiresome ecclesiastical constraints and death struck him down at an early age.

At one time, when I was more ambitious than I am now, I thought of trying to write a book about him myself. If I had done so, my ambition would have been to write such a book as Sister Leonard has now produced, based as it is on a thorough familiarity with his writings and sympathy with his cast of mind. In my judgement, all that she says about Tyrrell himself is exceedingly perceptive and clarifying; the contribution he made to the modernist movement at the beginning of this century is well brought out and rightly assessed; and the lasting value and the present relevance of his vision of the Catholic Church are made evident.

While, for obvious reasons, Tyrrell's life and work are primarily of interest to Roman Catholics, other Churches too are still having to meet the challenges that he boldly and prophetically faced in his time, and all Christians have much to learn from his responses to them. I warmly commend this book both for the way in which it brings Tyrrell himself to life and for the light it throws on the modernist movement which was condemned by Pope Pius x but which has to a large extent come into its own since Vatican ii.

Alec Vidler
Honorary Fellow
King's College
Cambridge

Introduction

George Tyrrell does not strike us as a consistent and systematic theologian. The studies examining his views on theological topics such as faith or revelation have brought out that he changed his mind many times. In every book he seems to create new theological concepts. In the present study, however, Ellen Leonard demonstrates that Tyrrell was in fact engaged in a consistent and sustained theological endeavour. Leonard shows that if we read Tyrrell's writing from a particular perspective, then we discover that despite the changing theological concepts his writings are all concerned with the identical theological issue, with an intellectual effort from which Tyrrell never swerved, namely the clarification of what Catholicism means or could mean in the modern world. To bring to light the true meaning of Catholicism was Tyrrell's great intellectual passion. He loved the Church. His entire theology was inspired by this spiritual and pastoral intention.

Tyrrell firmly believed that the official Roman definition of Catholicism was a grave distortion. Catholicism was here defined in terms of a highly conceptual understanding of truth, an administrative concept of unity and a repressive view of authority. Rome still defined Catholicism in the categories with which it defended it against Protestantism in the sixteenth and against liberal society in the nineteenth century. The Roman version of Catholicism was frozen in the past. It had acquired wholly static features and therefore differed from the Catholicism of antiquity and the middle ages as well as from the living Catholicism that was being born in Tyrrell's day in response to the modern age.

Against this deformation, protected by Roman power, Tyrrell proposed a new vision of Catholicism, the universal religion, indeed a religion of tradition, dogma and authority, but one that was alive, ever renewed through the religious experiences of the people, a dynamic movement that could respond creatively to the challenges of the modern age. Tyrrell believed that living Catholicism could be at one and the same time faithful to the ancient tradition and open to the intellectual aspirations of modernity.

Ellen Leonard has placed Tyrrell's effort to define the nature of Catholicism in the wider discussion carried on among European intellectuals who saw Catholicism as a phenomenon of the past. Protestant scholars tended to look upon it as a stage in the history of Christianity which had long been superseded. Others sought the origin of Catholicism in popular and pagan influences that very early in Christian history distorted the evangelical message. Secular scholars for whom the enlightenment represented liberation from past ignorance looked upon Catholicism as the religion of the feudal-aristocratic age, based on hierarchical control and supported by the credulity of the masses, now mortally afraid of modern scholarship and critical analysis. Against these secular trends Tyrrell was the great apologist of Catholicism. He tried to show that Catholicism was a living reality, the bearer of divine revelation through history, a cosmic religion, the sacramental key to the mystery of the universe, alive through the religious experiences and the religious practice of the people, and—in this modern age—open to historical scholarship and critical analysis.

George Tyrrell failed. Rome suppressed the modernist movement and reaffirmed its perception of Catholicism. What Tyrrell had not clearly seen was that the Roman version of Catholicism was not simply the delayed presence of an earlier phase; it was a counter-definition, a reaction against modernity. Whenever a religion vehemently rejects modern society, it integrates certain elements of modernity into the new form of orthodoxy. The highly conceptual understanding of truth which Tyrrell criticized was not unrelated to the positivism of the nineteenth century. The *via negativa* and the 'analogy of being' of medieval theology were largely forgotten. Doctrine was understood in terms of clear and distinct ideas. It was therefore possible for an administration to evaluate and control the truth. Similarly the bureaucratic control which Tyrrell lamented was not traditional but peculiarly modern. As the European monarchies and empires strove for greater centralization and at the same time found themselves opposed by popular movements, they perfected their administrative apparatus so as to cover and survey all aspects of social life, including scholarly research. Rome was not only traditional, it was also modern.

While Tyrrell and the modernists failed—their positions were not carefully thought through and they appeared more as isolated scholars than as pastors identified with their flocks—the questions they raised did not go away. The problems posed by the culture to which a religion belongs do not disappear; they can be disregarded for a time, but they shall return. Movements of renewal continued in the Catholic Church, each in a specific area, attempting critically to adapt Catholic life and thought to the changed cultural and social conditions of modernity. Vatican Council II, convoked by Pope John XXIII, permitted these movements to come to the surface and influence the making of public policy. At Vatican Council II Catholicism tried to redefine itself. It stressed the principle of collegiality over against the monocratic models of the past; it advocated co-operation and co-responsibility over against authoritarianism; it promoted pluralism in the Church over against enforced uniformity; it presented the sacraments as worship and celebration over against ritual observance accompanied by individualistic piety; it allowed openness to research and critical scholarship over against the control of ideas by an administrative magistery. The achievement of Vatican II was extraordinary. The transformation which it initiated in the Church is only partial. The old perception of Catholicism, which Tyrrell denounced and often caricatured in his writings, has not altogether disappeared. A centralized bureaucracy still sees itself as the principal embodiment of Catholicism.

George Tyrrell was a precursor of Vatican II only in a very remote way. For while he sought a new image of Catholicism, he was caught in a cultural Toryism that made him accept hierarchy in Church and society as part of the world God had created. The renewal movements that led up to Vatican II and that continue today record a much more egalitarian cultural experience, liberal or socialist. At Vatican II, despite the new emphasis on 'people of God' and 'community of the Spirit', the Church still presents itself as an 'unequal society'. But since the Church, as sign and sacrament of redeemed humanity, should manifest in visible fashion what the human community is meant to be and in particular demonstrate that in Jesus Christ the subordinations created by a sinful world have been overcome, it becomes increasingly difficult to justify a hierarchical structure that excludes the vast number of the faithful from decision-making and excludes on principle all women from the ordained priesthood. Can such a society be the sign and sacrament of human destiny? Is it really God's plan for humanity to become an unequal people? It will eventually become necessary to rethink papacy and episcopacy so as to make them responsible to the people and allow them to become organs through which the Spirit speaking in the people, finds public expression.

Ellen Leonard's study is timely. It reveals the freedom within the ever-unfolding Catholicism and the spiritual creativity that enables it to become the religion of humanity in every age, including the present.

Gregory G. Baum
Professor of Religious Studies
St. Michael's College
University of Toronto

1

The Tradition and Its Reinterpretation

What is Catholicism? Does it have a place in the modern world? In this ecumenical age, is it not sufficient to be simply 'Christian'? These are some of the questions which inspired this book. My own interests are primarily in Catholicism today and tomorrow, and yet the book begins by looking at the Catholic tradition at the beginning of this century. It does this precisely in order to try to understand Catholicism today. While recognizing that Catholicism is a larger reality than Roman Catholicism, this larger reality is viewed from a Roman Catholic perspective.

The events which have taken place within the Roman Catholic Church during the past twenty years have evoked many different responses. For some these years have marked the end of Catholicism, at least of the Catholicism which they knew. They miss the beautiful Latin mass, the plain chant, the aura of mystery. It seems to them that real Catholicism has almost disappeared. For others Catholicism has taken on new life. Vatican II was experienced as a breath of fresh air, perhaps even as a new Pentecost. Yet many of the hopes inspired by Vatican II have still to come to birth.

We can better understand what has happened within the Roman Catholic Church during the past twenty years by considering what happened at the beginning of this century during the so-called modernist period (*c*. 1900–10). It is a period which faced many of the religious problems which still challenge the Church as well as the individual believer. Ambiguity surrounds both the period and the principal characters involved in it. The very word 'modernist' is itself ambiguous. For some it conjures up a vision of heresy tearing the Church apart from within. For others it is seen as a movement within the Church which tried to respond to some of the challenges facing the Church at the turn of the century. For Pius x in his encyclical *Pascendi* (1907) it referred to a clearly defined

1

heretical system. In the reaction which followed the encyclical, the word was often used as a label for anyone who did not adhere to a strictly conservative position within the Church. For those who think of modernism as a heresy, or in the words of the encyclical 'the synthesis of all heresies', any suggestion that Vatican II was in some ways a fulfilment of the hopes of a least some of the modernists is repugnant. For those who understand modernism as an attempt, perhaps a premature one, to bring the Church into dialogue with the modern world, Vatican II does seem in some ways to be a fulfilment of the unrealized hopes of some of the so-called modernists.[1]

Ambiguity surrounds not only the modernist period. Our own period is equally ambiguous. We do not have the historical distance to see it objectively. Vatican II itself is open to a number of interpretations. Was it primarily an end, or was it a beginning? Was it in fact both an end and a beginning? In many ways it seems to have been an end. It closed the period of Counter-Reformation Catholicism with its polemic attitudes. It brought to an end the identification of Catholicism with its neo-scholastic formulation. It finally accepted biblical and historical critical method as a legitimate way to do theology. It completed the study of the Church begun at Vatican I. Finally, it may be seen, as Nicholas Lash suggests, as the end of a heroic attempt to bring Catholicism up to date with the world that came to birth between the seventeenth and nineteenth centuries. This attempt began with the modernist crisis and ended with Vatican II.[2]

Yet Vatican II can also be seen as a beginning, the beginning of a new openness to Christians of other traditions, to non-Christians, to all of humankind. Rahner maintains that Vatican II was the first major event in which the Church actualized itself as a world Church, although it did so only in an initial and diffident way. He compares this move from a Western Church to a world Church with the transition from Jewish to Gentile Christianity. But Vatican II was only a beginning. The implications of what it means to be a world Church have yet to be developed.[3]

As we reflect on the various interpretations of both modernism and Vatican II, it is fascinating to look at the one in the light of the other. One way to do this is to enter into dialogue with George

Tyrrell (1861–1909), a man who played an important part in the modernist period.

As a young man, Tyrrell was obsessed with the question of truth. His searching finally led him into the Roman Catholic Church. Convinced that somehow Catholicism was the answer to his religious questions, he desired to share this conviction with others. He tried to do this as a priest and as a writer. Catholicism began as the answer to Tyrrell's questions but it soon became itself *the* question. What is Catholicism? What does it mean to be a Catholic? The question plagued Tyrrell as he became aware of what he considered the inadequacies of the neo-scholastic, Roman-dominated Catholicism of his day. Was there another way to understand Catholicism, a way that was open to the modern world? Tyrrell believed that another interpretation was not only possible but necessary if the Catholic Church were to take its place in the twentieth century. His life's work may be seen as an attempt to provide a reinterpretation of Catholicism. His efforts were unacceptable at the time. Finally he found himself cut off from the Church he loved, alone and rejected by all but a handful of loyal friends.

In many ways Tyrrell was a tragic figure. He was not a great scholar. He referred to his own work as one of 'vulgarisation'.[4] He did not claim to offer answers to theological questions, but rather to make tentative suggestions as to directions in which solutions might be sought. Most of his contemporaries and those who lived in the shadow of the condemnation of modernism could not hear him. Perhaps at last he can be heard. His life, his writings, his vision, even his limitations can speak to us about the Catholic tradition.

Many Roman Catholics in the last fifteen years have found themselves in a situation somewhat similar to Tyrrell's. Brought up in a Catholicism shaped by neo-scholasticism and highly centralized authoritarian structures, they now find themselves in a Church which has opened itself to other possibilities. In this context what does it mean to be a Catholic? The question is asked by ordinary Catholics and by theologians, by members of Catholic institutions concerned about their identity as well as by ecumenical groups. It is a perennial question, but one which each age experiences in its own way. The reader is invited to enter into Tyrrell's world, to consider the question of Catholicism as he perceived it and to listen to his response.

During the nineteenth century Christianity found itself confronted by a new order. Tyrrell described it as 'a battle between Authority and Liberty; between Dogma and Science'.[5] The new order was characterized by the scientific spirit and the democratic movement, 'a new conception of truth and a new conception of authority and government'.[6] Both characteristics were threatening to all Christian Churches, but, as Tyrrell pointed out, the opposition between the Churches and the new order was more precise and acute in the Roman Church than in any other. 'If Rome dies, other churches may order their coffins.'[7]

The new scientific spirit took the form of biblical and historical criticism. It struck at the very heart of Christianity—the Bible and the Church. Both could be interpreted by the historical method. Questions were raised about Catholicism by nineteenth-century Protestant scholars as they applied the tools of biblical and historical criticism to the New Testament and to the history of the Christian Church. What is Catholicism, and how did it develop? Is it simply a stage in the development of the human spirit? Did it disfigure Christianity, making authentic Christianity obscure? Has it any enduring value? At the same time questions were being asked about the relationship between Christianity and other religions. Is Christianity only one among many religions and Catholicism a sect within Christianity?

Perhaps even more threatening to Catholicism was the new conception of authority. People realized that they were called to autonomy, to freedom, to the development of themselves as individuals. They refused to be treated as children, told what to believe and what to do by their elders. They wanted to take responsibility for their world and to share in its direction. Any institution which seemed to reject what the modern world perceived as values was suspect. Catholicism appeared to many at the time as totally out of touch with contemporary life and thought. Its dogmas, cult and rigid ecclesiastical structures seemed wedded to a medieval worldview. Pius IX, with his 'Syllabus of Errors', and Vatican I, with its decrees *Dei Filius* on the Catholic faith and *Pastor Aeternus* on the primacy and infallibility of the Roman Pontiff, presented a Catholicism which was clearly defensive and increasingly authoritarian.

4

All too easily it could be viewed as a reactionary force and used by those who wished to preserve the old order. Was there room in the post-enlightenment world for a dogmatic religion? Did Catholicism have any place in a world where democracy was replacing absolutism? Was there still a place for a spiritual absolutism?

Contemporary neo-scholasticism, based on a classical world-view, was unable to respond to these challenges offered by 'modernity'.[8] An approach was needed which would recognize the new historical consciousness, as well as such characteristic values of the modern age as autonomy, freedom, individualism and democracy. A small number of Catholics, including Tyrrell, tried to find ways of presenting Catholicism in response to this challenge. Using the tools of historical criticism, they tried to show that Catholicism was not a corruption but the faithful development of the gospel and of early Christianity. At the same time, they pointed out the historical conditioning of all the forms in which Catholicism found expression: its dogmas, its worship, its ecclesiastical structures. Since these had developed in response to the needs of a particular age, they could be reinterpreted to meet the needs of the new age.

Tyrrell was not himself a historian, but he was sensitive to the historical problem. Convinced that the conflict was more between criticism and an obsolete philosophical system than between criticism and Catholicism, he refused to identify Catholicism with the dominant theological system of his day or with its authoritarian structures. He believed that Catholicism could be understood in a way that was faithful to its own tradition and yet adapted to the modern mind, a way that did not ignore or deny the difficulties raised by historical criticism and a modern world-view. For him the Catholic 'idea' contained within itself the power to revise its categories, to renew its structures.

Tyrrell urged Catholicism to move beyond its defensive post-Reformation attitudes to a new self-understanding. He tried to show Catholicism in all the richness of its tradition, constantly pointing out that it was not limited to the ultramontane interpretation of his time, nor to the common conceptions or misconceptions prevalent among his contemporaries. He hoped that there was room in Catholicism for freedom as well as authority, for the individual as well as the community, for mysticism as well as the general teachings of the Church. His writings constantly point towards the wider dimensions of Catholicism.

This work of reinterpretation begun in a tentative way by people like Tyrrell has been courageously carried on by people like Adam and de Lubac, Chenu and Congar, Rahner and Schillebeeckx. At Vatican II the Church in an official way expressed an understanding of itself that was neither scholastic nor ultramontane.[9] In the documents we find a new emphasis on freedom, the rights of the individual, and personal response to God, as well as an openness to the modern world. Much of post-Vatican II theology is an attempt to express this new self-understanding of the Catholic Church. The task of reinterpretation is important not only for the Roman Catholic Church but for the future of Christianity. As Langdon Gilkey points out:

> If Christianity is to survive and be vital, that is authentic, it will only be because Catholicism has survived and become authentic. If Catholicism is to prosper creatively, it is essential that she reinterpret her own institutional structures and reshape them into forms appropriate and meaningful to modernity and powerful in our time—much as theology must reinterpret and reshape its symbols. This is also a creative and risky task, to uncover what a twentieth-century institutional form of Catholicism is and can be; and it requires the most fundamental criticism, creative rethinking, and practical work on every basic structure of that institution.[10]

This 'creative and risky task' faces the Church today. Perhaps we can learn from Tyrrell's insights and struggles. As Ronald Chapman rightly described him, he was 'a man of our time, questioning everything, courageously following the truth wherever it might lead'.[11]

2

Tyrrell and Catholicism

Biography provides much of the material from which theologians create their theology, and this was obviously true in Tyrrell's case.[1] What he wrote flowed from what was happening in his life and in the life of the Church. His understanding of Catholicism can only be appreciated against the background of his life. For him Catholicism was not simply an intellectual question. It was more like a love affair, and indeed he often referred to Catholicism in this way. The Church was his *donna gentile*, his Beatrice.[2] She was 'the woman'; he could live neither with her nor without her.[3] He was deeply involved in the religious struggles of his age, not as a spectator nor as a detached observer, but as a participant. Much of what he wrote was written quickly as a response to particular events and controversies. As Ronald Chapman observed: 'Tyrrell's thought is the expression of the man—all parts of his complex character contribute to the diversified picture of Catholicism which was his religion. The key to his thought is the man, not the reverse.'[4]

It is not easy to understand this complex character. Tyrrell wrote his own self-portrait for the first twenty-three years of his life.[5] In it he reflected upon his early religious development, his conversion to Roman Catholicism and his entrance into and early training in the Society of Jesus, events which set the stage for the struggles which characterized the rest of his life. Written when he was forty, the autobiography expresses some of the disillusionment of his later years. Both the reflections and the disillusionment give us an insight into the man.

The story of the second half of Tyrrell's life is told by Maude Petre, Tyrrell's friend and literary executor. Her objective was to continue Tyrrell's story, using the autobiography as a model. She wanted Tyrrell to appear as he was, '. . . with his strength and his weakness, his greatness and his littleness, his sweetness and his

7

bitterness, his utter truthfulness and what he himself calls his "duplicity," his generosity and his ruthlessness, his tenderness and his hardness, his faith and his scepticism'.[6]

Does the *Autobiography and Life of George Tyrrell* reveal the real person? Wilfrid Ward, who knew Tyrrell well, considered that the autobiography showed the writer's faults rather than himself. 'He was a far better man than he paints himself.'[7] Maude Petre tried to be objective, but the fact that the work was compiled by a close friend very soon after Tyrrell's death should not be overlooked. As Loome pointed out in 1971, the Tyrrell who was presented was Tyrrell as perceived by Maude Petre. She published what she considered important.[8] The situation is changing as letters and other material become available. Loome's extensive bibliographical work has contributed to this change.[9] However, a full-length biography which does justice to the man has yet to be undertaken. In the meantime, in spite of its limitations, the *Autobiography and Life* does enable us to meet Tyrrell. Letters provide other glimpses into this complex personality and at times provide a corrective to Maude Petre's presentation. Finally, there are his writings, which reveal both the breadth of his interests and the depth of his spirituality. Tyrrell emerges as a brilliant, impetuous, inquisitive man whose interest was directed from an early age towards the religious problem. This problem became the driving force of his life.

SEARCH FOR A SYSTEM:
CONVERSION TO ROMAN CATHOLICISM

Tyrrell was born in Dublin in February 1861. His spiritual odyssey began with his baptism in the Anglican Church. His father died a short time before he was born, leaving his mother with three small children and very little money. Tyrrell experienced an unsettled childhood, moving constantly from place to place. As the result of these moves, he was exposed to a variety of religious traditions, including Methodism, Calvinism and Evangelicalism. In his autobiography he described some of the early influences on his religious development: the simple piety of his mother, the agnosticism of his older brother Willie and Willie's death in 1876, the reading of Butler's *Analogy Of Religion*, which convinced him 'that religion could be soberly defended on a rational basis', and a certain fasci-

8

nation with Roman Catholicism as a paradox and a novelty.[10] All these experiences left their mark on the young boy. Rejecting the imaginary God of early childhood and strongly influenced by Willie, Tyrrell considered himself to have been an unbeliever from the age of ten to fourteen. He continued to be fascinated by religion and had a strong 'wish to believe'. He began with what he called 'the very fringe and extreme outskirts of Christianity', and from there he was driven relentlessly to the core. At fourteen his search brought him to Grangegorman, a High Church in Dublin. Recalling his first experience of Catholic worship, he wrote: '. . . I felt instinctively what I, long afterwards, understood clearly, namely: that the difference between an altar and a communion table was infinite; that it meant a totally different religion, another order of things altogether, of which I had no experience.'[11] Having been brought up to believe that Protestantism was 'the only authorized and tenable form of Christianity', his interest in Catholicism at first seemed almost sinful. Yet gradually he was led step by step to Catholicism as the solution to the religious problem.

A Protestant friend of Tyrrell's boyhood admitted that 'for Tyrrell, his change of religion was a necessary precondition to his gaining of his soul spiritually or intellectually'.[12] Christianity transformed Tyrrell's life, but as his friend noted it was not the form of Christianity in which he had been brought up: 'The truth is that he had not as a boy assimilated the saving truths of the Gospel as presented by Protestantism. The Protestantism he saw around him would not have retained the allegiance of his type of mind to orthodox Christianity.'[13]

Catholicism was Tyrrell's way to Christianity and to belief in God. His conversion was, as Tyrrell himself pointed out, in marked contrast with that of Newman. Whereas Newman began with a belief in God's presence in the voice of conscience, which led him ultimately to a belief in Catholicism, Tyrrell began with Catholicism, which led him to a belief in Christianity and then to theism.[14]

Those who knew Tyrrell at Grangegorman hoped that he might find his spiritual home within the Anglo-Catholic Church. It was with this prospect in mind that he was encouraged to leave Ireland and to go to London. There he would live with his friend Robert Dolling, who was involved in a social project undertaken by St Alban's High Anglican Church. Tyrrell arrived in London on

1 April 1879. Very soon both Dolling and Tyrrell realized that for Tyrrell it had to be 'Rome or nothing'.

It seems to have been particularly the sense of tradition and continuity that attracted Tyrrell to the Roman Church. He experienced this in a dramatic way on his first Sunday in London. He attended the Palm Sunday service at St Alban's and then wandered into the crypt of St Etheldreda's Roman Catholic Church. In St Alban's, in spite of the beauty of the service, he had a sense of unreality. Rather than being 'the utterance of the great communion of the faithful, past and present, of all ages and nations', it seemed to him to be the act of 'a few irresponsible agents acting in defiance of the community to which they belonged'. In contrast, at St Etheldreda's he experienced a strong sense of tradition. 'Here was the old business, being carried on by the old firm, in the old ways; here was continuity, that took one back to the catacombs; here was no need of, and therefore no suspicion of pose or theatrical parade.'[15]

Tyrrell was also looking for an authoritative religion. He found it in the Roman Church with its claim to an infallible teaching authority. This claim, as expressed in a syllogism, finally brought him into the Roman Church. 'Given that there must be a Church on earth claiming infallibility, no body that disclaims it can be that Church; and if only one body claims it, that must be the Church.'[16] The argument satisfied the eighteen-year-old Tyrrell, desperately looking for a system of belief. He was officially received into the Roman Church on 18 May 1879.

Reflecting upon his conversion many years later, Tyrrell was very conscious of the ambiguities which surrounded his acceptance of Roman Catholicism. He described his journey in his usual colourful style:

> I drifted into the Church for a thousand paltry motives and reasons; some good, some bad; some true, some false or fallacious—much as an ignorant and drunken navigator gets his vessel into the right port by a mere fluke. I am more satisfied to think, as I fondly perhaps do, that my lots were in other hands—at least I still hope so.[17]

EARLY INFLUENCES ON
TYRRELL'S UNDERSTANDING OF CATHOLICISM

Tyrrell's early experience of Catholicism was shaped by his entrance into the Society of Jesus and by his study of scholasticism.[18] These were formative factors in the development of his understanding of Catholicism. Although he later rejected the Society and scholasticism, both had an enduring influence on his life and thought.

Tyrrell had a strong sense of mission, a conviction that his search was not for himself alone. He often expressed an indifference in regard to himself and a lack of concern for his own salvation.[19] His concern was for others who were experiencing the same darkness through which he had come. Having embraced Catholicism as the answer to his search, he determined to 'live wholly for the Catholic cause'.[20] The means through which he hoped to do so was the Society of Jesus. He believed that the Society was militantly involved in the cause of Catholicism and would be the vehicle through which he could lead others to the truth which he had painfully discovered. Thus upon joining the Roman Catholic Church, he immediately applied for admission to the Society of Jesus. After a year living and teaching with a Jesuit community first in Cyprus and then in Malta, he was admitted to the novitiate in September 1880. Since he embraced Roman Catholicism and the Society of Jesus almost simultaneously, his understanding of Catholicism was initially shaped by his life in the Society.

In his autobiography Tyrrell described his efforts to accept a rigid way of life which he called 'Jesuitism'.[21] This way of life included a certain view of Catholicism which Tyrrell later realized was 'only a view, and not the only view'.[22] However, during his formation period in the Society it was the only view. It stressed uniformity, centralization and a blind obedience to authority.

How much of the disillusionment with the Society of Jesus which is expressed in his autobiography was the experience of the young postulant and novice, and how much that of the middle-aged man, is difficult to discern. Tyrrell's experience in the Society certainly did not correspond to his romanticized vision based on Paul Féval's *Jésuites*, a work which he had read before becoming a Catholic. The nineteen-year-old Tyrrell found the novitiate geared more to young schoolboys than to mature men. In many ways the system seemed to him, at least in retrospect, to be destructive. Yet, in spite of his difficulties, and some questions on the part of his superiors concerning the suitability of this critical young man for life in the Society, Tyrrell continued through the various stages of training, struggling to accept the system in its totality. He was allowed to make his religious profession in 1882.

Along with Tyrrell's initial acceptance of Catholicism and Jesuitism was his acceptance of scholasticism. He had been told by his novice-master that the study of scholasticism would be a remedy for the questioning and dissatisfaction which he experienced even during his novitiate. He therefore entered whole-heartedly into this study. Scholasticism was presented as *the* Catholic philosophy by which Catholicism must either stand or fall. Every other philosophical position was considered un-Catholic and heretical. While recognizing the advantages that the study of such a comprehensive system afforded, Tyrrell became increasingly critical of the way in which it was imposed as practically infallible.

During Tyrrell's student days there was a conflict in the Society concerning the way in which St Thomas should be studied. Some insisted that Leo XIII's *Aeterni Patris* (1879) allowed Thomas to be taught in the Society's traditional way using Suarez. Others, including Tyrrell, maintained that this was contrary to the Pope's directives. Tyrrell was grateful that he had the opportunity to study Thomas directly, rather than through his Jesuit commentators.[23]

Tyrrell continued throughout his life to express his appreciation for St Thomas: 'Whatever order or method there is in my thought, whatever real faculty of reasoning and distinguishing I have acquired, I owe it to St. Thomas. He first started me on the inevitable, impossible, and yet not all-fruitless quest of a complete and harmonious system of thought.'[24]

REJECTION OF JESUITISM AND SCHOLASTICISM

At an early age, and not without considerable difficulty, Tyrrell embraced Catholicism, Jesuitism and scholasticism. These were the structures which formed the background for his life and thought. He himself imputed his willingness to accept them to his desire for a system. The three systems were closely knit together and presented in an absolute way. Tyrrell's naturally critical mind and spirit soon made him aware of the inadequacies of each as a system. Gradually he recognized the need for a richer understanding and expression of Catholicism than that of the Jesuitized Roman Church of his day, with its insistence on scholasticism. He became convinced that the centralization of authority in one person, and the demand for unquestioning obedience and absolute uniformity, were distortions of true Catholicism.

By the time Tyrrell wrote his autobiography in 1901, he interpreted most of his experience in the Society, including his scholastic education, in a negative way. The spirit in the Society seemed to him to be contrary to the true spirit of Ignatius, which Tyrrell described as a spirit of elasticity and innovation. A rigidity and conformity had set in, which caused Tyrrell to wonder if it would be better for religious orders not to survive their early charismatic stage.[25]

Convinced that the originality of Ignatius lay in his willingness to adapt new means to meet the needs of his time, Tyrrell believed that the Jesuits could be once more a vital force for renewal in the Church by going back to the original spirit of their founder.[26] As a means towards the revival of this spirit, Tyrrell worked on what he called a 'Tyrrellian Commentary' on the *Spiritual Exercises*. Through it he hoped to present the message of Ignatius in a way that would speak to modern men and women, and which would emphasize the mystical aspect of Catholicism, which seemed to have been almost forgotten within the Catholic Church. Gradually Tyrrell lost hope that a revival of the spirit of Ignatius could take place within the Society. It had become the maintainer of the *status quo*, rather than an innovative force within the Church. Tyrrell abandoned his work on the *Spiritual Exercises*.[27] However, the influence of Ignatius, and through him of the Catholic mystical tradition, is evident in much of his writing.[28]

Tyrrell lamented the fact that Jesuitism had been imposed on the universal Church. Through the influence of the Society on other religious orders, on the education of both clergy and laity, and on Vatican policy in the post-Reformation period, a particular interpretation of Catholicism had become the only accepted one. The teaching of Ignatius on obedience and authority had been used by his followers to support what Tyrrell called the 'Divine Teacher fallacy'. The obedience due to Christ and the apostles was extended to all superiors. Divine authority was attributed to superiors in virtue of their office. According to Tyrrell this exaggerated conception of authority almost prevailed at the Vatican Council. Through the efforts of Jesuit theologians it subsequently became the official interpretation of papal authority.[29] Miraculous authority was attributed to the pope as God's vicar, while the bishops as delegates of the pope became 'ornamental nonentities'.[30] They could be compared to Jesuit provincials, whose authority is delegated by the General of the Society.[31] Tyrrell saw this interpretation as an abuse of the Catholic principle of authority. He rejected Jesuitism many years before he was dismissed from the Society.[32]

Tyrrell's rejection of scholasticism followed a similar pattern. In his early writings he defended the proper use of scholasticism as a vehicle for expressing the truths of faith, but pointed out its abuse.[33] He gradually became aware of its shortcomings, especially its inability to address itself to the modern world. While recognizing the service it had rendered to the Church, Tyrrell objected to its identification with Catholicism.

Just as the spirit of Ignatius had been destroyed by his followers, Tyrrell considered that Thomas had suffered a similar fate. He recognized the need to do for the twentieth century what Thomas had done for the thirteenth century. The study of Thomas 'not as an authority, but critically and historically as a genius' could be helpful.

> The fact is that Aquinas represents a far less developed theology than that of the later schoolmen, and by going back to him one escapes from many of the superstructures of his more narrow-minded successors, and thus gets liberty to unravel and reconstruct on more sympathetic lines. I would thus use the neo-scholastic movement to defeat the spirit which animates many of its promoters. . . . In a word, I would study Aquinas as I would study Dante, in order that knowing the mind of another age we might know the mind of our own more intelligently.[34]

Tyrrell attempted to promote this critical approach to Thomas when he was professor of philosophy at Stonyhurst (1894–6). His efforts to defend his approach against the one used within the Society led to his dismissal from teaching after only two years, an event which marks the beginning of Tyrrell's disillusionment and growing estrangement within the Society. Reflecting on this episode Tyrrell wrote: 'I cannot fail to recognize that being enlisted on the side of Thomism and the Pope, and against the dominant and domestic tradition of the Society, gave birth to those first feelings of disaffection and distrust towards the Order which have since ripened into a profound dislike of its sectarian egotism.'[35] A recent study of the Roman Archives of the Society of Jesus reveals the significance of this dispute on Thomism both from the point of view of Tyrrell and of his superiors. Tyrrell's letters express his pain at not being trusted while those of his superiors express their concern about this 'eminently gifted and well intentioned' man who dared to question the Jesuit method of teaching.[36]

Jesuitism and scholasticism had been the original foundation for Tyrrell's understanding of Catholicism. However, this foundation soon collapsed. The rest of Tyrrell's life, and much of his writings, may be interpreted as a search for an alternative basis for his understanding of Catholicism. Tyrrell hoped for a Catholicism which would no longer be identified with the existing Roman authoritarian model which he linked with Jesuitism, or with scholasticism, which he considered an obsolete theological system. Catholicism offered an answer to the problem of religious truth, but the particular expression which it had assumed in the late nineteenth and early twentieth centuries seemed too restricted for an age of freedom and scientific inquiry. Catholicism should not be inseparably united to any one system of thought or of ecclesiastical government. Tyrrell longed to burst the wine-skins, to find new forms for the new spirit at work in the Church and in the world. This seemed to him to be his mission within the Church.

NEW INFLUENCES ON
TYRRELL'S UNDERSTANDING OF CATHOLICISM

John Henry Newman: A New Spirit and a New Method

The gradual rejection of Jesuitism and scholasticism as old wine-skins, no longer adequate to hold the treasures of Catholicism, challenged Tyrrell to find or to create a new basis for his understanding of Catholicism. With gratitude he turned to John Henry Newman as a way of breaking out of the restrictions of scholasticism.

15

In him he found an Englishman, a Catholic scholar, a cardinal of the Roman Catholic Church, who offered an alternative approach to theology.

Newman had worked out his own apologetic for Catholicism, one which had led him into the Roman Catholic Church. In spite of a short stay in Rome and a brief exposure to contemporary neo-scholasticism, he was never at home in that system. His attitude towards the Roman theologians is revealed in this quotation from his letters:

> They know nothing at all of heretics as realities—they live, at least in Rome, in a place whose boast is that it has never given birth to heresy, and they think proofs ought to be convincing which in fact are not. Hence they are accustomed to speak of the argument for Catholicism as a demonstration, and to see no force in objections to it, and to admit no perplexity of intellect which is not directly and immediately wilful.[37]

Newman understood the English character and mentality. He could speak as an Englishman to the English. As both a believer and a man of culture, he upheld the independence and freedom of both faith and science. While recognizing the need for the infallible teaching authority of the Church, he opposed all authoritarianism, emphasized the primacy of conscience and recommended that the laity should be consulted in matters of faith. His apologetic was addressed to the whole person, to the feelings and imagination as well as to the intellect. However, it was especially Newman's recognition of the importance of history and his use of the historical method to support Roman Catholicism which offered Tyrrell a tool which he could use in his own efforts to understand Catholicism.

Tyrrell read and reread Newman's *Apologia, Essay on the Development of Christian Doctrine* and *Grammar of Assent*. The influence of these works may be detected in many of Tyrrell's writings. He was inspired by Newman's spirit even after he became aware of what he considered the limitations of Newman's 'system'. Although Tyrrell never considered himself to be a disciple of Newman, Newman did show Tyrrell new possibilities for a contemporary understanding of Catholicism. Newman may have had a greater influence on Tyrrell than the latter himself realized.[38]

Friedrich von Hügel: New Data

The person who made Tyrrell aware of the complexities of the question of Catholicism at the end of the nineteenth century was Friedrich von Hügel. Through von Hügel, Tyrrell was introduced to the works of many scholars, both Catholic and Protestant. He became increasingly aware of the challenges offered by biblical and historical criticism to the generally accepted view of Catholicism. It was only after meeting von Hügel in October 1897 that Tyrrell became involved in the question of Catholicism in the light of biblical and historical criticism. With von Hügel's encouragement, Tyrrell became familiar with the arguments of a number of important scholars such as Harnack, Sohm, Hatch, Sabatier, Weiss and Schweitzer. He also read the works of those who were trying to provide a Catholic response to the challenges offered by criticism, particularly Loisy and Blondel.[39]

Tyrrell described the effect of von Hügel's friendship: 'All the vast help you have given me—and surely I have grown from a boy to a man since I knew you—has been in opening my eyes to an ever fuller and deeper knowledge of the data of the great problem of life.'[40] The admiration was mutual. Von Hügel wrote to Tyrrell: 'I can say in all simple truth that, since Newman's death, there has been no English-speaking Catholic whose work appeals to me, and pierces, I think, to the very centre of questions, to a degree at all comparable to yours.'[41] Maude Petre regretted that Tyrrell's attention was directed more and more towards historical criticism. Her own conviction was that Tyrrell was not equipped for this kind of study, and that his proper field was spirituality.[42] However, once Tyrrell, with von Hügel's encouragement, became involved in the questions raised by biblical and historical criticism, he could not ignore them. They were part of the 'data of the great problem of life'.

Von Hügel and Tyrrell shared a deep interest in mysticism.[43] This interest is particularly evident in Tyrrell's early works. Both men recognized the need to emphasize the mystical aspect of Catholicism, which seemed to have been largely forgotten in the Catholic Church of the eighteenth and nineteenth centuries. Both believed that religion must maintain the balance of the historical or institutional, the philosophical or speculative, and the mystical or

17

intuitive.[44] The two men worked closely together, supporting and encouraging one another in their writing and in personal difficulties. Although in many ways they were very different, they shared with each other the passion of their lives, Catholic Christianity.

TYRRELL'S MISSION:
THE REINTERPRETATION OF CATHOLICISM

Von Hügel was an instrument in making Tyrrell aware of the challenges facing Catholicism, and some of the directions in which he might look for a solution to the 'problem of life'. Another factor that stimulated Tyrrell's own restless search was his pastoral ministry. With the exception of one year spent in a poor parish in Lancashire (1893–4), followed by two years teaching philosophy to Jesuit scholastics (1894–6), Tyrrell's ministry took the form of writing and spiritual direction. In 1896 he was assigned to the staff of *The Month*, a Jesuit periodical. Through his writing he became widely known. Many, especially from among the more intelligent and better educated Catholics, wrote to him or came to him for spiritual direction. In response to their needs, as well as his own, Tyrrell was led more deeply into the questions: What is Catholicism? Does it have a place in the modern world? Tyrrell attempted to respond to these questions through personal direction and through his writings.

Tyrrell's earliest writings reveal a certain 'militant orthodoxy' in the defence of Catholicism. However, he soon recognized the need for a 'change of tactics'. Controversial and polemic methods should be replaced by 'a clear manifestation of the Catholic religion in its ethical and intellectual beauty; not as *a* religion, but as eminently *the* religion of mankind'.[45] It seemed to him imperative that the Church should do what it had done in the past: 'address the intelligence of these times in its own language and on its own presuppositions'.[46] Much of his writing was an attempt to do so.

Some of Tyrrell's works were intended as 'strong medicine' for the few rather than for the many. In the Introduction to *A Much-Abused Letter*, he described those for whom such medicine was directed:

It is just those whose mentality is specifically modern, whose minds are well knit together and unified by the categories and methods of current thought, who will necessarily realize the difficulty of assimilating a theology fabricated to suit the mentality of an earlier day, and couched in conceptual language many of whose terms have either become obsolete or, still worse, have so shifted their meaning as to be positively misleading.[47]

Tyrrell's efforts to prescribe for such persons soon led him into trouble with the censors, with his own religious superiors and with the Roman authorities.

The focus for Tyrrell's work was not that of the scholar, as in the case of Loisy, but of the spiritual director. His interest was religion, devotion, the spiritual and mystical life. His involvement in the problems raised by biblical and historical research, and his criticism of the contemporary expression of Catholicism, were means towards an end. The end was the Christian life.[48] This spiritual focus is more evident in his early works, such as *Nova et Vetera, Hard Sayings* and *Oil and Wine*. However, it is also present in later works, such as *Lex Orandi, Lex Credendi, A Much-Abused Letter*, and even in his last critical work, *Christianity at the Cross-Roads*.[49]

Tyrrell saw his mission in relationship to Catholicism. He had entered the Catholic Church and the Society of Jesus with the determination 'to live wholly for the Catholic cause'. He became more and more convinced of the need to reinterpret Catholicism for his age and for Anglo-Saxons. He also recognized the need for Catholics to be in dialogue with other religious thinkers. From 1898 to 1904 he was an active member of the Synthetic Society, an interdenominational philosophical and religious discussion society.[50] In 1904 he joined the new London Society for the Study of Religion. Through his membership in these societies, Tyrrell came into contact with the religious thinkers of his day and established a number of lasting friendships. This ecumenical experience had an effect on Tyrrell's understanding of Catholicism. His reinterpretation of Catholicism had to be open to all of humankind.

STRUGGLES WITH SUPERIORS

Since the official Church appeared to be wedded to a particular theological system and a particular understanding and exercise of

19

authority, it is not surprising that Tyrrell's efforts to present a wider understanding of Catholicism involved him in a bitter conflict with religious and ecclesiastical superiors. It was these struggles which compelled Tyrrell to reflect upon the principle of authority within Catholicism.

The turn of the century marked a turn in Tyrrell's attitude towards authority. The question of authority became a personal one. Tyrrell had already experienced some problems with his superiors concerning his method of teaching philosophy. Now a more serious difficulty arose over his article on hell entitled 'A Perverted Devotion' which appeared in the *Weekly Register* of 16 December 1899.[51] The article shows the influence of Mother Juliana of Norwich and her revelation that the Lord 'shall make well all that is not well', although we do not know how this shall occur.[52] Before the mystery of God's love and his justice, Tyrrell suggested a 'certain temperate agnosticism' as one of the essentials of intelligent faith.

The problems over this article revealed the difference in outlook between the authorities in Rome and those in England. The English censors had found the article 'theologically blameless and calculated to do good', while the Roman censors objected to its anti-rational tone, and the General of the Society of Jesus found it 'offensive to pious ears'. The latter was concerned that the English Jesuits were 'too anxious to conciliate the enemies of religion' and were not 'speaking boldly and strongly enough in condemnation of heretics and unbelievers'. These differences of opinion convinced Tyrrell of the weakness of Roman centralization. Neither the General nor the Roman censors understood the situation in England. Tyrrell wrote to von Hügel: '. . . the whole incident reduces this Roman centralization to an absurdity. We are not even allowed to know England and English as well as Italians and Spanish do.'[53]

As a result of Tyrrell's difficulties over this article he was sent, in the summer of 1900, to a quiet Jesuit mission in Richmond, where he spent the rest of his life as a Jesuit. Removed from the many demands which had been placed upon him in London, Tyrrell was able to spend his days in reading, studying and writing. Unfortunately he was not able to do so in peace. The next six years were years of almost constant struggle between Tyrrell and his superiors, both religious and ecclesiastical.

There were long letters from Tyrrell to the General, and from the General to Tyrrell, communications with the Provincial and with Cardinal Vaughan concerning the imprimatur for some of Tyrrell's works, letters to his friends in which he poured out his anger and frustration.[54] It was particularly the process by which Roman authorities judged writers and their works that Tyrrell found objectionable. He complained to Cardinal Vaughan of 'this unmanly unchristian system of government by secret tattling and organized slander'. Tyrrell considered the whole process to be 'unEnglish', and he expressed a hope that the Cardinal as an Englishman would feel the same way.[55]

Tyrrell's struggles with ecclesiastical authorities, while curtailing his activities, did not reduce him to silence. Maude Petre described the situation: '. . . the difficulties that now beset any kind of publication conduced, not to the arresting of his work but only to the suppression of his own personality; they drove him into anonymity and pseudonymity, but not into silence'.[56] Tyrrell has been criticized for writing in this way, but he considered it necessary. In doing so, he was continuing to respond to those who were seeking help while not implicating the Society in the ideas that he expressed. In December 1901 he wrote to Bremond:

I met so many moribund Catholics in London in search of a *modus vivendi* that I determined on a book or series of reflections for the spiritual help of people in that condition. On the analogy of 'How to live on sixpence a day,' this might be entitled 'How to live on the minimum of faith'.[57]

A Much-Abused Letter and *Religion as a Factor of Life* were written in response to this need.

Tyrrell was a born fighter. His own relentless search had led him into deep waters. He became aware of many problems raised by biblical and historical criticism which should be studied. The refusal of the Catholic Church of his day even to admit that there were problems angered him. He could not remain silent. He felt compelled to point out the dangers that threatened the Church by its intransigence.

Tyrrell's efforts were neither appreciated nor understood. Difficulties with superiors over censorship, his removal from the ministry of preaching and other restrictions strained his relationship with the Society. In a letter written in August 1905, Tyrrell explained his situation to the General:

> The Society has become an avowedly reactionary institution; I am, and always will be, impenitently progressive. As such, my position in her ranks is dishonest; unfair to her and to myself. That I believe myself true in principle to St. Ignatius is neither here nor there; for my duty is to the actual and living Society and to her interpretation of St. Ignatius.[58]

Tyrrell hesitated to leave the Society for fear of scandalizing those who depended upon him. He was finally dismissed in February 1906, on the grounds that the excerpts of his 'Letter to a Professor', which had been published without his consent in the Italian newspaper *Corriere della Sera*, had given scandal.

Tyrrell hoped to achieve a separation from the Society which would not bring him into conflict with the Roman officials. However, he discovered that the two authorities operated as one. He objected to this identification of the Church and the Society, and their interdependence, but there was little he could do in a Church which seemed to him to have been 'Jesuitized'. In a letter to his Superior General, Reverend L. Martin, in December 1905, he wrote: 'In the name of Catholic liberty, of the other religious Orders, and of the original hierarchy of the Church, I protest against this identification; but I acknowledge it as a fact and have long been prepared for its unpleasant consequences.'[59]

Tyrrell, as well as a number of his friends, tried to find a bishop who would accept him into a diocese. In a letter to Bremond, Tyrrell mentioned that the Archbishop of San Francisco, Patrick Riordan, had indicated a willingness to accept him.[60] Cardinal Mercier of Malines in Belgium also expressed an offer. However, the conditions imposed by the Roman authorities 'neither to publish anything on religious questions nor to hold epistolary correspondence without the previous approbation of a competent person appointed by the Archbishop' were unacceptable to Tyrrell. As he wrote to a friend, it was more important for him to write than to say mass.[61]

In the midst of his own problems, Tyrrell was concerned about others who were experiencing similar difficulties. He was particularly sympathetic towards Loisy, whose work he admired. Tyrrell

saw Loisy as an important figure in the movement towards a reinterpretation of Catholicism.[62] Loisy's difficulties with ecclesiastical
authority, as well as his own struggles with superiors, had a cu-
mulative effect on Tyrrell. They led him to criticize the existing
hierarchical structures, which seemed to him an abuse rather than
a faithful exercise of the Catholic principle of authority. They also
impelled him to develop his own theory of authority.[63]

STRUGGLES WITHIN THE ROMAN CATHOLIC CHURCH

Interpretation of Vatican I

Tyrrell's struggle with authority must be seen as part of a larger
struggle within the Roman Catholic Church during his lifetime.
Tyrrell had become a Catholic less than ten years after Vatican I.
The Church was still divided over the interpretation of the council
decrees.[64] The extreme ultramontanes, such as Manning, did not
give up after the council. They strove to promulgate a maximalist
interpretation of the council's decrees. Their influence was felt,
especially on seminary education and catechetical instruction.
Others followed a moderate interpretation, such as that presented
by Newman in his 'Letter to the Duke of Norfolk'.[65] Tyrrell adopted
this latter view. He insisted that ultramontanism was not Catholicism, or at least not the only expression of Catholicism.

The extreme interpretation considered the pope to be not only
the infallible interpreter of the mind of the Church, but the very
mind of the Church. His doctrinal statements were practically independent of the sense of the faithful, of the investigations of theologians, and even of the deliberations of councils. Tyrrell believed
that this view had been rejected by the council in favour of a more
limited view whereby the pope discerns and articulates the mind of
the Church. He is not the mind, but merely the voice of that mind.
The interpretation of Vatican I, and especially of its decree on
infallibility, became a focus for much of Tyrrell's thought and writing on the question of authority.[66]

Joint Pastoral

The Joint Pastoral Letter of the English Roman Catholic hierarchy,
'The Church and Liberal Catholicism', has been seen as a

turning-point in Tyrrell's approach to the question of Catholicism.[67] Previously he had seen himself in a mediating position between the extreme right and the extreme left. He explained his position to Wilfrid Ward: 'My position is not a half-way house. My aim or programme is, whatever *unknown* issue may come forth from the working of the opposed but complementary tendencies, Right and Left, to prevent the catastrophe of the exclusive predominance of either, which would result from a schism.'[68] The pastoral seems to have been the cause of Tyrrell's shift from this mediating position to a more militant one. In reacting against what he considered an abuse of authority and a heretical view of Church, Tyrrell was impelled to work out his own understanding of authority and the nature of the Church.

The pastoral began by stating: 'It has become a dominant principle in England that all power and authority in civic, political, and religious matters are ultimately vested in the people.' In such an atmosphere it was not surprising that some Catholics had been 'infected by the critical spirit of private judgment'. The pastoral sought to correct these 'liberal Catholics' who freely expressed their own opinions on Church doctrine, theology and government without reference to ecclesiastical authority.[69]

The bishops emphasized that the teaching authority of the Church resided in the hierarchy. God is the 'Divine Teacher' who spoke through Jesus Christ, then through Peter and the apostles, and now through their legitimate successors, the pope and the bishops. The visible Church is composed of two orders of persons: the small body of chosen men assisted by the Holy Spirit who represent the authority of Christ, and the large body of the faithful who are taught by the 'Divine Teacher' speaking through the smaller body. The former, consisting of the pope and bishops in union with him, is the *ecclesia docens*; the latter, consisting of laity, ecclesiastics and bishops as private individuals, is the *ecclesia discens*. All Catholics are obliged to think as the Church thinks and to give assent to whatever she presents for acceptance. The pastoral referred to the 'assent of faith' to be given to revelation and dogma, and the 'assent of religious obedience' to be given to the ordinary teaching of the Church. Such 'ordinary teaching' would include pastoral letters of bishops, diocesan and provincial decrees, many acts of the pope and all decisions of the Roman congregations.

The general tone of the pastoral was negative. The only suggestion that it offered to those who saw problems within the Church and wanted to do something about them was 'greater self-restraint, a more docile spirit'. For Tyrrell and a number of other Catholic writers, it was a serious blow. Tyrrell summed up the directives of the bishops: 'Don't look, don't read, don't think; listen to us; we know *a priori* there are no difficulties; still don't look or you might see something.'[70]

Tyrrell considered that the pastoral presented a heretical view of ecclesiastical authority.

> It implies a conception of Church-authority that can in no sense be explained away as a 'development', but imports a wholesale innovation—a living, active *Ecclesia docens*, and a purely dead and passive *Ecclesia discens*—the Pope is not the *inherent* head of the organism, a part of that whole which is the spouse of Christ; but he is vicariously the spouse of the Church, an *alter Christus*, a distinct personality outside and above the Church. This is heresy. Also there is no limit assigned to his vicarious powers; he is pleni-potentiary; not a divinely-assisted teacher, but a divine teacher. The Pope is Peter; Peter is Christ, and Christ is God, and there is no more to be said but *Venite adoremus!*[71]

Tyrrell's response to the joint pastoral took the form of a number of newspaper articles. The most important of these appeared in *The Nineteenth Century*, over the signature of Lord Halifax.[72] In it Tyrrell assumed the position of an Anglican asking for clarification on the precise limits of the infallible teaching authority claimed by the pope, and on the non-infallible teachings of the pope, bishops, congregations and other components of the *ecclesia docens*. In this article Tyrrell pointed out the false transition of the term 'Divine Teacher' from God to the Church. 'The implied argument is that the Pope is Peter, Peter is Christ, Christ is God; therefore the Pope or the Church is God.'[73] Tyrrell insisted that the pope and bishops are not 'inspired' but 'assisted'.[74] He then presented two ways of considering papal authority: as an extension of the infallibility of ecumenical councils, and exercised under the same conditions, that is as an ultimate principle of unity; or the view adopted by the pastoral, which considered the pope as the 'Divine Teacher' standing outside and above the Church. For Tyrrell the question concerned the very constitution of the Church.[75]

The controversy over the joint pastoral raised many questions: Was the pope part of the Church or above the Church? Who has authority in the Church to formulate religious beliefs and to impose them on the whole Church? Was absolutism the only response to anarchy? The result of Tyrrell's reflections on these questions was *The Church and the Future*, which appeared in 1903 under the pseudonym Hilaire Bourdon. It presented two views of Catholicism: Catholicism as officially stated, and a 'liberal' restatement, which Tyrrell argued was faithful at least to the spirit of the Vatican Council.[76]

Condemnation of Modernism

Even more disturbing to Tyrrell than the joint pastoral of 1901 were the decrees of 1907 condemning modernism. *Lamentabili Sane*, with its sixty-five condemned statements, was issued with the approval of Pius x in July. It was followed in September by the encyclical *Pascendi Dominici Gregis*, addressed by Pius x to the bishops of the world.[77] Both documents took ideas from the writings of a number of authors, including Loisy and Tyrrell. *Lamentabili* simply condemned isolated statements from these writings. *Pascendi* developed these ideas into a system which it labelled 'modernism'. It presented a systematic analysis of the 'modernist teaching', outlined the sources of the errors and prescribed remedies for averting the evil. The impression given by the encyclical was that an organized movement within the Roman Catholic Church threatened its very life.

Studies on modernism today point out that there was no 'modernist movement' as such. There were a few Catholic scholars who had some contact with each other, mainly through the tireless efforts of von Hügel. As Loome remarks: 'Even if certain elements within the "system" had been taught by one or the other individual scholar, the "system" as such was the product of Rome's imagination.'[78] However, at the time and for many years, the view of modernism presented by the encyclical was widely accepted. Gabriel Daly suggests that 'it is high time for Roman Catholic theologians to cease making ritual obeisances towards the myth of a concerted modernist threat to the unity, orthodoxy, and stability of the Church'.[79]

Whether the encyclical was a response to a real or to an imagined threat to the Church, its effect on the Church was very real. Tyrrell's reactions were published in the *Giornale d'Italia* and *The Times*.[80] He argued that no theologian would consider it infallible. 'It is a disciplinary measure preceded by a catena of the personal opinions of Pius x and his immediate entourage.'[81] The *Tablet* took Tyrrell to task for his lack of 'Catholic obedience and decorum' in criticizing the Pope publicly. It argued that the encyclical was not 'a newly-made infallible judgment', but that it was 'infallible with the infallibility of the several judgments already made, which it solemnly proclaims and applies'.[82]

Tyrrell strongly objected to the encyclical's identification of Catholicism with its scholastic interpretation. The encyclical 'tries to show the Modernist that he is no Catholic'; it succeeds only 'in showing him he is no scholastic'.[83] In a letter to Dr Amigo, Bishop of Southwark, Tyrrell referred to the encyclical as a 'document destructive of the only possible defence of Catholicism and of every reason for submitting within due limits, to ecclesiastical authority'.[84]

Tyrrell was aware that his action was 'ecclesiastical suicide'. Yet he felt compelled to respond in this way. As he was already suspended, he had less to lose than other priests. He also considered he had a responsibility to those whom he had influenced:

> . . . all whom I had ever brought to or kept in the Church would have been scandalised had I silently accepted a document denying every reason I had given them. I felt I should show them that I could reject that document and yet remain a Roman Catholic. Again, I felt it would be better to come out in public, and act as my own accuser and defender, than wait to be tracked down by inquisitors and be condemned for some outrageous travesty of my position.[85]

Tyrrell had already lived for a number of years with the threat of possible excommunication. He accepted it as part of the price he had to pay in order to be faithful to his convictions. In 1904 he had written an article, '*Beati Excommunicati*', in which he suggested that the claims of conscience and inward sincerity may require the Catholic to resist Peter to his face and to endure patiently the consequent excommunication. Such a person cannot suffer a complete spiritual excommunication. The article ended with a quotation from St Augustine concerning the excommunication of good men.[86] In his *Times* article, Tyrrell expressed the need to stand firm as a Catholic, even if one should suffer excommunication. 'No Modernist will be moved from his Catholicism by any act of juridical violence of which he may be the object. His faith is not something that can be annihilated in a moment by the word of an angry Bishop.' [87] Tyrrell did not have long to wait before hearing from his bishop. Amigo reported Tyrrell's *Times* article to Rome. Rome ordered that he should be deprived of the sacraments and his case reserved to the Holy See. Tyrrell understood this to be excommunication, although, as Amigo pointed out to the press, Tyrrell was not formally excommunicated, but only forbidden to receive the sacraments.[88]

Tyrrell tried to show that Newman was also condemned by the writers of the encyclical, who 'not without some foundation, look on the anti-liberal, patristic, Conservative Newman as the founder of a theological method which others have legitimately worked out to conclusions at which he would have shuddered'.[89] Rome sent assurances that Newman was not included among those whose positions were condemned.

In his Lenten Pastoral of 1908 Cardinal Mercier, who two years before had offered Tyrrell a place in his diocese, singled him out as the leading modernist: 'The most penetrating observer of the present Modernist movement—the one most alive to its tendencies, who has best divined its spirit, and is perhaps more imbued with it than any other, is the English priest Tyrrell.' [90] Tyrrell's response to the Cardinal was *Medievalism*. In it he presented two conceptions of Catholicism, including two ways of understanding authority: Mercier's view and Tyrrell's. Mercier considered Tyrrell's view to be modernism, not Catholicism. Tyrrell considered Mercier's view to be Vaticanism or medievalism, not Catholicism. According to Mercier, Tyrrell had no right to continue to call himself a Catholic: '*La prétension d'être Moderniste et de rester, après l'encyclique Pascendi, Catholique, ne peut reposer que sur une équivoque. La loyauté bannit l'équivoque.*' [91]

But for Tyrrell, his Catholicism was not '*une équivoque*'. The condemnation of modernism, and his own condemnation, led him to reflect more deeply on the question of Catholicism. *Medievalism* was his passionate, personal response to that question. In his conclusion to Mercier, he wrote: 'As long as I think thus, it seems to me I must hold to the Roman Church. And if I will to do so, "Who shall separate us?" not twenty Popes nor a hundred excommunications.' [92]

TYRRELL'S FINAL STRUGGLE

The final period of Tyrrell's life was a sad one. No longer allowed to carry out his priestly ministry nor even to receive the sacraments, he was in many ways a man without a home, a vagabond. Fortunately he had a number of good friends who were very devoted to him and who welcomed him into their homes. His time was divided between visits to his friend Bremond in France, prolonged stays in London at the home of the Shelley family and periods at Storrington, where he stayed first at the Priory of the Premonstratensians and later in a cottage provided by Maude Petre.[93] He continued to work on his reinterpretation of Catholicism, resolutely refusing either to 'give up' or to 'give in'. Although he was attracted to Anglicanism, the Church of his baptism, and was in contact with the Old Catholics, he persevered in what he called his 'doorstep policy'. He had written to a friend in March 1907 concerning his plan of action: '. . . I will not join any existing body nor help to form a new one, but will stand on the doorstep and knock and ring and make myself a nuisance in every possible way.' [94] In doing this he saw himself following in the tradition of Döllinger and Acton.[95] It was his way of drawing attention to what he considered the evils of Vaticanism. Tyrrell recognized that this was a position of 'great spiritual danger and difficulty'.[96] Yet he saw it as his vocation within the Church.

For many years Tyrrell had suffered from severe migraine headaches, and during his final years from Bright's disease. How much this affected his conduct and writings during the last few years of his life has been debated. Some have used his sickness to excuse behaviour which they consider inappropriate.[97] There can be no doubt that Tyrrell's physical condition did have an effect on his writing. It was the reason for the haste with which he undertook his literary work. As early as November 1901 he wrote: 'I am always hurried to get things in before death overtakes me, and am restless while anything is unfinished that I have once begun. Could I feel sure of a year . . . but I always think it may be in a week.' [98] This sense of urgency characterizes all of Tyrrell's work. Rather than take the time to work out a systematic response to a problem, he tried to clarify the question and offer some tentative suggestions as to the direction in which solutions might be found. It is necessary to consider the context of Tyrrell's words in order to separate his convictions from his emotional responses to particular situations.

The struggle between Tyrrell and his ecclesiastical superiors continued even beyond his death, which took place in Storrington, 15 July 1909.[99] Those who knew him best understood his desire to receive the sacraments, but not at the price of a retraction which would deny what he had stood for during the last few years of his life. Although he received conditional absolution and was anointed, he was refused Catholic burial because he had made no formal retraction. Von Hügel, Maude Petre and William Tyrrell made every possible effort to obtain a Catholic funeral. Maude Petre explained later:

> Not to have done so would have been to give the lie to his life, and to accept the notion that official, sectarian, ultramontane Catholicism was true Catholicism. If he was not to lie in Catholic ground then it must be made plain that it was certainly through the actions of ecclesiastical authorities.[100]

Tyrrell was buried in the churchyard of St Mary's, Storrington. His friend Abbé Bremond addressed the small gathering of mourners and blessed his grave, an action considered by Amigo to be one of disobedience and for which Bremond was suspended from his priestly duties until he retracted his errors. Barmann calls these events surrounding Tyrrell's death 'the triumph of Vatican policy'. At the same time they are consistent with Tyrrell's life, and particularly with his understanding of Catholicism. In January 1909 he had written:

> If I decline the ministration of a Roman Catholic Priest at my death-bed, it is solely because I wish to give no basis for the rumour that I made any sort of retraction of those Catholic

principles which I have defended against the Vatican heresies. If no priest will bury me, let me be buried in perfect silence. If a stone is put over me, let it state that I was a Catholic Priest, and bear the usual emblematic chalice and host. No notes or comments.[101]

Tyrrell was willing to die as he had lived, trusting in the loving mercy of God.

In his address at the graveside, Bremond commented on the significance of the location 'half-way between the two Churches, the one in which he died and the other in which he was born'.[102] There, according to Tyrrell's request, his tombstone bears the emblem of the chalice and the host and the words: 'Of your charity pray for the soul of George Tyrrell Catholic Priest who died July 15 1909. Aged 48 years. Fortified by the Rites of the Church. R. I. P.'

The press cuttings, carefully preserved in scrapbooks by Maude Petre, reveal the ambiguity which surrounded Tyrrell's life and death.[103] There are many beautiful tributes to Tyrrell as a man of faith and courage. There are also expressions of anger at the bishop's refusal of Catholic burial as well as statements which support the bishop's position. An article in the *Guardian*, 20 October 1909, 'The Late Father Tyrrell and the Old Catholics', was seen by the *Tablet* to justify Rome's action against Tyrrell. Tyrrell had written to Bishop Herzog in November 1908: '. . . I entirely deny the ecumenical authority of the exclusively Western Councils of Trent and the Vatican and the whole medieval development of the Papacy so far as claiming more than a primacy of honour for the Bishop of Rome.' Such a statement was considered proof enough that George Tyrrell had ceased to be a Catholic.[104]

A few months after Tyrrell's death his last book, *Christianity at the Cross-Roads*, was published. Once more the ambiguity of Tyrrell's position was evident. Many saw it as a statement of faith and Tyrrell's final response to the question of Catholicism. Representative of many enthusiastic reviews was that in the *London Quarterly Review*:

Never again will it [Tyrrell's voice] be lifted in eloquent, poignant tones pleading that the best in Roman Catholicism should be liberated from Pope and Curia and Congregations of Cardinals, and be allowed to speak for itself, for its faith and for its Master.

This last utterance of Father Tyrrell is to us very touching, and the echoes of this swan-song of a noble martyr for the faith that was in him will not soon die away.[105]

Others were disappointed in his polemic against Liberal Protestantism as well as against the official interpretation of Catholicism. But Tyrrell was never one who sought to please. What he did try to do was to express the truth as he saw it.

CONCLUSION

Tyrrell's understanding of Catholicism must be seen against the events of his life and his own personality. His early life was unstable. As a youth he searched relentlessly for a system which would satisfy his questioning mind. Catholicism seemed to provide an answer, but it was a Catholicism shaped by what Tyrrell labelled Jesuitism and scholasticism. Could Catholicism be salvaged from what he came to see as an outmoded expression? Could it be reinterpreted in a way that was open to what he considered 'the assured results of criticism' and the legitimate demands of the age? Tyrrell was convinced that such an expression not only could be found but must be found, if Catholicism were to be true to itself.

The latter part of Tyrrell's life was dominated by a struggle against negative aspects of Catholicism which Tyrrell considered to be abuses of true Catholicism.[106] He had been attracted to Catholicism as a dogmatic religion, a religion of authority, but he soon experienced the misuse of the principle of authority. He observed how Catholicism as a way of life easily deteriorated into ritualism, sacerdotalism or legalism. The Catholic stress on tradition and continuity, instead of acting as a principle of life, could lead to decay and death. He believed that this had happened in the Roman Church. The real error of the day for Tyrrell was not 'modernism' but 'medievalism', the refusal to face contemporary problems, and the binding of Catholicism to sixteenth-century thought-forms. Through his writings he tried to expose these abuses of true Catholicism in order to awaken the Church to the need for renewal.

In his struggle to find a new understanding of Catholicism and to point out what he considered abuses within the Church, Tyrrell was in opposition to the highest authorities within the Roman Church. His conclusion was that he had not left the Church; the Church had left him.

Tyrrell continued to consider himself a Catholic and to work for a new understanding and expression of Catholicism. He had a vision of what Catholicism could be and of what he believed it had to become if it were really to live in the twentieth century. His vision, in spite of its limitations, can still be a source of enlightenment and inspiration.

3

The Question of Catholicism: A New Context

Every age presents its own challenge to Christianity. The nineteenth century confronted Christianity with a new order, characterized by a new scientific spirit which took the form of biblical and historical criticism and a new conception of authority. A number of Protestant scholars responded to this challenge. Using the tools of historical criticism, they presented their interpretation of the biblical and historical data in support of Protestant Christianity. At the same time they pointed out the weaknesses of the Catholic claim to be the one, true Church of Jesus Christ. These critics argued that Catholicism had developed at a particular period in the history of Christianity in response to particular events. Its origin and development could be traced in the same way as that of other institutions. In the light of historical criticism, they judged the claims of Catholicism to be untenable; in the light of the 'modern' spirit, they considered Catholicism to be an anachronism.

The official Roman Catholic Church chose either to ignore or to condemn the work of the critics. However, Catholics like von Hügel, Loisy, Blondel and Tyrrell were convinced that the question of Catholicism must be faced and answered in its new context. Their efforts can only be understood and appreciated in the light of the contemporary neo-scholastic position.

THE NEO-SCHOLASTIC UNDERSTANDING OF CATHOLICISM

The generally accepted self-understanding of the Roman Catholic Church at the end of the nineteenth century, as it was expressed in seminary manuals and catechisms, might be summed up as follows: Jesus Christ founded the Church on Peter and the twelve apostles. The pope, the bishop of Rome, is the direct successor of Peter and is therefore the head of the Church on earth. He is the vicar of Christ, with authority over the entire Church and with power to speak infallibly in matters of faith and morals. The bishops are the true successors of the apostles, continuing their work of teaching, and governing their dioceses in the name of Christ and under the leadership of the pope. The Church is a visible kingdom with world-wide jurisdiction, deriving its authority from Christ, who entrusted to it the preaching of the gospel to all nations. It is a divine institution through which Christ continues to act in human history. Only the Catholic Church is the true Church founded by Christ on Peter and the apostles, and continuing virtually unchanged through nineteen hundred years.

The documents of Vatican I reflected this understanding of Catholicism. They, as well as the seminary manuals, bore the stamp of the Roman theologians.[1] The emphasis was on the Church as teacher. *Dei Filius* stated:

> In order that we may be able to satisfy the obligation of embracing the true faith, and of persevering in it firmly, God established the Church through His only-begotten Son, and provided her with clear signs of her establishment; so that she can be recognized by all men as the guardian and teacher of the revealed word. For the Catholic Church alone possesses all those numerous and wonderful signs that are divinely arranged to make clear the credibility of the Christian faith.[2]

It was presumed that persons of good will would see the truth of Catholicism and embrace it. Loyal Catholics would accept unquestioningly the teaching of the Church.

Tyrrell in his theology classes at St Beuno's was exposed to this neo-scholastic understanding of Catholicism—an understanding which depended solely on the teaching authority of the Church. The new age, with its historical consciousness and its questioning of authority, challenged this understanding of Catholicism, especially in regard to its origin and its authoritative claims.

THE CHALLENGE OF HISTORICAL CRITICISM

The historical-critical method was itself a challenge to nineteenth-century Christianity. To apply the scientific method to the documents of the Church, and even to the inspired writings of Scripture, seemed to many Christians almost a denial of their Christian faith. Maude Petre, writing many years later, emphasized the devastating effect that historical criticism had on many sincere Christians: 'The present generation can scarcely conceive the effect on traditional belief of the—almost sudden—emergence of a new historical conception of the documents of Christianity.' [3]

Two great Christian scholars, Ferdinand Christian Baur and Adolf Harnack, saw that the new scientific method could be applied to the New Testament and to later church documents in a way that supported Christian faith. They insisted that Christianity must be understood as a historical movement, and that it must be interpreted by the historical method. Older church historians had described doctrines and institutions with respect to their historical manifestation. Baur and Harnack wanted to understand how these doctrines and institutions originated and developed. The method they used and the questions they asked set the pattern for historical theology in the generations which followed. [4]

Raising the Question

Ferdinand Christian Baur raised the question of the origin of Catholicism. Using Hegelian dialectic, he interpreted the development of Catholic Christianity in the second century as the outcome of a conflict between Jewish Christianity and Gentile Christianity. Catholic Christianity was the synthesis of these two elements.

Harnack gave Baur credit for raising the right question, the question of the development of Catholicism from primitive Christianity. [5] However, Harnack disagreed with the interpretation of Baur and the Tübingen school, pointing out that Jewish Christianity was no longer a factor in the second century. A new element, the Greek spirit, was at work as early as the first century. It could be traced to Paul, who translated the gospel into Greek modes of thought for his Gentile converts. The task for historical criticism, according to Harnack, was to show that 'the Catholic process of formation was nothing else than a building up of the ancient world on the ground of the Gospel'.[6]

It was to this task that Harnack and other critics directed their attention. Following the pattern set by Baur, they focused on the origin and development of Catholicism.

Catholicism: the Deification of Tradition?

The most impressive and influential study of the origin and development of Catholicism was that of Adolf Harnack.[7] Using the historical-critical method, Harnack believed that it was possible to discover the 'kernel' or 'essence' of Christianity. This 'kernel' is the 'gospel'. The gospel may, and indeed must, be expressed in different historical forms, but it must not become identified with any form, not even its original form. Harnack based his idea of the gospel on what he considered to be the main teachings of Jesus: the kingdom of God and its coming, God the Father and the infinite value of the human soul, the higher righteousness and the commandment of love. These three points are closely related, each containing in itself the whole 'gospel' and the 'essence' of Christianity. Harnack used his conception of the gospel as the norm by which he judged the whole history of Christianity. The fundamental proposition which he adopted was: 'That only is Christian which can be established authoritatively by the Gospel.'[8]

Harnack carefully traced the origin and the development of the institutions and dogmas of Christianity, showing how these developed in response to historical situations and were conditioned by these situations. For Harnack, Catholicism was the result of the blending of Christianity with the ideas of antiquity. He admitted that this process saved the gospel and Christianity, as well as much that was valuable in antiquity, but 'in throwing a protective covering around the Gospel, Catholicism also obscured it'.[9]

In the light of his historical study, Harnack objected to the Catholic Church's claim that its teaching and ecclesiastical organization were apostolic. Harnack called this the 'deification of tradition'. For him this was the 'essence' of Catholicism. 'The declaration that the empirical institutions of the Church, created for and necessary to this purpose, are apostolic, a declaration which amalgamates them with the essence and content of the Gospel and places them beyond all criticism, is the peculiarly "Catholic" feature.' [10]

This 'deification of tradition' may be seen in the history of the special relation between 'Roman' and 'Catholic'.[11] The world, which had become used to receiving law from Rome, readily accepted the Church of Rome as the guardian of unity. Gradually the Roman Church took over the administrative role of the empire and assumed leadership over the other Churches as the *ecclesia principalis*. At first it was the Roman Church which claimed primacy, but this primacy soon centred on the Roman bishop, who gradually took the place of the emperor. The final result was an ecclesiastical system which continued the old Roman empire in a new form, and which replaced earlier dogmatic Christianity. Obedience to ecclesiastical authority took the place of faith, and all authority, even the authority of dogma, was concentrated in one infallible authority. 'The Church itself is the living tradition; the Church, however, is the Pope.' [12] Harnack interpreted this process as a continuation of the de-Christianizing and secularizing of the Christian religion which had characterized Catholicism from the earliest times, and which reached its logical outcome in Vatican I with its declaration of papal infallibility.

Harnack suggested, as a remote possibility, that the decree of 1870 might provide a way by which the Church could free itself from its own history and move into a new era of Catholicism. In the future the pope might find a way of renouncing his 'fictitious divine dignity'. However, the 'signs of the times' seemed to him to point to an ever greater exercise of papal infallibility, an infallibility which threatened dogma, since the pope had supreme authority to define the doctrine concerning faith and morals to be held by the entire Church.[13]

Although Harnack was, at times, devastating in his criticism of Roman Catholicism, nevertheless he regarded the Roman Catholic Church as the most impressive product of Christian history.[14] He also recognized that at all times within both the Greek and Roman Churches there had been, and still were, saints who responded to the gospel in spite of the political forms which obscured it. Although individuals might be faithful to the gospel, he considered the Church itself to be unfaithful. He saw the Roman Church as 'part of the history of the Roman World-Empire', while the Eastern Church was 'part of the history of Greek religion'.[15]

It was not only Harnack and the German critics who challenged the Catholic understanding of the Church. Similar arguments were used by Edwin Hatch, the Anglican divine who shared Harnack's conviction that history offered a true apologia for Christianity.[16] Intrigued by the shift which had taken place from Christianity as a way of life based on the teachings of Jesus, to Christianity as assent to a metaphysical creed, Hatch tried to show that it was the nature of Christianity to assume different cultural forms in order to meet the needs of successive ages. For Hatch, this power to change confirmed that God was acting in human history.

Hatch showed how all-pervasive the Greek influence had been on the Christian Church in every facet of its life. How much of what had been assimilated should be retained? Hatch suggested two possible courses of action. Christianity, which began without the Greek elements, might throw off Hellenism and stand in its original splendour; or it might be argued that Christianity was meant to be a development, and that each succeeding age must accept the developments of the past and do its part to bring on the development of the future. In either case, much of the Greek element might be abandoned. In the first, the Greek elements are not essential since they are not found in primitive Christianity. In the second, they are part of an incomplete development and should therefore be abandoned if they no longer meet the needs of contemporary Christianity. The study of history is the tool by which the Church can discern what Christianity has been in the past and what it should be in the future.[17]

Like Harnack, Hatch emphasized the evil of divinizing what had developed in history as the result of Greek or Roman influences. Referring to metaphysical theology which had arisen due to the Greek tendency to define and to speculate, he wrote: 'The belief that metaphysical theology is more than this, is the chief bequest of Greece to religious thought, and it has been a *damnosa hereditas.*' [18] Hatch was convinced that the Spirit of God continued to speak to the Church and called it to interpret the present as well as the past. He suggested that the time had come 'to transcend the assumptions of Greek speculation by new assumptions, which will lead us to a diviner knowledge and the sense of a diviner life'.[19] Christianity might then become once more what it was intended to be, a way of life based on the Sermon on the Mount, rather than assent to a body of doctrines. In assuming new forms the Church would be faithful to God, who had placed the organization of the Church in human hands.

These ideas of Harnack and Hatch challenged the Catholic teaching concerning the origin and development of its institutions, its doctrines and its form of worship. If all of these could be shown to have developed in response to needs and to have been influenced by existing cultural forms, how can the Church claim that they are divine? In deifying its traditions, had Catholicism distorted the gospel?

Catholicism: the Institutionalization of Christianity?

Rudolf Sohm identified the origin of Catholicism with the institutionalization of Christianity. As a jurist, Sohm was interested in the origin of church law and church organization. He saw the Church as a spiritual reality, the Body of Christ, ruled by the Holy Spirit. There was no room for law in his understanding of Church.[20] The early Christians had enjoyed the freedom of the gospel. Whatever organization was required was based on charism. Human nature, however, strives against this freedom and longs for a religion of law. 'From these impulses of the natural man, born at once of his longing for the gospel and his despair of attaining it, Catholicism has arisen.' [21]

The 'catholicizing' of Christianity took place as Christianity moved from its charismatic to its institutional phase. As communities became larger, there was need for a president to preside over the eucharist, and for a fixed order. Gradually the Church was no longer the place where two or three gathered in Jesus' name, but the place where the bishop and presbyters were. Communion with Christ became dependent upon outward forms and conditions. The Church was no longer founded on the community of believers, but on the episcopal office. Thus, by the end of the first century, Catholicism was born.

An authoritative power became even more necessary as the Church faced the false doctrine of Gnosticism and the prophetic

enthusiasm of Montanism. By establishing a monarchical constitution the Church was able to withstand the storms which threatened her again and again through the course of her history.
Gradually the Church was no longer seen as the Body of Christ, a
non-terrestrial reality ruled by the inspirations of the Holy Spirit,
but as an earthly society, a corporation ruled by the pope. For
Sohm, the essence of Catholicism was this identification of the
Church of Christ with a legal institution which claimed to regulate
the lives of Christians.

Harnack and Sohm recognized a mutual dependence upon one
another. However, neither believed that the theory of the other was
adequate to explain the essence and origin of Catholicism. Sohm
admitted that hellenization was one of the factors which led to
Catholicism, but it did not explain Catholicism itself. Harnack
admitted that law was an important element in Catholicism, but it
could not explain the rise of Catholicism nor be considered its
essence. For Harnack, the essence of Catholicism was the deification
of tradition in general, a tradition which included not only law, but
the whole life of the empirical Church as it actually exists. According
to Harnack, Sohm was right in what he maintained, but wrong in
what he rejected.[22] However, Harnack agreed that Sohm had the
right starting-point, and in seeing the Catholic Church as an apos-
tasy gave the sharpest conceivable contrast to the Catholic view.[23]

Sohm's extreme view of law as incompatible with the true nature
of the Church was a challenge to the Catholic Church, an institution
based on a definite hierarchical order and a highly organized juridical system. Sohm believed that the Roman Catholic Church
hindered, or even annihilated, the religious life of the individual,
since only the pope had an immediate relationship to God. All
others were second-class citizens. His conclusion was that neither
faith nor the science of historical criticism supported the Catholic
claim to be the Church of Jesus Christ.

Catholicism: a Phase in Christianity?

A number of Protestant scholars interpreted Catholicism as a phase
through which Christianity has passed. It was not the 'essence' of
Christianity. However, this phase served a purpose at the time, and
should therefore be considered providential. It made Christianity

a universal religion, and at the same time preserved much of the Graeco-Roman world which might otherwise have been lost. One of the most eloquent proponents of this theory was Auguste Sabatier, a Huguenot, the founder and later the dean of the Protestant Faculty of Theology at Paris.[24]

Sabatier studied the psychological origin of religion and its evolution through the ages. Moving from religion in general to Christianity, he illustrated how the origins of the gospel are to be found in Hebraism, and how Jesus is the fulfilment of the religious development of Israel. Like Harnack, Sabatier looked for the 'essence' of Christianity and found it in the relationship of the soul with God as Father, a relationship which achieved its perfection in the person of Jesus. The gospel translated this filial consciousness of Jesus to the social milieu in which he lived. From the Fatherhood of God flows the ideal of the brotherhood of men. Sabatier distinguished between the purely moral essence of Christianity and all its historical expressions. Religion in general, and Christianity in particular, is a life which can only manifest itself in the organisms which it creates; but it must never become identified with these organisms. This is true even with the gospel itself, in which it is necessary to distinguish the life principle from its Hebraic soil. Like a leaven or a seed, the Christian principle was 'thrown into a gross, heavy mass of anterior traditions which it was meant to raise and to transform'.[25] Christianity not only transformed these anterior traditions of Judaism and paganism, but it was also transformed by them. Historical criticism makes it possible to distinguish the Christian principle from its various historical and contingent forms.

Sabatier described how Christianity has passed through three distinct phases and assumed three essentially different forms: the Jewish or messianic phase, in which the Christian principle grew in the soil of Hebraism, the Graeco-Roman or Catholic phase, in which Christianity was transplanted into the rich soil of Graeco-Roman civilization, and the Protestant or modern phase, in which there was a return to the primitive sources of the gospel. The Jewish phase marked the infancy of Christianity, the Catholic phase corresponded to its adolescence, and Protestantism marked the age of autonomy. Unfortunately Protestantism, which had broken away from the authority of the Church, made of the Bible another religion of authority. Thus the true Christianity, the religion of the Spirit, lay in the future.

Sabatier compared the evolution of humanity from authority to autonomy with that of the individual from infancy to adulthood. External authority must be internalized and thus become transformed into autonomy. In the case of religion, authority claims to be divine. In the Roman Catholic Church this divine authority resides in a supernatural institution, infallible in its teaching, while in Protestantism authority resides in the Bible, which is also claimed to be infallible. The Church and the Bible, rather than simply helping the Christian to discover the truth, have claimed to be truth itself. Through historical criticism, Sabatier illustrated how these dogmas of Roman Catholicism and Protestantism had developed. He revealed their inadequacies and pointed to the direction which he believed religion should take in the future.

Sabatier was convinced that Christianity was a religion of the Spirit. Hitherto it had taken on the authoritative forms of the religions which it had replaced, that is the forms of Judaism and of paganism. Authoritative forms had been necessary as Christianity passed through childhood and adolescence. However, the truly Christian period was about to begin. 'The religion of the priesthood and the religion of the letter are outworn and dying before our eyes, making way for the religion of the Spirit.'[26] The religions of authority are like old wine-skins which can no longer hold the Christian principle. The overcoming of the religions of authority by the religion of the Spirit would complete the Reformation begun in the sixteenth century and be a faithful response to the intent of Christ.

Sabatier referred to the Catholic interpretation of the history of Christianity as 'a tissue of legends'.

> Being unable to admit that Catholicism is not the work of Christ and the apostles, or that the Church has varied its dogma or its institutions, Catholic theologians naively imagine that the first Christian communities of Jerusalem and Antioch resemble those of Rome, Milan and Lyons in the fourth century; that Peter was the first of the popes and exercised for five-and-twenty years the supreme pontificate; that the apostles appointed bishops everywhere as their successors and the heirs of their power.[27]

In contrast with these 'legends', Sabatier presented his interpretation of how Catholicism developed. He placed the birth of Catholicism in the second century, when the Christian principle became imprisoned in a visible institution. The central dogma for Sabatier was the dogma of the Church, with its claim to divine origin, supernatural powers, infallibility and continuity. This dogma reached its logical completion in the decrees of Vatican I, which concentrated all authority in the person of the pope.

The antithesis between Christianity and Catholicism, worked out by historical critics such as Harnack, Sohm and Sabatier, threatened the very existence of Catholicism. Scientific scholarship seemed to support their position. In the light of historical criticism, could the Catholic Church maintain its claim to be the true Church founded by Christ upon the apostles?

THE CHALLENGE OF BIBLICAL CRITICISM

The historical-critical method was applied to the New Testament as well as to later church documents. In their effort to discern the 'essence' of Christianity, critics such as Harnack and Sabatier focused on the person of Jesus and on his teaching. The picture that emerged has been called the 'Liberal Protestant Christ'. This picture was challenged by the eschatological interpretation of the New Testament worked out by Johannes Weiss and Albert Schweitzer. Both the Liberal Protestant view and the eshatological view challenged the Catholic understanding of Christ and his teaching.

The Liberal Protestant View

The real focus of the gospel for Liberal Protestant scholars was the good news that God is Father and that every individual soul is of infinite value. Faith in God as Father is accompanied by faith in Jesus Christ, who knows the Father and who reveals him. Jesus declared himself to be the Messiah, the one through whom the kingdom comes. Faith in Christ demands an ethical response, a new righteousness. For Harnack and other Liberal Protestant thinkers, it was no depreciation of the gospel to represent it as an ethical message. Rather it indicated the great value of Christianity which brought to humanity the ideal of brotherhood and love for one's neighbour, as exemplified in the teaching but more concretely in the life and death of Jesus of Nazareth.

The Liberal Protestant view emphasized the spiritual nature of the kingdom of God. While recognizing that Jesus and his disciples used apocalyptic language when they spoke of the kingdom, and of Jesus' relationship to the kingdom, this way of speaking was considered to be the Jewish soil into which the gospel was sown. Although Jesus preached the coming of the kingdom of God in power in the near future, he also recognized that the kingdom was already present in his own person and in his ministry of preaching, healing and forgiving. He was conscious of his messianic vocation, but was not limited by the popular messianism of his day. He shared the apocalyptic hopes of his contemporaries, but he transformed these hopes, giving them a deeper, spiritual meaning. Jesus' message might be clothed in apocalyptic imagery, but his real concern was for individuals and their relationship with God.

Jesus was able to use apocalyptic language while at the same time transcending it. The disciples were less successful in this regard. They stressed the future coming of Christ in glory, but neglected Jesus' teaching on the kingdom as already present in his earthly life. For this reason, belief in the imminent return of Christ played an important part in New Testament writings.

The expectation of the imminent return of Jesus in glory was a mistaken idea, but it did provide a powerful motivation for the early Christian communities. Since the Old Testament did not refer to a second advent of the Messiah, this was a specifically Christian belief added onto Jewish eschatology. However, the gospel was not inseparably connected with the eschatological beliefs of Judaism or of the early Church. With the hellenization of Christianity, the idea of salvation changed. Christians no longer looked forward to the imminent return of Christ and the establishment of the kingdom of God. Salvation came to mean a knowledge of God in this life which leads to eternal blessedness in the next.

The Eschatological View

A very different interpretation was presented in the works of Johannes Weiss and Albert Schweitzer.[28] These men, working independently, came to the same conclusions concerning Jesus' understanding of the kingdom and his consciousness of himself as the Messiah.[29] Whereas Liberal Protestantism interpreted the kingdom of God as an inner reality, the rule of God in the hearts of men, and the Catholic Church claimed to be the kingdom of God on earth, united with the kingdom of God in heaven, Weiss and Schweitzer were convinced as the result of their study of the New Testament that the kingdom of God, as understood and preached by Jesus, was neither of these. It was a transcendent reality that Jesus expected to take place during his own life-time. This kingdom would come from God himself, not from human efforts. Not even Jesus could establish the kingdom. All he could do was to prepare for it. Jesus believed that the kingdom was imminent, that this world was soon passing away, to be replaced by the kingdom of God. At moments of prophetic vision, it seemed that the kingdom was actually dawning. Initially, Jesus hoped that the kingdom would arrive during his own life-time, but he gradually realized that he must first die, and then return as Messiah.

For both Weiss and Schweitzer, kingdom and Messiah were correlative terms. If the kingdom had not come, Jesus was not yet Messiah. He would become Messiah or Son of Man when the kingdom arrived. From the time of his baptism, Jesus had a messianic consciousness which he kept secret except from the Twelve. He understood his vocation to be one of preparation for the kingdom in which he would be the Messiah. Schweitzer stressed the temporal-causal connection between Jesus' passion and the eschatological dawning of the kingdom. Through his suffering and death Jesus hoped that the kingdom would come. According to Schweitzer, it was this secret, that the kingdom was very near and that Jesus would be the Messiah, that Judas gave to the Sanhedrin, thus bringing about Jesus' arrest and condemnation.

Jesus' belief in a future objective messianic kingdom which would replace this present world was soon modified. The death of Jesus, which was a transitional event leading to the dawn of the kingdom, became the central fact upon which a new non-eschatological view was built. After the resurrection of Jesus, Paul and the other New Testament writers lost sight of the fact that in the preaching of Jesus his Messiahship and the kingdom were future events. In their writings and in the early preaching, the office and dignity of the risen Lord is combined with the historical personality of Jesus of

Nazareth. Jesus is presented as Messiah during his earthly life. This de-eschatologizing finds its logical conclusion in the fourth gospel, which presents Jesus as the Messiah come down to earth. Those who believe in him already belong to his spiritual kingdom.

Weiss and Schweitzer dealt a death blow to the Liberal Protestant interpretation of Jesus as the great moral teacher and exemplar, although it took a number of years before their message was heard.[30] According to Schweitzer,

> The Jesus of Nazareth who came forward publicly as the Messiah, who preached the ethic of the Kingdom of Heaven upon earth, and died to give His work its final consecration, never had any existence. He is a figure designed by rationalism, endowed with life by liberalism, and clothed by modern theology in an historical garb.[31]

In contrast, the Jesus of Weiss and Schweitzer was a first-century Jewish apocalyptic preacher whose whole preaching and ministry centred on the imminence of the coming of the kingdom of God. The ethics which he taught was an interim ethics: 'This world is quickly passing away; time is short. Repent, because the kingdom of God is near.' The nearness of the kingdom was the motive for the ethical life and demanded a new righteousness. The kingdom was not, as Liberal Protestantism suggested, the goal of an ethical life, for the kingdom is super-moral. It will be brought about by a cosmic catastrophe in which evil is completely overcome.

Both Weiss and Schweitzer recognized the gulf between the world-view of Jesus and that of their contemporaries. Nevertheless, they insisted that Jesus must be seen in his own setting. Any other Jesus is a distortion, a fabrication. Jesus left in his eschatological world is greater than any modern Jesus that human beings could create. This does not, however, imply that theology is bound to retain the world-view of Jesus. In fact, by his death Jesus destroyed the form of his *Weltanschauung*. 'Thereby he gives to all peoples and to all times the right to apprehend him in terms of their thoughts and conceptions, in order that his spirit may pervade their "Weltanschauung" as it quickened and transfigured the Jewish eschatology.'[32] Theology should recognize that the expression 'kingdom of God', as used in theology, means something very different from the original historical meaning that these words had for Jesus.

Christianity is then free to found itself on the super-human personality of Jesus, irrespective of the form in which it was first expressed.

Weiss and Schweitzer forced theologians, both Protestant and Catholic, to recognize the importance of eschatology in the New Testament and stimulated further study in this area.[33] Although their exclusively futuristic interpretation might be rejected, it could not be ignored. It was to have a profound influence on the work of Loisy and Tyrrell, both of whom found the eschatological interpretation to be more faithful to the New Testament data, and more easily reconcilable with a 'Catholic' interpretation than with the Liberal Protestant view.[34]

THE CHALLENGE OF
THE COMPARATIVE STUDY OF RELIGIONS

The new scientific study of Christianity was accompanied by the study of other religions. Using the same historical-critical method, scholars undertook the empirical investigation of all religions, from those of advanced cultures to those of non-literate groups.[35] Such study raised the question of the relationship between Christianity and these other religions. The claim of Christianity to be 'absolute' had to be reinterpreted in the light of the new historical consciousness. It could no longer be based on the infallible statements of the pope, or on the inspiration of the Bible.

The problem was articulated by Ernst Troeltsch, along with suggestions for a reinterpretation of Christianity's claim to absoluteness.[36] If Christianity is a genuinely historical phenomenon, it is subject to all the limitations of historical phenomena. Absolute truth lies outside history. God alone is absolute, but humanity has access to the absolute only through history. To wish to possess the absolute in an absolute way at a particular point in history is an illusion.[37] 'Absoluteness' for Troeltsch was simply the highest value discernible in history, and the certainty of having found the way that leads to perfect truth. This certainty depended on personal conviction based on comparative observation.

Troeltsch saw Christianity not as the absolute religion, but as the normative religion for the individual and for all history up to the present. Christianity itself is the combination of many strands: Israelite prophecy, the preaching of Jesus, the mysticism of Paul, the idealism of Platonism and Stoicism, the integration of medieval European culture, the individualism of Luther, the conscientiousness and activism of Protestantism. It is possible that new combinations may arise in the future. Christianity may be seen as a culminating point in the history of religions. However, it must be viewed within history, not outside history.

The challenge of historical and biblical criticism and the comparative study of religions raised new questions. The old answers were no longer convincing. As Tyrrell pointed out, historical criticism was no longer confined to the study. It had 'reached the street and the railway bookstall'.[38] The solution was not to try to keep people ignorant of the results of criticism, but to help them to learn how to integrate these results with their Catholic faith. At least this was the conviction of some Catholic scholars. The Catholic Church at the time generally looked upon historical criticism with indifference, suspicion or hostility.

THE 'MODERN' SPIRIT

Catholicism was threatened not only by the scientific study of religion, but by the whole spirit of the age, an age characterized by individualism, democracy and freedom. Catholicism seemed to stand for collectivism, absolutism and unquestioning obedience to authority. As such, it was out of step with the age. Kings and queens had fallen out of favour. The emphasis was on the rights and the freedom of the individual. An authoritarian, dogmatic religion was considered by many as suited to the Middle Ages rather than to the post-enlightenment era.

Liberal Protestantism presented a view of Christianity which seemed more in tune with the new age. By attempting to reduce Christianity to its 'essence', it was possible to eliminate those elements which were irrelevant or distateful to nineteenth-century men and women. At the same time, by linking Catholicism with a particular phase in the history of Christianity, Harnack and others implied that Catholicism belonged to the past. The Catholic form of Christianity had served a purpose, but new forms were necessary to respond to the needs of the late nineteenth and twentieth centuries. The Catholic Church had had its moment in history. It was still a political reality which ruled over more than one-third of Christendom. However, many predicted that it would be more and more difficult for the Catholic Church to retain its power. Could a Church which stressed obedience to one infallible authority survive in an age of individual freedom and democracy? The new age called for a new understanding of authority.

It also demanded a new approach to dogma. The nineteenth century could accept Christianity as a religion of morality, but had difficulty accepting a dogmatic religion. Critics such as Matthew Arnold tried to free Christianity from the *Aberglaube*, the extra belief added on to the true religion of the Bible, a religion centred on righteousness.[39] Jesus was seen as the great moral teacher. Whatever could not be supported by reason and experience should be eliminated. Other critics recognized the need for dogma but insisted on its interpretation. Sabatier suggested the form this interpretation should take. Convinced that scholastic theology, based on authority, could not survive for long in the modern world, he proposed that a scientific theology, based on the new method of observation and experiment, could take its place alongside the other sciences. The task of scientific theology would be the interpretation of dogma.

Sabatier's ideas on dogma are important as a response to the 'modern' spirit and as a reflection of that spirit.[40] Within dogma he distinguished three elements: a religious element, an intellectual or philosophical element and an element of authority.[41] History shows how dogmas have evolved, and how they bear the characteristics of the particular period in which they developed. The object of criticism is to discover the religious element or living principle, and to free this from intellectual forms which are no longer suitable. In order to be faithful to the religious element, some alteration in the intellectual expression is necessary. New forms need to evolve which harmonize with modern culture.

Sabatier was conscious of the inadequacy of all religious concepts and the symbolic character of the terms in which these concepts are expressed. Opposed to the idea of an external revelation, Sabatier understood revelation as taking place within the subject, through the action of the Spirit of God. God is known only in relation to humanity. This experience of God must be expressed in symbol, the only language suited to religion. Symbols develop within the collective consciousness of a people and become the tradition of that people. Dogmatics is the study of that tradition from the symbolic point of view, as the objective revelation of the inner life of the Church.

Sabatier opposed both orthodoxy and rationalism. Orthodoxy denied that dogmas were historically and psychologically conditioned, while rationalism denied that there was any permanent and divine element expressed in dogma. Dogmas are necessary since without them religious life cannot be communicated. However, it is important to recognize their symbolic character. The criterion to be used in judging the value of a dogma is its moral value. Sabatier called his doctrinal theory 'critical symbolism', a theory which combined veneration for traditional symbols with the right to assimilate and adapt symbols to the experience of believers. Through the application of critical methods to dogma, the Church would be freed from old outmoded forms and the way prepared for a renewed Christian life.[42]

These ideas were diametrically opposed to the Catholic understanding of dogma. Vatican I had stated:

> For the teaching of faith, which God has revealed, has not been proposed as a philosophical discovery to be perfected by human ingenuity, but as a divine deposit handed over to the Spouse of Christ to be guarded faithfully and to be explained infallibly. Hence that meaning of sacred dogmas must perpetually be retained which Holy Mother Church has once declared; nor is that meaning ever to be abandoned under pretext and name of a more profound comprehension.[43]

The approach adopted by the council and reflected in contemporary neo-scholasticism was ahistorical and highly rational. Faith was the 'full submission of intellect and will to God when he reveals something'.[44] It could never be reduced to a sentiment or feeling. Since God willed to be revealed through a Church, individualism was an evil to be avoided. Authority within the Church was increasingly centralized and provided infallible guidance. Obedient response to ecclesiastical authority brought with it the assurance of eternal salvation.

CONCLUSION

The results of scientific research applied to the history of religion, and especially to the origin of Christianity and its subsequent development, raised many questions for Christianity, and particularly for Catholicism. Was Catholicism the synthesis of Jewish and Gentile Christianity as Baur proposed? Was it the deification of tradition as Harnack and Hatch suggested? Was it the institutionalization of Christianity as Sohm maintained, or an adolescent phase in the history of Christianity as Sabatier insisted? Was Christianity only one among many religions, and Catholicism a sect within Christianity? What was the connection between the gospel and the Church? What was the relationship between Jesus and the gospel? Neo-scholasticism, with its ahistorical approach, could not respond adequately to these questions. Only a theory which could justify the historical developments which had occurred, and at the same time maintain their continuity with the original Christian faith, could offer a response to these questions. A few Catholic scholars faced the questions and offered the beginnings of a response.

4

The Beginnings of a Catholic Response

The beginnings of a response to the question of Catholicism as it emerged in the late nineteenth century may be found in the works of two scholars who were very different in their methodology as well as in their personalities: Alfred Loisy, the historian, and Maurice Blondel, the philosopher. Both offered an apology for Catholicism which responded to contemporary challenges. Loisy used the theme of development; Blondel worked out his view of tradition as the life of the Church and his 'way of immanence'. Tyrrell drew on the work of both as he tried to find his own response.

THE THEME OF DEVELOPMENT

The theme of development evokes the name of John Henry Newman. His theory of doctrinal development had led him to accept Roman Catholicism. It is understandable that those who saw the need for a new apologetic for Catholicism should look to Newman and particularly to his theory of development as an alternative to the ahistorical, neo-scholastic theology of the day. However, as both Loisy and Tyrrell pointed out, it was a new world since Newman's time, and there were new questions to face.[1] Newman wanted to determine which form of nineteenth-century Christianity could be considered the Church of the Fathers. Through his study of history he came to the conclusion that it was the Roman Church. The problem in the late nineteenth century was not the development of early Catholicism into contemporary Catholicism, but the transition from Christ to Catholicism. Alfred Loisy attempted to respond to that problem.

Loisy acknowledged his indebtedness to Newman. However, he extended Newman's theory of development back into the New Testament and applied it to biblical revelation as well as to the history of religion since the origin of humankind. Loisy was convinced that Newman's theory of development could provide a satisfactory explanation of the changes which had produced Catholicism, and thus would provide an answer to Harnack and Sabatier.

The relationship between Loisy's notion of development and Newman's has been a subject of debate. Did Loisy just use Newman's name in order to make his own theory acceptable? Newman scholars have made this accusation but, as Lash points out, 'to accuse Loisy of deliberately distorting Newman's thought, simply because his own concerns were significantly different, and because he only took over from Newman those aspects of his thought which seemed helpful to him, is unjust'.[2] Loisy found in Newman a method to be used in developing a new apologetic for Catholicism.

It seemed to Loisy that Harnack and Sabatier, in their efforts to reconcile Christian faith with the claims of science, had reduced Christianity to a sentiment. Using the same historical-critical method, Loisy believed that he could demonstrate the weakness of the Liberal Protestant position and present a Catholic interpretation which was compatible with the findings of historical criticism.[3]

Loisy insisted that he was presenting a historical study. His aim was 'to catch the point of view of history' in order to show the historical connection between the gospel and the Church. He claimed that he was not considering the gospels or the teachings of the Church from the point of view of faith, but simply as historical documents.[4] To study the historical life of Jesus and the development of the Church with its doctrines, organizations and sacraments is not to deny either the divinity of Christ or the Catholic doctrine regarding the divine institution of the Church. Since these are matters of faith rather than of history, they can neither be proven nor disproven by means of historical study.

The focal point for Loisy's critique of Harnack and Sabatier was their use of the historical method to reduce Christianity to a single principle from the gospel: faith in God the Father as revealed by Jesus Christ. This in turn became for them the touchstone for testing the whole development of Christianity.[5] Loisy considered such a reduction of Christianity to be unfaithful to the facts of history. The gospel has an existence independent of those who study it. It cannot be interpreted in the light of the preferences and needs of later ages. To regard as non-essential whatever seems uncertain or unacceptable to one's contemporaries is contrary to the rules of historical criticism. The essence of the gospel of Jesus includes all the ideas which he taught and for which he died.

For Loisy, if there were an essence in the gospel which could be detected by the the historian, it was Jesus' teaching concerning the kingdom of heaven, a kingdom which Loisy understood in the same way as did Weiss and Schweitzer, that is as a future objective reality. The gospel was the immediate and direct preparation for the kingdom and as such was subservient to the kingdom. Jesus inaugurated the kingdom in its preparation, not in its fulfilment. Loisy found no support in the gospels for Harnack's thesis that the kingdom of heaven referred to the soul's union with God and was a present reality. The historian must resist the temptation to modernize the conception of the kingdom as preached by Jesus. Because Jesus was convinced that this world was soon to come to an end, he did not lay down rules for a society. The work of adapting Jesus' teaching to a situation different from that of Jesus and his contemporaries has been necessary since the earliest times and is seen in the New Testament itself. The gospel is not an absolute doctrine, but a living faith which must continue to evolve. This faith first took shape in the idea of the kingdom of heaven. Theologians who interpret Jesus' teaching for their contemporaries must not confuse their commentary with the primitive meaning of the gospel texts.

It is unhistorical to take some aspects of Jesus' teaching as absolute and other aspects as relative. All of the gospel is bound to a conception of the world, and of history, that belonged to a particular period and therefore must be adapted to subsequent epochs. Jesus was the great representative of faith. But faith must always be expressed in symbols. These symbols are related to a particular stage in the evolution of faith and religion. Jesus, as a Jew, used the Jewish symbols of kingdom and Messiah. He built upon the faith of the Jewish people. The early Christian communities interpreted these symbols in the light of their faith in the resurrection of Christ. The faith which comes to us from Jesus is not a simple deposit to be guarded by subsequent generations, but a living faith which continues to live and grow after Jesus, just as it had lived and grown before him in the faith of Israel.

The truly evangelical part of Christianity today, is not that which has never changed, for, in a sense, all has changed and has never ceased to change, but that which in spite of all external changes proceeds from the impulse given by Christ, and is inspired by His Spirit, serves the same ideal and the same hope.[6]

For Loisy everything changes. The essence of Christianity is the fullness and totality of its life, a life that flows from Jesus. Just as the essence of a tree is not in the seed but in the tree itself, the essence of Christianity is not in the seed but in the religion which grew like the mustard tree from its small beginning.

In his consideration of the Church, Loisy stressed that from the beginning the Church was a visible reality of those who had received the gospel. The Church proceeded from the gospel and continued the gospel. Unlike Harnack, whom Loisy accused of placing the whole development of the Church outside true Christianity and interpreting it as a progressive abasement of religion, Loisy justified the way that the Church developed. 'The Church can fairly say that, in order to be at all times what Jesus desired the society of His friends to be, it had to become what it has become: for it has become what it had to be to save the gospel by saving itself.'[7] Jesus did not lay down a constitution for the Church. His mission was to announce the kingdom of heaven. In Loisy's often quoted words: 'Jesus foretold the kingdom, and it was the Church that came; she came, enlarging the form of the gospel, which it was impossible to preserve as it was, as soon as the Passion closed the ministry of Jesus.'[8]

Loisy saw in the Catholic Church a continuation of the ideas of Jesus concerning the kingdom. The Church is a provisional institution still preparing and hoping for the coming of the kingdom of heaven. The Church is not the kingdom, nor is it the gospel. But Church and gospel stand in an identical relationship with the kingdom. The Church continues the ministry of Jesus, a ministry devoted to the proclamation of the coming kingdom. Thus the history of the Church is the history of the gospel in the world. The Church has constantly adapted to the needs of each age. In spite of all the changes that have occurred, there is a continuity between the community of the first disciples and the present Catholic Church, a continuity that Loisy compared to the development from child to adult.

The Church is founded on Christ, rather than by Christ. Since it is founded on belief in the divinity of Christ and his resurrection, belief in the divine institution of the Church is the object of faith rather than of history. Just as the resurrection of Jesus is a supra-historical event that cannot be demonstrated by history independent of the witness of faith, the same is true for the institution of the Church. For the historian it is faith in Christ which has founded the Church; for the believer it is Christ himself, who lives and continues his work through his Church.

In the same way Loisy showed how the exercise of authority within the Church, especially the position of the Roman pontiff, cannot be supported by a few scriptural texts, all of them proceeding from the faith of the first Christian communities, but only by faith in the living tradition of the Church. Loisy justified the manner of exercising authority which the Church had assumed in the past as necessary to meet the needs of the time. However, he suggested that the time had come for the Church to change its manner of governing in a way that would be more faithful to the New Testament idea of authority as service and to the aspiration of contemporary society. The Catholic Church had fallen out of touch with the modern world and needed to be reconciled with contemporary society.

The gospel lives in dogma as well as in the Church. Since everything in the gospel must be interpreted, the question for Loisy was whether 'the commentary is homogeneous with the text or hetero-geneous'.[9] Loisy agreed with Harnack's emphasis on the influence of Greek philosophy on Christian dogma. He considered this adjustment to have been necessary if Christianity were to become a universal religion rather than remain a Jewish sect. However, he argued that the primitive Christian tradition was never exchanged for philosophy. The dogmas that developed were not philosophical dogmas, but religious dogmas which made use of certain philosophical elements in order to interpret the gospel for Greek converts. The starting point for dogma was the gospel and the apostolic tradition. Loisy then traced the development of the main Christian dogmas and concluded:

The conceptions that the Church presents as revealed dogmas

are not truths fallen from heaven, and preserved by religious tradition in the precise form in which they first appeared. The historian sees in them the interpretation of religious facts, acquired by a laborious effort of theological thought. Though the dogmas may be Divine in origin and substance, they are human in structure and composition. It is inconceivable that their future should not correspond to their past.[10]

Loisy admitted that the Catholic Church had not recognized the development of dogma and emphasized the need for it to accept the idea of development. He also suggested that the intellectual form in which a belief is expressed might need to be changed. 'Truth alone is unchangeable, but not its image in our minds.' [11] The object of faith is God himself, Christ and his work, but dogmatic formulas are necessary in order to express and communicate this faith. In contrast with the traditional Catholic idea of dogma as revealed truth which is immutable and divinely authorized, Loisy presented his understanding of the nature of human knowledge and of revelation. Our perception of truth is always conditioned and relative, always perfectible, and at the same time susceptible to diminution. Revelation takes place in the human person, but it is the work of God. It has for its object the assertions of faith which subsist in the dogmas of the Church. These dogmatic statements are necessarily conditioned by the age in which they developed, and are always inadequate to express the living faith of the Church. They are 'the least imperfect expression that is morally possible' of the truth which can never be expressed in its fullness.[12] To suggest that the idea of the relativity of dogma is a Protestant infiltration is no more true than to say that the idolatry of dogmatic formulas is truly Catholic.[13] The true spirit of Catholicism does not consider dogmas as the absolute rule of faith. Rather it insists on the need for a living Church constantly to interpret the gospel.

For Loisy, the main point at issue between Catholic and Protestant theologians was whether the gospel of Jesus was, in principle, individualist or collectivist. Loisy was firmly convinced that it was collectivist and that it continued to live only in and through the Catholic Church. Harnack and the Liberal Protestants stressed the importance of the individual's relationship with God and read the gospel in this light. Loisy, on the other hand, interpreted the gospel

58

as primarily concerned with the approaching kingdom, a concern which has been carried on by the Catholic Church. Both Harnack and Loisy appealed to history, but with very different results. Glick sums up the difference between the two historians:

> For Loisy the history was borne by the tradition, and inevitably it must be understood through the tradition. Harnack described this as 'overcoming history by dogma'. For Harnack the history was hidden behind the tradition, as a kernel is hidden by husk. Loisy characterized this as a systematic method of investigation, but not the definition of a historical reality.[14]

For Loisy, the Catholic Church alone can claim to be the historically legitimate continuation of the gospel, but in the words of Poulat it is '*un catholicisme éclairé, purgé de l'autoritarisme qui le vicie, mais préservé de l'individualisme qui le tuerait et où Loisy n'est pas loin de voir l'hérésie majeure du christianisme*'.[15]

Loisy's apologetic for Catholicism was not acceptable to the ecclesiastical authorities. While willing to recognize the development from an implicit to an explicit expression of belief, they were opposed to the theory of development proposed by Loisy. For him, development meant essential change. Although there is continuity, the tree is different from the seed; the adult is different from the infant; Catholicism is different from the gospel. There is no unchanging 'essence' which can be expressed in different forms throughout the ages. In Tyrrell's words: 'Rome (profoundly ignorant of the critical movement, its currents and tendencies) thought that even a victory over the Protestant might be purchased at too great a cost, and repudiated a notion of development different from that of her theological dialecticians, and disastrous to their idea of orthodoxy.'[16]

It has been argued that Loisy's response was not really a 'Catholic' response, since he admitted that by 1885 he saw the need to reshape the entire Catholic system. He wanted 'to adapt the theory of Catholicism to the facts of history, and the practice of Catholicism to the realities of contemporary life'.[17] He was aware that 'official Catholicism' opposed such adaptation, but he believed that it was necessary for the life of the Church. Loisy's experience as chaplain in a girls' school convinced him that not only intellectuals but simple believers recognized the incompatibility between the statements in the catechism and the contemporary world-view.[18] Rather than disturbing the faith of believers, Loisy believed that a historical study of the relationship between the gospel of Jesus and the Church would strengthen faith and assure the believer that Catholicism is compatible with the full use of human reason and of modern scientific methods. Although both his personal faith and his sincerity have been questioned, it seems that when he wrote his two little books he was sincere in his faith and in his desire to serve the Church.[19]

TRADITION AS THE LIFE OF THE CHURCH

Another response to the question of Catholicism in the context of the challenges presented in the late nineteenth century was suggested by Maurice Blondel, one of the most interesting figures of the modernist period. Like Loisy and Tyrrell, he recognized the need for a renewed apologetic, but unlike Loisy and Tyrrell, in spite of some misunderstanding, he escaped official condemnation and was able to continue to contribute to a renewed understanding of Catholicism.

Blondel and Loisy responded, each in his own way, to the same question: How can Christianity, and particularly Catholicism, address itself to contemporary men and women? Loisy answered as a historian, Blondel as a philosopher. While agreeing with many of Loisy's ideas, Blondel could not accept Loisy's response. The correspondence between them reveals the struggle Blondel went through in trying to understand Loisy's arguments.[20] Blondel asked Loisy: Is it legitimate to pretend to do pure history? If the historian is also a Christian, can he separate his historical knowledge from his faith? Is not the autonomy of history a doctrine which replaces other doctrines? Is it not a virtual denial of positive revelation and the supernatural to pretend to base the preambles of a Christology and of an authentic Christianity on the ordinary given of history? Blondel feared that Loisy had diminished and relativized Christ and Christianity. James M. Somerville summed up Blondel's position:

> He could understand Loisy's impatience with those who had little sense of the work of history in the clarification of religious truth,

but he could not accept his positivistic reductionism, which made the Christ of history into a powder of crumbling papyri and turned the Christ of faith into a purely subjective projection of an ideal.[21]

Loisy's response to these difficulties of Blondel was: '*Vous me reprochez surtout de n'avoir pas mis votre philosophie dans mon histoire.*' [22] He also tried to show Blondel that he did not understand the historical significance of the gospels. Loisy pointed out that Blondel read later understandings into the gospel texts and used extra-historical means in order to define historically the knowledge of Jesus. This was to be unfaithful to the methods of historical criticism.

'*Histoire et dogme. Les lacunes philosophiques de l'exégèse moderne*', was Blondel's response to the challenge of biblical and historical criticism.[23] While disclaiming any intention of criticizing a particular writer, '*Histoire et dogme*' is usually considered a critique of Loisy's response. In it Blondel described what seemed to him to be two inadequate solutions to the problem of the relationship between history and dogma, and then presented his own solution to the problem. The first solution, extrinsicism, linked history to dogma only in an extrinsic and accidental way. New knowledge of history threatened this position. Equally inadequate, from Blondel's perspective, was what he called historicism, the position of Loisy. If extrinsicism made it impossible to pass from faith to history, historicism made it impossible to pass from history to faith. Blondel criticized from a philosophical point of view an 'apologetics through history alone'. History is not an independent science, but depends on many other sciences. It has a word to say, but this is not the last word. Blondel contrasted what he referred to as 'scientific history' with what he called 'real history'. Real history is the life of humanity. For Blondel, historicism reduced reality to what could be known scientifically. It tended to mistake the portrait for the living person.

Blondel posed the question: Did the early Church attach itself to the real Christ or to the historical Christ?[24] To found Christianity on a few of the early synoptic texts seemed to Blondel to confuse a portrait of Christ with the living reality of Christ as he has been known and loved throughout the ages. For Blondel, Christianity must be based on the Christ who knew himself to be human and divine, the Christ who continues to live in the Church and in the hearts of believers. The history of Christianity cannot be explained as simply a natural development, nor its dogmas considered merely 'the adaptation of Christian facts and feelings to the eternal themes of philosophical thought'.[25]

Blondel disagreed with Loisy on the centrality of the parousia in the teaching of Jesus and the early Church.[26] He suggested that the expectation of the parousia was only a first imaginative synthesis of Christianity, suited to the first followers of Jesus. The gospel was much more than simply the expectation of Jesus' return in glory. In fact the early Christians experienced the presence of Christ in the Church even more than if he had returned in glory. The explanations offered by historicism were for Blondel not only inadequate, but even destructive of true Christian faith.

Blondel sought a link, a principle which would effect a synthesis between history and dogma, while respecting their relative independence. He found this link in tradition. Tradition includes the whole collective life of the Church. It is not only concerned with the conservation of truth, but with its discovery. It is a power of development and expansion which gives the Church the freedom to regard as figurative what had been considered literal. With the help of the past, the Church can be freed from the limitations and illusions of the present. Animated by the Spirit of Christ, the Church can continue to grow.

THE WAY OF IMMANENCE

Loisy's evolutionary theory of development and Blondel's developmental theory of tradition as the whole life of the Church, were attempts to respond to the challenge posed by the new scientific study of religion. The way of immanence proposed by Blondel was an attempt to respond to the 'modern' spirit, to come to grips with modern philosophical thought.

Blondel had a positive view of the development of modern thought. He was convinced that only a thorough renewal of philosophical method and doctrine could take advantage of the great movements of human thought of the past five centuries. He believed that modern philosophy, if it were faithful to its own principles, could find in its fully developed conclusions 'a wonderful conformity with the Christian spirit'.[27] He was also aware of the difficulties involved in the kind of renewal which he envisaged:

> It is true that one cannot touch these outworn envelopes without seeming to lay violent hands on those essential truths which, for the time being, they happen to contain and without making oneself an object of suspicion for so many people who confuse their scholastic prejudices with the cause of which they make themselves the privileged champions.[28]

Blondel later qualified his criticism of traditional apologetics by admitting that it was not the true features of scholasticism but its caricature which his criticism envisaged. However, he insisted that Catholicism must learn to communicate with contemporary thinkers. He suggested that the time had come 'for the truly Catholic idea to show its power and to promote a philosophy which is the more appropriate to it the more autonomous it is'.[29]

Blondel believed that it was possible to have a philosophy which might 'coexist in our consciousness as in our life, with the most intrepid criticism and the most authentic Catholicism'.[30] He devoted his life to this task, considering it his vocation to present the gospel to contemporary men and women, to show that Catholic thought was not sterile and to provide a philosophical foundation for Christianity. Although strongly attracted to the priesthood, he decided that his vocation as a philosopher could best be fulfilled as a layman.[31]

Blondel realized the inadequacies of the various methods used by apologetics. He was convinced that a new philosophical basis needed to be developed if Christianity were to answer the needs and desires of contemporary men and women. This foundation should be rooted in life itself. It should not be imposed upon the subject from the outside, nor should it proceed solely from either the mind or the will. Rather it should proceed from the whole person, from the experience of life, from what Blondel called 'action'. It is in action that the core of life may be found. Here one experiences the need for another order which cannot be reached by oneself, and yet which must be reached if one is to be whole. Although his purpose was apologetic, Blondel's method was strictly philosophical. He wanted to show by philosophical methods that philosophy, by itself, is insufficient to explain the deepest human experiences. Reason or philosophy cannot give divine life, but in recognizing its insufficiency, one can be opened to God's gift. Using the way of immanence, Blondel demonstrated the incompleteness of philosophy, and the necessity as well as the inaccessibility of the supernatural, which can be discovered by reflecting on one's own experience of life. In his consideration of human action, Blondel perceived an openness to transcendent truths immanent in life itself. The way of immanence for Blondel led to a doctrine of transcendence.

Traditional apologetics had been concerned with the object of faith and had neglected the one who is invited to faith. Blondel directed his apologetic towards the subject:

> We must not exhaust ourselves refurbishing old arguments and presenting an *object* for acceptance while the *subject* is not disposed to listen. It is not divine truth which is at fault but human preparation, and it is here that our efforts should be concentrated. And it is not just an affair of adaptation or temporary expediency; for this function of subjective preparation is of the first importance; it is essential and permanent, if it is true that man's action co-operates all along the line with that of God.[32]

Blondel's 'shift to the subject' has had a profound effect on twentieth-century theology. Through the way of immanence, he suggested an approach to apologetics which took seriously contemporary philosophical thought, while at the same time remaining faithful to the Catholic tradition.

At the time, Blondel experienced opposition from two fronts: the philosophers, who needed to be persuaded that action was worthy of philosophical reflection and that he had not gone beyond human reason in showing the insufficiency of philosophy, and the Catholic theologians, who needed to be assured that he was not turning Christianity into a philosophy, but providing a philosophical basis upon which an apologetic for Christianity could be developed. In succeeding ages his work has been appreciated by both philosophers and theologians.

CONCLUSION

Loisy and Blondel suggested directions in which Catholicism could move in response to the legitimate demands of the age. Rather than rejecting contemporary methods, they were both convinced that these methods could be used in a way that supported Catholicism. Thirteenth-century methods could be replaced by new ones. Although their approaches were different and they failed to reach an agreement, they seem to have shared a common concern for the future of Catholicism.

This concern was also Tyrrell's. Under von Hügel's tutorage the problems raised by historical criticism and the proposed responses became his own as he pursued his search for an understanding of Catholicism which would replace the Jesuit, neo-scholastic understanding which he had rejected. The method by which he arrived at his own synthesis and the reinterpretation which he suggested form the subject of the following chapter.

5

Tyrrell's Contribution: His Idea of Catholicism

As a result of his own search and in response to the needs of those who came to him for direction, Tyrrell became increasingly aware of the question of Catholicism in its new context. It became *his* question. He was convinced that Catholicism could adapt itself to the new age and could absorb the true values of the age, including the scientific approach to religion. To do so it would be necessary for him to criticize both Catholicism and the age. Tyrrell was not a promoter of progress in an uncritical way. He insisted that the Church should neither identify with 'progress' nor isolate herself from it. 'Her attitude must always be the difficult and uncomfortable one of partial agreement and partial dissent.'[1]

Tyrrell steadfastly refused to identify Catholicism with the dominant theological system or ecclesiastical structures of his day. If Catholicism were to address itself to his contemporaries within or without the Roman Church, it had to be viewed beyond the limits of the past three centuries and of the Latin peoples.[2] Catholics in England were a weak minority, often sectarian in their own understanding of Catholicism and misunderstood by their fellow citizens who thought of a Catholic as 'one who lives by authority, seeks salvation in externals, worships the Virgin and the Saints'.[3] Tyrrell emphasized the need 'to distinguish between what is *per se* and *per accidens*; what is to be ascribed to Catholics as such, and what to their local, national or individual circumstances and peculiarities; what is due to the use, what to the abuse, of principles and laws'.[4] For Tyrrell, Catholicism could not be one of many versions of Christianity, nor could it be identified with one particular form. It had to be 'the one great human-hearted Church of humanity, who is "the mother of us all" '.[5]

In an essay written in 1896, Tyrrell expressed the need as he perceived it:

What is needed before all things is a clear manifestation of the Catholic religion in its ethical and intellectual beauty; not as *a* religion, but as eminently *the* religion of mankind; as the complement of human nature, the 'desire of the nations'; as the one God-given answer to the problem of life and the social problem. For this we need interpreters or go-betweens; men, that is, who know and sympathize with both sides, who have at once a comprehensive grasp of the 'idea' of Catholicism and are possessed with its spirit, and who are no less in touch with the spirit of their own country and age, its strength and its weakness; who can understand and speak both languages, and recognizing unity of thought under diversity of expression, can translate from one into the other, interpreting the age to the Church and the Church to the age.[6]

This quotation may be considered a description of Tyrrell's vocation as he perceived it and attempted to live it.[7]

A new understanding of Catholicism was necessary. Scholasticism had served the Church well at a particular period in its history. However, the abuse of scholasticism had led to a narrow rationalism which was destructive of faith.[8] An apologetic, addressed to the whole person, to the heart as well as the mind, would restore the balance disrupted by an overly rationalistic approach to religion. Before the mind can look for reasons to believe, the heart must 'wish to believe'. Tyrrell realized that his own 'wish to believe' had been a powerful motivation in his acceptance of Catholicism. By revealing the beauty of the Catholic 'idea', Tyrrell hoped that prejudices would break down and a desire to believe would be awakened.

At the same time, a new understanding of Catholicism would try to respond to the problems raised by historical criticism. Tyrrell was convinced that the results of historical criticism could not simply be ignored. In *Medievalism*, he enumerated some of the problem areas:

It is the irresistible facts concerning the origin and composition of the Old and New Testaments; concerning the origin of the Christian Church, of its hierarchy, its institutions, its dogmas; concerning the gradual development of the Papacy; concerning the history of religion in general—that create a difficulty against which the synthesis of scholastic theology must be and is already shattered to pieces.[9]

The task of finding solutions to the problems raised by historical criticism belonged to the Church, which in every age must respond to the questions of the age. Tyrrell attempted to clarify the issues and to offer suggestions as to the direction that might be taken in working out a solution. He admitted that his work was more the popularizing of the scholarly work of others than original scholarship. His originality seems to consist in his ability to take the ideas of others and put them into a new synthesis which he then presented in a popular style. As Daly pointed out, this was itself original at the time. 'He was a serious theological essayist, and a good one, many years before the *genre* had become fashionable, at least among Catholics.' [10]

TYRRELL'S METHOD

Tyrrell's method was eclectic. Reflection on his own life provided much of the material for his writings on Catholicism. He also drew extensively from the writings of others. This approach is common to all writers but is particularly evident in Tyrrell's case. After he broke away from neo-scholasticism, be belonged to no school. He read widely, absorbing much of what he read into his own thought. From a vast array of Protestant and Catholic authors, he used whatever seemed helpful for his particular purpose. Since he was neither a scripture scholar nor a historian, he had to rely upon the work of others. He accepted the method and many of the results of historical criticism, but he tried to interpret them in a way which would be acceptable to the Catholic position and which would support that position.

Tyrrell referred to himself as 'a weaver of materials'.[11] It is impossible to separate the strands which he picked up from many and varied sources, although certain strong influences can be detected.[12] Many of the ideas of Protestant critics such as Harnack, Hatch, Sohm, Sabatier, Weiss and Schweitzer became part of his way of thinking. He often disagreed strongly with them, and yet there are many similarities between their writings and his. He accepted many of their theories as 'facts'. In *Christianity at the Cross-Roads*, he described his method: 'In these pages I have asked myself frankly what I should consider the essence of Christianity were I not acquainted with the results of criticism; and how much of criticism I should admit if I cared nothing for Christianity.'[13] He then attempted to work out a synthesis between the essentials of Christianity and the 'assured results of criticism'. The same approach may be seen in a number of his other works.

Tyrrell accepted a great deal from the critics. Their ideas appear in various forms throughout his writings: Harnack's emphasis on the Graeco-Roman influence on Catholicism; Sohm's views on the 'catholicizing' of Christianity; Sabatier's ideas on revelation, theology and dogma; the apocalyptic view of Weiss and Schweitzer; Troeltsch's position concerning the absoluteness of Christianity. All find an echo in Tyrrell's works.

At times Tyrrell expressed concern about the integrity of his position. Had he accepted too much from the critics? After reading Sabatier's *Les Religions d'Autorité et la Religion de l'Esprit* he wrote to a friend: 'Am I implicitly a liberal Protestant; or is Sabatier implicitly a liberal Catholic? Or is there still an irreducible difference of principle between us?'[14] Towards the end of his life he rejected the Liberal Protestant interpretation of the New Testament in favour of the apocalyptic view of Weiss and Schweitzer. Looking back on his life he realized how influenced he had been by Liberal Protestantism. 'I hope I am wrong; but I feel I have been reading the Gospel all my life through nineteenth-century eyes.' [15]

Yet in all his writings Tyrrell had his own perspective, a profoundly Catholic perspective. He made use of what he considered the 'facts' of historical criticism, but he placed them within a Catholic framework. In this he was helped by his friend von Hügel and by the works of Loisy and Blondel. Although he was not a historian like Loisy nor a philosopher like Blondel, Tyrrell was able to build upon their responses to the question of Catholicism. He took the results of their scholarly work and presented them in a more popular style. After carefully studying *L'Action*, Tyrrell wrote to von Hügel that he and Blondel had reached

... most identical conclusions independently, and from most opposite approaches—a fact which vouches for the 'naturalness' of those conclusions far more than had we followed the same methods. To put it more truly he reaches by a methodical research what I stumble on by luck, or, at best, by instinct. Hence it is a great strength to me to discover that I have been unconsciously talking philosophy.[16]

Along with Loisy and Blondel, Tyrrell accepted a developmental pattern. His vision, like theirs, was communal rather than individual. Whereas Liberal Protestantism stressed personal experience of God, Tyrrell emphasized the community's experience throughout the ages. He recognized that faith is mediated to the individual through the community. In all of this Tyrrell was profoundly 'Catholic' in his approach.

Tyrrell's method was indirect. He offered suggestions, asked questions, indicated directions instead of working out a systematic response to a theological question. Knox and Vidler suggest that his method was dictated, at least in part, by his desire to postpone the inevitable clash with authority.[17] Tyrrell also chose this method because he believed that the time was not yet ripe for a systematic response to many of the questions facing the Church at the beginning of the twentieth century.[18]

Tyrrell used the results of biblical and historical criticism, philosophy and psychology, but his approach was basically phenomenological, based on his own experience and on the experience of humanity, past and present. The Catholicism which he presented was not that of the theological manual, but the living Catholicism of experience, particularly the experience of the saints throughout the ages. He stressed the mystical element which he considered an essential but often overlooked ingredient of Catholicism. Tyrrell's idea of Catholicism provided a response to the question of Catholicism in the context of the early twentieth century, but it also has relevance for the late twentieth century.

TYRRELL'S IDEA OF CATHOLICISM

Tyrrell's basic insights into the idea of Catholicism are woven throughout his writings from his earliest spiritual conferences to his last critical work, *Christianity at the Cross-Roads*, completed just two weeks before his death. They recur again and again in his numerous essays and in his correspondence. Of course there is a development of these insights as Tyrrell continued his own education and tried to respond to 'the assured results of criticism'.

Although Tyrrell often referred to the idea of Catholicism, even in his early writings, it was only in *Christianity at the Cross-Roads* that he clarified what he meant by 'idea'. He distinguished between the substance or content of an idea and its form or expression:

> As we use the word here an 'idea' is a concrete end, whose realization is the term of a process of action and endeavour. It is akin to that Augustinian *notio* (or *ratio*) *seminalis*, with which every living germ seems to be animated, and which works itself out to full expression through a process of growth and development. It does not change in itself, but is the cause of change in its embodiment. Transferred from the realm of organic life to that of human activity, an 'idea' is still a good or end to be realized and brought to perfect expression. But it is rather a volition than a concept.[19]

Jesus embodied the religious idea at a certain stage of development. Tyrrell saw Catholicism as a continuation of this idea of Jesus, expressed in different forms throughout the ages. No one mind could ever hope to grasp the Catholic idea in its entirety. The constant danger is that the idea of Catholicism becomes identified with a particular expression which it assumes in a particular mind, or nationality, or period. It is necessary to 'purify the Catholic idea more and more from all foreign admixture and build it up member by member, nearing, yet never reaching, a perfect disclosure of its organic unity, its simplicity in complexity, its transcendent beauty'.[20]

Catholicism As the Religion of Humanity

Basic to Tyrrell's idea of Catholicism was his conviction that it is *the* religion of humanity. To support this view, he used the results of the comparative study of religions. These studies emphasize that humanity is basically religious. Religion is natural to human beings. Just as languages and social customs have developed throughout the ages to fulfil human needs, so have religions developed. Catholicism has grown as a 'natural' religion, following the laws of growth of 'natural' religions, in contrast to systems of thought developed through human effort. The fact that Catholicism can be shown to follow the psychological laws that govern the growth of 'natural' religions points to its divine origin, since these natural laws are the laws of God, not the result of human efforts.[21] The comparative study of religions pointed out the affinities between Catholicism and universal religion. Rather than accepting this as an argument against Catholicism, Tyrrell used it to support Catholicism as the 'divinely conceived fulfilment of all man's natural religious instincts'.[22] He presented Catholicism as the correction and fulfilment of all other religions, including in itself all that is good in the other religions. For Tyrrell,

> to have thus recognized the 'natural' character of religion and of Christianity and of Catholicism is no novelty, but only an 'explicitation' of the thought of the greater prophets, of Christ, of St. Paul, of Tertullian, of Origen, of Clement of Alexandria—a thought which had to struggle long with opposing tendencies, traditional opinions and sentiments that have only gradually yielded and made way for its full manifestation in these latter days.[23]

Tyrrell accepted the 'historical facts' presented by Harnack, Hatch, Sohm and Sabatier concerning the influence of Greek and Roman culture on Christianity, but he interpreted this influence as an indication of the adaptability of Christianity and a proof of its divinity. He freely admitted the influence of paganism on Catholicism. In fact, he saw paganism as very much part of Catholicism, going back even before the time of Christ. In this sense, as a 'natural' religion, Catholicism is as old as humanity itself. There are no new religions, just as there are no new languages. Even Christianity was not a new religion; it grew out of Judaism. Christianized Judaism flowed into the religions of the Graeco-Roman empire, forming Catholicism. In entering into the Gentile religion, Christianized Judaism lost nearly all of its exclusively Judaic elements. Christianity adapted itself and 'transubstantiated' paganism, keeping the accidents while changing the substance. Tyrrell described the process:

> It adopts the institutions, rites, and terminology of the empire-

religion as far as it can, and much further perhaps than it ought; it finds for them a new significance in its own interests; it uses them as a fuller and richer vehicle of self-expression than Judaism could ever have been.[24]

The adaptation was not perfect; the struggle between paganism and Christianity continues within Catholicism to the present day.

The recognition of Catholicism as Christianized paganism or world-religion rather than as the Christianized Judaism of the New Testament seemed to Tyrrell to be 'a liberation and spiritual gain—a change from tight clothes to elastic'. He saw it as an intuition which put Harnack and others 'out of court finally'.[25] Tyrrell loved the image of the new wine bursting the old wine-skins. The new spirit of Christ could not be cramped into the Old Testament categories. New vessels were needed. These were borrowed from the Gentiles. When larger vessels are available these too will be filled.[26] The synthesis which is Catholicism is still in the making. Its very incoherencies and inconsistencies are a sign of its natural life and growth. Like civilization itself, of which it is a factor, Catholicism is a concrete living reality. Rather than standing for a set of theses and propositions, it is a living social organism with two thousand years of world-wide experience of human nature applied to the principles of the gospel, while its roots go back to the very beginning of humanity.

> Catholicism is but the most fully developed branch of a tree that springs from the very roots of humanity, and bears traces and proofs of its kinship with every other branch of the religious process. Its paganisms bear testimony not only to its antiquity and universality, but still more to the strength and vigour of the Christian spirit, which can subdue all things to its own ends and uses.[27]

Tyrrell returned to the conception of Catholicism as the religion of humanity in the last section of *Christianity at the Cross-Roads*. Other Christian sects have retained certain elements of Catholicism but have cut off too much that cannot be taken on again. Catholic Christianity, on the other hand, has not cut away anything which may be needed. For this reason it is

... more nearly a microcosm of the world of religions than any other known form; where we find nearly every form of religious expression, from the lowest to the highest, pressed together and straining towards unification and coherence; where the ideal of universal and perpetual validity has ever been an explicit aim; where, moreover, this ideal is clothed in a form that cannot possibly endure the test of history and science and must undergo some transformation.[28]

Tyrrell believed that Catholicism had the power to undergo this transformation, and he continued to hope that it would take place within the Roman Catholic Church. In the last page of his last work, Tyrrell asked:

> . . . why should the Modernist leave his Church? Where else will he find the true Catholicism of which he dreams? In this or that body he may find some neglected principle of Catholicism, emphasized and developed, but in isolation from the rest and at the cost of integral Christianity. He would find a religion as little, or less, Catholic in fact, and far less in potentiality.[29]

It was this catholic or universal aspect that Tyrrell emphasized in all his writings. Catholicism as the religion of humanity appeals to all classes, to all cultures, to all ages, to all stages of religious development, to all of one's religious needs. It is the religion of the masses, and yet it is also the religion of the intellectual, the mystic, the saint.

It seemed to Tyrrell that Protestantism had no place for the majority of ordinary people, while Catholicism supported even those who were naturally irreligious and those too weak to stand alone. 'Anglicanism is too academic, too educated; Protestantism, in some of its forms, is only for a spiritual aristocracy, for the naturally religious, for the elect or the converted; Catholicism it is which appeals to the mediocre millions.'[30] Although Tyrrell's ministry was primarily to the educated, he was always aware of the poor and the uneducated. A religion for the elite would not be Catholic. The bread needed to be broken for the multitude. It is important for the Church to address the educated because they are the ones who form and guide the opinions of the multitude. They should be the ones to break the bread and distribute it to the many.

Unity of faith and diversity of form is one of the principles of

Catholicism. Tyrrell referred to Pentecost as the 'birth-day of Catholicism in religion and also the death-day of nationalism in religion', when the Holy Spirit found utterance in many tongues.[31]

> To speak to each man, each class, each people, each age, in its own language, on its own presuppositions—scientific, historical, philosophical, nay, even religious—so far from being contrary to, is altogether consonant with, the democratic spirit of the Gospel. The truth spoken is the same, and the whole endeavour of accommodation is inspired by the wish to speak it as fully as the hearer can hear it.[32]

This vision of a truly 'catholic' religion, speaking to all humanity, at all times and in all circumstances, had been distorted by an exclusiveness, a sectarian spirit and a rationalistic approach which had developed within Roman Catholicism as the result of centuries of controversy. Too easily Catholicism appeared to be a theological system, or the religion of a particular time or place. Over against such a narrow Catholicism, Tyrrell proposed his vision of a Catholicism based on 'reasons of life and experience'.[33]

Catholicism As a Way of Life

Describing his initial attraction to Catholic Christianity, Tyrrell wrote: 'I cared for it more as a life, and less merely as a truth.'[34] This appreciation for Catholicism as a life to be lived underlies Tyrrell's understanding of Catholicism. It was this aspect which first attracted people to Tyrrell and his writings.

Tyrrell was convinced that the rationalistic Catholicism of his day had forgotten the truth that Catholicism is primarily a life to be lived. He insisted that we can live Catholicism without being able to say what it is. In fact it is an illusion to think that we can ever adequately describe it. We should look at the life of Christ and the lives of Christians throughout the ages. It is this life and spirit which has been entrusted to the Church rather than a body of doctrines. The doctrines are the intellectual formulations of the truth which help us to live according to the spirit of Christ. Catholicism is a matter of experience. It is something to be lived rather than to be analysed and discussed.

Catholicism is the life of a people. For Tyrrell, as for Loisy, the essential difference between Catholicism and Protestantism is the Catholic emphasis on the communal, as opposed to the Protestant stress on the individual. However, Tyrrell insisted that there was, and always had been, room for the individual within Catholicism.[35] The individual is saved and sanctified, not as an individual but as a member of the Body of Christ. No single individual can adequately or independently contain the spirit of Christ. Only the whole body of Christians, past and present, can be a vehicle for that spirit. Tyrrell's writings abound in beautiful passages describing our union in Christ with one another.

> We are not united to God singly and independently as rays which converge to a common centre and yet do not touch one another on the road, but we are first knit together into one living organic body under the Man Christ as our Head, and then with Him and through Him united to the very Godhead, whose life and beatitude flows down to the least and furthest member of that living thing.[36]

This mediatorial character of Catholicism along with the communal distinguishes Catholicism from Protestantism. Protestantism stresses the individual's direct relationship with God. The Catholic approaches God 'hand in hand with Christ and His faithful'.[37] In the Preface to *Oil and Wine*, he wrote:

> We are Catholics because we know that the organ in which the embodied Spirit of Truth and Righteousness gradually reveals itself and works out its fuller manifestation is not the individual but the community; because we subject the limited infallibility of our own mental processes, to that of a social experience and reflection—to an infallibility which is higher according to the width, the depth, the antiquity of that stream of collective experience.[38]

In religion, as in other areas of life, we depend upon society. For Tyrrell this dependence was in keeping with the psychological laws of spiritual development, laws which depend upon the wisdom of God working through nature. To cut oneself off from one's fellow human beings is to cut oneself off from God. This sense of solidarity with the whole human race, past and present, has been preserved, although imperfectly, in Catholicism. By belonging to this 'world-wide, authentic, and original Christian society', one enters into the collective life of 'all those millions who have ever borne, or bear, or shall yet bear the name of Catholic, and who have in any degree lived worthy of that name'.[39]

Tyrrell opposed schism as an unsatisfactory solution to difficulties facing individuals or groups within the Church. It separated the schismatic body or individual from the living organism of the Church, and from its historic past. Tyrrell described it as '. . . an impoverishment of the sense of continuity and a narrowing of the field of collective experience, from which the collective spirit is taught and nourished'.[40] The break of communion with the past seemed to Tyrrell to be even more impoverishing than the break with the life of the present community. At the same time the Church itself is weakened. Schisms emphasize, or over-emphasize, one aspect of truth. This aspect is often lost when a group withdraws from the Church. Such was the case at the time of the Reformation. The Catholic Church, as well as the groups which withdrew, were poorer because of the break. Tyrrell believed that Erasmus was right and Luther was wrong. 'Had the reformers of the sixteenth century remained in the Church they might perhaps have effected a more tardy, but surely a more healthy, adjustment than was effected at Trent.' [41]

Tyrrell was convinced that efforts to create new religions were useless. It was necessary 'to continue, purify, widen, and deepen the process that was in possession before these schismatic movements took place'.[42] He believed that there was room in Catholicism for a great deal of variety. The Catholic Church had the duty to make room for all, even at a certain sacrifice of uniformity; all had the duty to make reciprocal efforts towards reunion, even at a certain sacrifice of their individual identity.[43]

Another way of referring to the collective life of the Church, past and present, is to speak of tradition. Tyrrell had a deep appreciation for the rich Catholic tradition, although he seems to have preferred to refer to it as 'life' rather than as 'tradition'. He was convinced that the new had to be made out of the old, and yet the past should not be imposed as a dead burden on the present. It must constantly be criticized in order to retain what is essential and to discard what is accidental. Tyrrell opposed any theory which would accept tradition *en bloc*. Tradition contains truth of all sorts, as gold in the ore.

It must be continually sifted and corrected. He insisted that '. . . the attitude of the Modernist, however critical, is one of attachment to, not of detachment from, the Church's tradition'.[44]

Mercier referred to the organ of transmission as tradition. Tyrrell argued that tradition referred rather to the process of transmission and to what is being transmitted.[45] For Tyrrell it is always life that is being transmitted. This is the life of the whole Church, not just of the hierarchy. The hierarchy has the task of gathering together the experience of the entire Church, past and present, and of criticizing this experience according to its practical value for the life of the whole Church. It is the official guardian of the tradition.

In all his works Tyrrell stressed the collective experience of the entire Church, which for him included in some way the religious experience of humanity. The sense of solidarity with humanity, past and present, was more important than the external structures which should reflect this communal approach to life and truth. In fact, the external structures of Roman Catholicism, as they existed and operated in Tyrrell's day, seemed to him to distort the Catholic idea by placing all authority in one person, rather than in the whole community. This was a form of individualism which Tyrrell considered contrary to the Catholic tradition which looked to the whole community, not to the individual, as the vehicle for the Christian spirit. In refusing to accept what he considered as the abuse of ecclesiastical authority, Tyrrell claimed to be faithful to a deeper and truer interpretation of Catholicism. Referring to what Catholicism really means, he wrote: 'It is no mere juridical bond to be snapped at the word of an angry bishop that makes him a Catholic, but a massive consciousness of solidarity with the whole Catholic communion, past and present, by whose spirit he is animated, whose beliefs, hopes, aspirations, and sentiments he shares.'[46]

Catholicism As a Creed

The relationship between Catholicism as a life and Catholicism as a creed occupied much of Tyrrell's theological reflection. He was convinced that contemporary Catholicism had rationalized religion. Too much emphasis was placed on particular ways of expressing the truth which were often unrelated to people's lives. Tyrrell argued that the truths we live by are few and simple. Catholicism is more than a system of truths or a theology. Faith is not orthodoxy, nor is revelation theology. For Tyrrell, truth was primarily to be lived, not to be analyzed. In his reaction to 'intellectualism', he sometimes fell into a 'voluntarism' which he himself recognized.[47] It seemed to him, however, to be a necessary corrective to the overly rationalistic approach of his time.

How then does Catholicism as a way of life relate to Catholicism as a creed? What is the meaning of revelation? What is the legitimate place of dogma in the Christian life? Tyrrell reflected deeply on these questions. In his search for answers he passed through a number of phases in the development of his thought. In the Introduction to *Through Scylla and Charybdis*, Tyrrell stated that he had arranged the essays in this work to show the process through which he had passed. He admitted that it appeared as a 'wavering, rather than a straight line' and that his conclusions had been reached 'through a series of blunderings and amendments'.[48] However, it is possible to detect four phases in his understanding of revelation and dogma.[49] Laubacher referred to these phases as a period of uncritical orthodoxy (1886–99), a period of transition (1899–1902), a period of restatement of Catholicism (1902–7) and a final period of further precision in the restatement (1907–9). Kilfoyle referred to the four phases as orthodoxy, liberalism, modernism and anti-Roman modernism. These phases overlap and subsume one another.

In the first phase Tyrrell accepted the scholastic view of the deposit of faith as a fixed body of revealed truths handed down from the apostles by the Church whose task it is to protect and interpret these truths for succeeding generations. In this task the Church is infallibly guided by the Holy Spirit. Later deductions were added to the original apostolic revelation, and these along with the original revealed truths form one vast theological system endowed with divine authority.

Representative of this first phase is Tyrrell's response to Sabatier's *The Vitality of Christian Dogma*.[50] Tyrrell rejected Sabatier's concept of revelation as a stirring up of feeling rather than an instruction of the mind, and faith as an internal sentiment rather than an assent to divine mysteries somehow revealed from outside. He considered Sabatier's position to be 'Protestantism worked out ruthlessly to its logical conclusion'.[51] In contrast, Tyrrell presented the Catholic position. Revelation is 'a supernatural instruction of the mind, in which the forms and images which constitute what might be called the "language" of the mind in question, are used by God (either directly or through some created agency) to express truths not known before, or not known in the same way'. Dogma is 'the spoken or written equivalent of that mental language in which Christ and His Church (divinely assisted) have embodied the truths of revelation'.[52] Tyrrell distinguished between the truth revealed, and the language in which this truth is expressed. Referring to the deposit of faith bequeathed to us by the apostles, he wrote: 'The language, philosophy, science, and imagery was their own, but the truth and its translation into that language was from God.'[53] Tyrrell compared this language and philosophy to a sacred vessel which contains a priceless gift. To recognize the inadequacy of the concepts used to express the truth is not to reduce them to symbols devoid of objective, representative value. These concepts are the 'form of sound words' which the Church ponders from century to century. Our understanding of revelation can become fuller and richer as the Church contemplates the deposit of faith.

It is the function of the Church to hold fast to the apostolic revelation, to guard against misinterpretation, to supervise and control the evolution of its meaning. The Church does this through its dogmatic teaching. The language of revelation is human, but divinely chosen and guaranteed; the language of dogma is humanly chosen but divinely guaranteed. The role of dogma is to protect the original deposit.

The inadequacies and abuses of this view soon became apparent to Tyrrell. The authority of revelation was extended to theology and to other fields of knowledge as well, such as science, history and philosophy. The believer felt bound to outmoded ways of thinking. Tyrrell could see that this problem would become an ever greater one for the educated Catholic. He also reacted against the rationalistic approach to revelation which characterized the scholastic view. Faith was more than the assent of the mind to information communicated to it by an external, infallible authority.

The inadequacies of scholasticism soon led Tyrrell to a second phase, a more liberal approach to revelation and the development of doctrine. Revelation is a present experience of the divine, expressed by each generation of believers in its own language. The deposit of faith is a spirit, a principle, an idea, implanted in the human spirit by God. The recipient of this 'deposit' is the collective mind of the Church, guided by the Spirit. Truth is judged by the Church in terms of its universal religious value. Faith is a person's response to the present experience of revelation by a life of love.

The modern Church does not understand revelation better than preceding generations did, but it understands it in a way better suited to the modern mind. In translating the message into the language of those to whom it speaks, it is following the example of Jesus, who translated the fundamental idea of the kingdom of God into the language of the Galilean peasantry of two thousand years ago. In Scripture we do not have a 'naked and absolute revelation of the Divine, but one that is clothed in the swaddling bands of human infirmity'.[54]

The creed is the record of the gradual unravelling of the meaning of humanity's relationship with God as it is lived out and reflected upon by the Church, guided by the Spirit of Christ. The criterion used by the Church in judging the truth of a doctrinal statement is its proved universal religious value, *semper, ubique, ab omnibus*. The rule of prayer is the rule of belief. The test of truth is spiritual fruitfulness. 'Life leads, and theory follows, and then fuller life and wider theory. The Church's life precedes and dictates her doctrine step by step.'[55] Doctrinal development will end only when the life of the Church comes to an end.

Gradually Tyrrell reached the conclusion that this view was not really faithful to the tradition, especially as it had been understood by the Fathers. It ignored the normative character of apostolic revelation and gave present and future generations an advantage over past generations. In trying to work out his own solution, Tyrrell was aware of the pitfalls of both scholasticism and the theology of thinkers such as Sabatier.[56] Scholasticism, with its fixed theology, clashed with scientific and historical knowledge and seemed to bind the believer to a particular set of philosophical categories. The theology of Sabatier and other liberal Protestants, while not necessarily denying belief in the miraculous and the supernatural, put aside such belief and applied modern scientific methods to the religions of humanity. Christianity was usually seen as the highest and fullest development of the religious spirit so far achieved, but as only one of many revelations which have been or may be made. The old theology cut the Catholic off from his own age. The new theology seemed irreconcilable with Catholicism. Some Catholics, such as Wilfrid Ward and Tyrrell himself, tried to find a way between Scylla and Charybdis, between the old theology and the new, by applying a theory of dogmatic development. Tyrrell gradually recognized that these attempts did not solve the dilemma.

In '*Semper Eadem* II' Tyrrell presented his understanding of Newman's theory of development, pointing out the ways in which it failed to provide a *via media* between the old theology and the new.[57] Tyrrell contrasted Newman's Anglican 'Theory of Developments of Religious Doctrine' as sketched in his *University Sermons* of 1843 with the application of the same theory in his *Essay on the Development of Christian Doctrine* (1845). In the *Sermon*, it seemed to Tyrrell that Newman's conception of doctrinal development, although applied to a supernatural revelation, was in principle identical with the new theology. In this view the subject-matter of development is not a formulation of the object revealed, but the object itself, ever present to experience. This is the 'idea' or 'sacred impression' which prior to its formulations acts upon the reasoning. For Tyrrell, Newman's 'idea' does not mean the mental formulation of an experienced object, but the object itself considered as apprehensible and intelligible.[58] Tyrrell considered that Newman 'is trying to see how far revelation may be regarded, not as a past event, living on only in its record, but as an ever-abiding perpetual experience of the Church'.[59] The criterion for judging present expressions of truth is not their identity with the past, but their conformity to the supernatural experience of the present. Tyrrell judged that Newman had the same theory of development in mind in his 1845 *Essay*, but that he applied it only so far as it was applicable to the actual history of Catholic theology.

In the *Essay*, Newman accepted the presupposition of the Tractarians that the deposit of faith is 'the communicable record and symbolic reconstruction of a revelation accorded to the Apostles alone'.[60] Newman then tried to show that if it were necessary to accept a principle of development in order to explain the Catholicism of the first four centuries, then this principle should be extended to the later centuries as well. Newman made earlier developments the criterion for later developments and thus subjected the present and future to the past. Newman's solution, as presented in the *Essay*, offered relief to a pressing problem of his time and suggested a method which might be used in handling such problems, but at the same time it raised or left unsolved other great difficulties. The problem at the beginning of the twentieth century was not to reconcile contemporary Catholicism with the Catholicism of earlier centuries, but to find in the earliest Catholicism a true development of the 'idea' of Christ.[61]

Tyrrell suggested that Newman's solution of 1845 really had more in common with scholastic theology than with the new theology.[62] He became convinced that the very conceptions of revelation, dogma and theology had to be re-evaluated. Some Catholics, such as Ward, had hoped that 'the categories of existing Catholicism were elastic enough to accommodate themselves to the latest results of historical and critical research and to the requirements of modern life—ethical, economic and social'.[63] But it was becoming more and more difficult to put the new wine into the old wine-skins. The solution was to criticize and revise the categories themselves: religion, revelation, institutionalism, sacramentalism, theology, authority, etc. It would involve a reconstruction of Catholicism.[64]

The third phase that is evident in Tyrrell's writings involves this work of reconstruction. He considered it to be a more conservative position than the second phase, since it included a return to the earlier view of the unchanging, unprogressive character of apostolic revelation. The classical or normative revelation is the experience given to the apostles through Christ. This is the fullest manifestation of the divine by which all other manifestations are to be tested. Revelation is a total experience in which God 'shows himself' and the recipient receives an impression. This first moment is followed by a second in which the impression is expressed in human imagery. Tyrrell used the word 'revelation' in reference to the total religious experience, as well as for the mental or imaginative element of the experience. He also referred to the inspired record of the experience as 'revelation' in a secondary sense. The unifying factor in the revelation experience is the spirit present in Christ, the Church and the individual. All our explanations of the spiritual world are inadequate and analogous, whether they are expressed in the prophetic language of Jesus or in philosophical language. It is the task of the Church to preserve the deposit of faith, the 'form of sound words', and to discern whether a particular expression is faithful to the normative apostolic revelation.[65]

Revelation takes place in every person who is religiously alive. Tyrrell distinguished a spiritual or mystical impulse and a moral impulse, which together form one's 'religious faculty'.[66] It is this capacity which is open to supernatural revelation. 'If supernatural relevation is an enlightenment of the spirit, there must be in us a capacity of enlightenment, which if it does not absolutely demand revelation is at least susceptible of it and proportioned to it.'[67] Revelation from outside must evoke a revelation within. Only because we have the spirit of Christ can we understand the apostolic revelation. Tyrrell liked to compare revelation to the experience of love. Only one who has loved can understand the language of love, a language which may use different images from age to age, but which does not develop as does scientific knowledge. The language used to express revelation also changes but does not develop.

In its first form the Christian revelation was apocalyptic, prophetic and visionary. The whole person responded to this self-manifestation of the divine. Gradually revelation was presented as a revealed theology to which the Christian was required to give intellectual assent. Tyrrell interpreted this process as part of the 'catholicizing' of Christianity. The identification of revelation and theology seemed to Tyrrell to be at the root of many of the problems facing the contemporary believer. By separating revelation from theology, by recognizing that they are two distinct ways of knowing, the one prophetic, the other scientific, one could preserve tradition and respect intellectual freedom. Tyrrell was aware of the difficulty involved in attempting to separate revelation and theology. Christian revelation has been presented in the language of theology, while theology has claimed to be divinely revealed. Only revelation belongs to the realm of faith; theology belongs to the realm of science. A recognition of the rights and limits of revelation and theology would enable the believer to be faithful to the tradition without being bound to outmoded categories of thought.

Theology develops, as do other sciences, by continual readjustment to new knowledge. While theology needs to be restated, the inspired language of revelation has a timelessness, like the language of love. Revelation is the substance of what is believed. The form in which it finds expression in the creed is the result of theological reflection. Faith lays hold of the substance of the creed, not its form.

We may content ourselves with Faith in the unbroken totality of revelation as presented to us in its original and essential form of 'prophetic truth'; and we may refuse to express any opinion on the various attempts which have been made, especially of late, to translate that prophecy into the language of exact thought.[68]

Tyrrell recognized the gospel as normative but understood the futility of trying to reproduce New Testament Christianity. It is the spirit of Christ which endures and continues to inspire those who follow Christ. The Church is the unfolding of the implications of this spirit. Ecclesiastical dogmas are a protective husk wrapped around the kernel of apostolic revelation. We would not have the kernel without the husk. Dogmatic decisions have a protective, but not a scientific infallibility. They are symbolic expressions by which successive ages have interpreted the apostolic revelation. They should not be interpreted as exact statements. Their value lies in their protective role.

A more radical understanding of dogma is evident in Tyrrell's last writings, which may be considered a fourth phase in the development of his thought. In a letter to von Hügel, Tyrrell explained his 'revolutionary view of dogma'.[69] Distinguishing again between revelation and theology, which tries to explain revelation, he stressed that revelation, which is prophetic in form and sense, involves an idealized reading of history, past and future. All the elements of that symbolic vision express one thing—the kingdom of God. It is not necessary to find an independent meaning in each element or to 'determine prematurely what elements are of literal, and what of purely symbolic value—which is the core of historic fact and which idealisation'.[70] Dogma is neither revelation nor theology; it is a protection for revelation.

Tyrrell distinguished between a dogma's obvious sense and its deeper sense, between its fact value and its religious value.

I believe the Church is precisely and only the guardian of the deposit of revelation and that she cannot add to it in any way; that her definitions are simply safeguards and protections of revealed truths. *What* she says is often absolutely wrong, but the truth in whose defence she says it is revealed, and to that truth alone we owe adhesion.[71]

As an example he used the Church's condemnation of Galileo. The Church was defending the inspiration of Scripture in its condemnation of heliocentricism. If the denial of the Virgin Birth would seem to destroy its religious value, the Church must affirm its historicity in order to affirm its religious value, which is the glory and dignity of Christ. 'In the implicit affirmation she is right of necessity; in the explicit protective affirmation she may be quite wrong.' [72] However, Tyrrell added that certain religious values depend not just on ideas and symbols of truth, but on their realization in history.

> The value of the Gospel is not that it gives us an ideal life, but that that life was actually lived. The historicity of His passion is all-important, the factualness of His resurrection equally so. But the mode, not equally so. What imports is the triumph of the Gospel through His death.[73]

Tyrrell realized that his view of dogma was not that of the Church, but he believed that the Church would eventually be forced to a new understanding of dogma.

In an address delivered before an audience of professors and students at King's College, London, 26 March 1909, Tyrrell clarified his ideas on 'Revelation As Experience'.[74] Rejecting the idea of a divine statement directly addressed to the prophet's intellect, Tyrrell insisted that revelation is the indwelling spirit of Christ, present to all people of all times. We use human statements to attempt to express a divinely given experience, but revelation itself is not the statement but the experience. The creeds of the Church are 'the creation of her collective human mind, but guided by her collective religious experience—by the spirit of Christ that is immanent in all her members'.[75] They are human statements inspired by divine experience. We test our interpretation of the Church's creeds by the criterion of spiritual life and fruitfulness, by the revelation of experience.

Tyrrell's final statement is his last book, *Christianity at the Cross-Roads*. It is interesting to speculate on the direction in which he might have moved if death had not intervened. In this last work he demonstrated that God has been revealed in a definitive way through 'the apocalyptic vision of Christ'. The Catholic Church has been faithful not only to the substance but to the form of Christ's apocalyptic vision. It has preserved the earthen vessel along with its heavenly treasure. Tyrrell asked: 'Ought we not to keep it while carefully distinguishing it from its contents?'[76] However, it should be recognized as a symbolic rather than a literal expression of the truth. He pointed out the dangers of a transitional state between consistent literalism and consistent symbolism. Tyrrell recommended that the symbolic character of the vision of Jesus be explicitly recognized and its meaning expressed by each age in its own language, with allowance always made for the inadequacy of any translation or interpretation. In this way the believer would be free to accept the prophetic truth of revelation without being bound to out-moded categories of thought.

Divine truth always comes to humankind in human thought-forms. The only test for revelation is the test of life. The creed is the collective result of the spiritual experience of Christians. It is the norm by which our own spiritual growth can be criticized. Its beliefs are in some sense sacramental. They express spiritual values under the form of historical or philosophical truth. The understanding attempts to reconcile these historical and philosophical assertions with the rest of human knowledge. However, more important than the intellectual form of a doctrine is its religious value. All forms are inadequate to express the mystery of the divine. It is only through analogies and symbols that we can express the inexpressible.

Catholicism As a Sacramental Religion

This awareness of the need to express the inexpressible in human ways gave Tyrrell a deep appreciation for the sacramental nature of Catholicism. In *External Religion: Its Use and Abuse*, a series of lectures to Catholic undergraduates given at Oxford in 1899, we have the clearest presentation of his understanding of Catholicism as a sacramental religion. Tyrrell probably would have changed and qualified many of his statements in these lectures, but he consistently maintained his basic argument in support of a sacramental religion in his later writings. His appreciation for the sacramental nature of Catholicism made his excommunication a particularly painful experience for him.

Tyrrell based his argument for a sacramental religion on the incarnation. God became man; the Word was made flesh; the invisible found expression in the visible. 'The sacred humanity of Christ is the sacrament of sacraments.'[77] He is for us what he reveals and signifies. Through his body, he redeemed the whole person, body as well as soul, the spirit through the flesh, the invisible through the visible. The Catholic Church is the religion of the incarnation, carrying on the work of redemption. The visible Church is an extension of the humanity of Christ, continuing his saving work by making use of the visible world, including the body with its senses and imagination as instruments of sanctification. Unlike some Puritan-type sects which condemn the material universe as evil, Catholicism embraces the material universe and uses it as a means of salvation. The Catholic Church continues the way chosen by God. 'As sacramental in principle, the religion of the Incarnation is consonant with the unchanging exigencies of human nature; it is the ideal religion of humanity.'[78]

A study of natural religions supports this need for religion to express the internal through the external. As a human being possesses a body and a soul, religions also need both the visible and the invisible. Attempts to develop merely spiritual or philosophical religions are unnatural. Every spiritual movement tends spontaneously to some kind of social institution. On the other hand, religions which stress the external can easily deteriorate into idolatry or superstition. Tyrrell argued that Catholicism is a supernatural religion built on humanity's natural religious instincts. It is of all religions the most human.

The need for both the internal and the external in religion is based on the very nature of the human person. Protestantism, with its stress on the principle of private inspiration and the liberty of the individual, tended to depreciate the visible Church through which Christ's teachings and sacraments come to each person. External aspects, such as dogmas, sacraments, rites, hierarchical order, were considered unnecessary or even harmful. All that was necessary was the soul and God. Tyrrell argued that this was not the way chosen by God and revealed in Christ. The visible Church is the divinely appointed instrument which mediates to us the mystical Christ. However, to emphasize only the external and to neglect the internal is an error, and one to which Catholicism is susceptible. The teachings of the Church and the administration of sacraments facilitate our approach to God. They do not excuse us from personal efforts. To use the external as an end in itself, and not as a means to the internal, is to abuse the sacramental principle.

Tyrrell distinguished between the invisible and the visible Church. The visible Church is the sacrament of the invisible Church. In *A Much-Abused Letter*, he referred to the visible Church as the 'effectual, if not altogether indispensible, sacrament' of the invisible Church.[79] The two are not coextensive. The invisible Church includes the whole communion of saints, 'the many-membered corporate Christ of all times and ages'.[80] All on earth who have Christ's spirit belong to this invisible Church. In his early writings, Tyrrell identified the visible Church with the Roman Catholic Church.

> It is the visible union of the faithful, under one visible head or government; understanding by the faithful those who with their lips and outward conduct subject themselves to the teaching and laws of the Church, in short, those who would be numbered in a census of Catholics. It is as definite an institution as the Roman or the British Empire, notorious in the history of the world for the last two thousand years.[81]

As the sacrament of the invisible Church, the visible Church symbolizes and effects incorporation with the invisible Church. It is a means, but not a guarantee, of union with the invisible Church. Through it we receive the Word of God and the sacraments. Tyrrell suggested that there can also be a membership of desire, similar to baptism of desire, through which the graces of actual membership in the visible Church may be secured by those outside the visible Church.[82]

In his later writings, Tyrrell was more aware of difficulties with the Roman Catholic claim to be the one, visible society through which all humanity can be incorporated into the invisible Church. He suggested that we learn to see in the Roman Catholic communion an 'as yet woefully abortive endeavour to bring forth this ideal of the "communion of Saints" made visible, made flesh'.[83]

Tyrrell grappled with the problem of how other Christian bodies and non-Christian religions are related to the Catholic Church. In *The Church and the Future* he asked: 'What is he [the Catholic] to think of the six-sevenths of the seeming religious life of the world that lies beyond that of his Church? Must he call it death?'[84] The traditional Catholic teaching, which made communion with the Catholic Church an essential condition for salvation, seemed intolerable. 'The same development of the Christian spirit itself, which makes intolerable the Calvinistic belief in the election by divine favouritism of a small handful from the reprobate multitudes of humanity, makes the official conception of Catholicism as the one and only religion equally intolerable.'[85]

This consideration led Tyrrell to examine other expressions of religious life. He accepted Harnack's assessment of the Eastern Churches as having an arrested development. They had been prevented from working out the Catholic principle to its logical conclusion because of their dependence upon the secular state. While keeping the Christian spirit alive, they did little to develop it.[86] Protestantism attempted to go back to the charismatic phase of Christianity, but to do so is to deny the reality of development. In rejecting institutional Christianity and accepting the Bible in place of the living Church, the past was made the rule for the present and the future. Tyrrell pointed out the inconsistency of rejecting the Church while accepting its view of the New Testament. In rejecting the collective mind of the Church and in stressing the freedom of the individual, Protestantism carried the principle of liberty to the point of contempt of authority. The result has been disintegration.[87] Anglicanism attempted unsuccessfully to work out a *via media* between Catholicism and Protestantism, between authority and liberty.[88] 'Official' Catholicism carried the principle of authority to the contempt of liberty.

Tyrrell continued to see in a reinterpreted Catholicism the ideal of a universal Christian society which could gather together the fragments of a shattered Christendom. While Christianity would see itself as the highest expression of the religious instinct of humanity, it would also recognize the right of other religions to exist. Absolute truth belongs to the future and lies outside history. The ideal of one universal religion must be as 'the thought of a land to which we ever journey, without hope of reaching it'.[89] The spirit of Christ is not limited to Christianity, nor to a visible Church. As the true light that enlightens every one who comes into the world, the spirit of Christ speaks to each person 'in the mysterious whisperings of conscience'.[90]

Although Christ does speak to each person in his or her own conscience, it is still important to belong to the visible Church in order to benefit from the collective spiritual experience of Christians past and present. Through the visible Church we are in contact with the whole mystical body. Christ lives on in the Church and finds in it a growing medium of self-utterance, ever complementing and correcting that of his mortal individuality.

> Thus it is through the instrumentality of the Church and its sacraments that His personality is renewed and strengthened in us; that the force of His spirit is transmitted and felt. The Church is not merely a society or school, but a mystery and sacrament; like the humanity of Christ of which it is an extension.[91]

As a sacrament, the Church is not invalidated by the 'beggarly elements' through which the spirit of Jesus is communicated.[92]

The sacramental nature of Catholicism should be seen as a sign of continuity with Jesus and the early Church. Jesus himself did not condemn all external worship, but only its abuse. He and his followers, as pious Jews, participated in the Jewish religion. When the early Christians were expelled from the synagogue, they did not cease to recognize the need for a visible expression of their religion. Borrowing from Jewish and Hellenic sources, the Catholic Church, like the creeds, is the fruit of the collective spiritual experience of past ages. The Church is the vehicle through which the individual can enter into this rich experience. It is not an end in itself, but a means towards union with the divine.

Catholicism As the Continuation of the Idea of Jesus

Historical criticism had raised the question: 'What is the relationship between Jesus as presented in the earliest New Testament writings and Catholicism?' There seemed little resemblance between the Roman Catholic Church and the Church of the New Testament, or between the Church of the New Testament and the ministry of Jesus and the Twelve. Tyrrell recognized the folly of attempting to go back to primitive Christianity, or of reducing Christianity to some supposed essence. He referred to the Liberal Protestant reduction of Christianity to 'the Fatherhood of God and the brotherhood of man' as 'Christianity in a nutshell'.[93] Tyrrell insisted that the kernel by itself was not enough; it had to grow throughout the ages, in order to meet the needs of different cultures. Critics, such as Harnack, Sohm and Sabatier, implied that Catholicism was in some sense a perversion of the gospel, necessary at the time, but nevertheless a departure from the original gospel. It was the husk which had grown around the kernel. In his colourful language Tyrrell described the Liberal Protestant view: 'The Pearl of Great Price fell into the dustheap of Catholicism, not without the wise permission of Providence, desirous to preserve it till the day when Germany should rediscover it and separate it from its useful but deplorable accretions.'[94] Tyrrell, like Loisy, tried to show that Catholicism is a true development of the idea of Jesus.

Modern scholarship had brought Christianity to a cross-roads. Liberal Protestantism was one response to the challenges facing Christianity. Tyrrell tried to work out a synthesis between the Liberal Protestant and the eschatological interpretations of the New Testament, or between what he called the inward-timeless view of the kingdom of God and the outward-future apocalyptic view. Gradually he became convinced, on critical grounds, that the eschatological school was historically correct, while the Liberal Protestant position was historically untenable. Tyrrell attempted to work out the implications of this conviction for Catholicism in *Christianity at the Cross-Roads*. In this last work, all the strands of his idea of Catholicism come together.

By setting the Christ of Liberal Protestantism over against the Christ of eschatology, Tyrrell tried to show that only the latter could be accepted on critical grounds. The Christ of eschatology expressed his idea in the form of an apocalyptic vision. Tyrrell asked whether the idea of Catholicism was a development of this idea:

> By the 'idea' of Jesus I mean, then, the religious idea in a certain stage of development, along a particular line. I ask myself: Is Catholic Christianity on the same line or, as Liberal Protestants suppose, on an entirely different line? Is it the outgrowth of the same branch, or did it fork off in the first century? Is it simply a Hellenic process, violently grafted into the Liberal Protestantism

of Jesus—the latter being interrupted at that point until the graft was broken off by criticism?[95]

Tyrrell set out certain similarities between the idea of Jesus and the idea of Catholicism. Both emphasized the other-worldly, the transcendental. Jesus had stressed the immediacy of the coming of the kingdom, an aspect which was necessarily dropped with the delay of the parousia. However, Tyrrell argued that this was more a stimulus than an essential element of the idea of Jesus. Catholicism continued to believe in the coming of the kingdom and to accept in a literal way the images of the Son of Man coming in glory. Both Jesus and Catholicism accepted the dualism of good and evil, of the kingdom of God and that of Satan. For Jesus and for Catholicism the material is the sacrament of the spiritual. Both accept the need for external worship. Eternal life is not a life of righteousness in this world, but a supermoral life in the next world. The moral life is but the condition for this supermoral life. Just as the Catholic expresses faith in the communion of saints, Jesus expressed his communion with Abraham, Isaac, Jacob, Moses, Elias and David. Jesus' understanding of his own nature, of his function, of miracles, of the eucharist are all similar to the Catholic understanding. Only one Catholic feature is missing in the teaching of Jesus, that is formal theology. Jesus expressed his idea in the form of an apocalyptic vision. The Church later translated this vision into conceptual form. Tyrrell concluded that in Catholicism all the leading ideas of Jesus, as these are determined by historical criticism, are to be found.[96]

The principal and original element of the gospel is the apocalyptic vision of Jesus. It is this which Catholicism has retained. The moral element, while contained within the gospel, is secondary and did not originate with Jesus. Liberal Protestantism is a continuation of the ethics adopted by Jesus. Catholicism is the continuation of the religious idea of Jesus. Jesus used the imagery of a first-century Jew. Catholicism has been faithful not only to the idea but even to the form used by Jesus. The refusal to recognize the symbolic character of the apocalyptic vision of Jesus had brought Catholicism into conflict with the modern mind. The Catholic modernist wanted its symbolic character to be recognized in a consistent way so that each age might embody the idea of Jesus in its own terms. The criterion for judging the fidelity of any embodiment is whether it preserves the idea of Jesus. Those who consider Jesus as a founder and teacher have been upset by attempts to put him back into the first-century Jewish milieu. However, those who possess his spirit can continue to recognize him as present throughout the ages. It is this spirit which is the true 'essence' of Christianity—this spirit which speaks to each person in his or her own conscience, is incarnate in Jesus and lives on in Catholicism.

TYRRELL'S IDEA OF
CATHOLICISM IN THE CONTEXT OF TODAY

In his earliest works, Tyrrell described his idea of Catholicism as a reality to be found in the Roman Catholic Church. As he became more aware of the problems raised by historical criticism, he offered his idea as an alternative interpretation for 'Catholicism as officially stated'. He argued that the wider interpretation was no less orthodox than the official one, while at the same time it was more in harmony with modern thought. His later experience with ecclesiastical authority destroyed his hope that such an interpretation would find acceptance in the Roman Catholic Church during his lifetime. However, he continued to hope that eventually it would be accepted. Towards the end of his life, Tyrrell presented the idea of Catholicism as an ideal struggling to come to birth. Only a complete transformation or a revolution could bring forth this ideal Catholicism from existing Catholicism. The spirit of Christ, which had saved the Church in the past from oppressors both within and without, could free the Church to be truly Catholic.

It seems that the Church in the last decades of the twentieth century is struggling to become 'truly Catholic'. As Rahner suggested, Vatican II can be interpreted as the first time the Roman Catholic Church expressed itself as a world Church.[97] However, the challenge that this entails confronts the Church at all levels and in all parts of the world. The ecumenical movement may also be interpreted as a struggle to reach a true Catholicity. Tyrrell's idea of Catholicism, presented in the context of the early twentieth century, can be helpful for the Church in the late twentieth century. The words of Karl Adam may well be applied to Tyrrell:

Though he be not understood by his own age, yet he is never

solitary. His thought, provided it be based on truth, will be taken into the life-stream of the Church and clarified in those pure waters, so that it may in some future time, in this stream and through it, become the fertilizing water of life for many souls.[98]

Tyrrell's method and much of his thought have entered into the life-stream of the Church. Whether this has happened because of Tyrrell, or in spite of him, is an interesting question and one which probably cannot be answered. However, it can be shown that a number of Tyrrell's questions and concerns are still with the Church today, and that the directions he suggested in which answers might be found are still worth exploring.

Tyrrell's method of using the scientific knowledge of his time, to support Christian faith while at the same time subjecting it to a critique, is used by many theologians today. Psychology and the social sciences are used as tools for reflecting on the experience of faith. Everything need not be accepted, but nothing should be excluded without testing its usefulness. Tyrrell's willingness to take from both the old and the new, to let go of the old when necessary and to live with a certain insecurity while working towards new answers can be helpful for those engaged in the theological enterprise today.

It is interesting to note that Rahner has suggested the same approach that Tyrrell used in addressing individuals, and for similar reasons. It is too soon to work out a complete systematic theology that is addressed to contemporary Christians; and yet questions need to be answered. An indirect method which can justify faith and respond to the demands of the individual conscience needs to be developed.[99] This task was what Tyrrell attempted in his *Much-Abused Letter*. Rahner uses this approach in his *Foundations of Christian Faith: An Introduction to the Idea of Christianity*, pointing out that from one point of view 'this indirect way is the more direct way because it proceeds more immediately from our own concrete and lived Christianity'.[100] Both Rahner and Tyrrell insist that one must begin with the person who is being addressed. Both express concern for 'Christians of tomorrow who already exist today'. These are not the cultural Christians of the past whose faith is supported by the sociological structures of society, but rather those who freely make a deliberate choice to believe.[101] Such persons need an intellectually honest justification for their Christian faith and for their Catholicism.

Tyrrell's conviction that Catholicism is *the* religion of humanity finds an echo in Henri de Lubac's excellent work, *Catholicism: A Study of Dogma in Relation to the Corporate Destiny of Mankind*. For de Lubac, as for Tyrrell, 'Catholicism is religion itself. It is the form that humanity must put on in order finally to be itself.' [102] Both refused to consider Catholicism as a sect. However, within Catholicism there can exist a great diversity. Tyrrell opposed any plan for reunion which would mean 'the formation of a gigantic sect leagued against the rest of the world, excluding and condemning five-sevenths of its religious life'.[103] He believed that the spirit of Christ was present among all peoples. It is a vision that found expression in Vatican II's *Dogmatic Constitution on the Church*:

> All men are called to be part of this catholic unity of the People of God, a unity which is harbinger of the universal peace it promotes. And there belong to it in various ways, the Catholic faithful as well as all who believe in Christ, and indeed the whole of mankind. For all men are called to salvation by the grace of God.[104]

Abandoning an exclusive, sectarian vision of Catholicism, Vatican II expressed the same view of Church which may be found in many of Tyrrell's writings. The Church as the Mystical Body of Christ, as the people of God, as the sacrament of salvation are all favourite images used by Tyrrell. They are basic in twentieth-century ecclesiology, but at the beginning of the century they were a refreshing change from the standard approach found in theological manuals.

Tyrrell's concern for the 'two-thirds of present humanity, and nine-tenths or far more of past humanity' who are not Christian was addressed by the Council Fathers.[105] The way in which God is already present among these people is a question which engages contemporary theologians. Rahner's 'anonymous Christianity' provides one approach to the question. It recognizes that most of the human family have only an implicit awareness of God's saving action through Christ and the Church which continues his mission, while Christians are those who know and can celebrate this salvation in Christ in an explicit way. Tyrrell expressed his solution to the problem: 'Hence all who are saved are saved through Christ, whose personality is that of the indwelling Spirit. Christianity has but brought the universal principle of salvation to its highest degree of force and explicitness.'[106]

Pope John XIII in his opening speech to the Council, delivered on 11 October 1962, distinguished between 'the substance of the ancient doctrine of the deposit of faith' and 'the way it is presented'.[107] One thinks of Tyrrell's efforts to separate revelation and theology. In its decree on 'Ecumenism', the Council Fathers refer to 'an order or "hierarchy" of truths, since they vary in their relationship to the foundation of the Christian faith'.[108] Again one thinks of Tyrrell, who wrote in his *Much-Abused Letter*, 'The truths by which you really live and grow are few and simple, and too fundamental to be involved in the fate of anything so contingent as a theological system.'[109]

Nicholas Lash, in his Introduction to his work, *Change in Focus: A Study of Doctrinal Change and Continuity*, writes: 'In a situation such as ours, it would be illusory to suppose that anyone has "the answers". It is enough for a pilgrim people, and it is no small thing, if we succeed in asking the right questions.'[110] A study of Tyrrell's understanding of revelation and dogma in the light of contemporary theology shows that he did ask the right questions. They are the questions with which the Council Fathers grappled in the *Dogmatic Constitution on Divine Revelation* and which have occupied the attention of theologians both before and after the Council. Tyrrell reminded the theologians of his day that all language is inadequate to express the mystery whom we call God. He insisted on the symbolic aspect of our religious language. He was concerned about the recipient of revelation and the relationship between the original revelation and our own Christian experience. He clearly recognized the need to distinguish between truth and its cultural expression, realizing that the conflict was between theology and the rest of knowledge, rather than between faith and knowledge. His solution was to separate revelation and theology, prophetic and scientific truth. He lacked the hermeneutical tools to work out an adequate solution, but he showed the need for a reinterpretation of doctrinal statements, a task which confronts theologians today.

In his Preface to *Christianity at the Cross-Roads*, Tyrrell wrote that the time had come 'for a criticism of categories—of the very ideas of religion, of revelation, of institutionalism, of sacramentalism, of theology, of authority, etc.'. It was his conviction that

> ... the Catholic Christian Idea contains, within itself, the power to revise its categories, and to shape its embodiment to its growth, and that such a transformation or revolution would be within the orderly process of its life—merely a step forward to a fuller and better self-consciousness from a confused and instinctive self-consciousness.[111]

Lash likewise suggests that we may have to integrate the concept of 'revolution', as well as 'evolution', in our understanding of the process of doctrinal development.[112]

Tyrrell took history seriously. As he wrote to von Hügel in March 1908: 'Our "Syntheses" and solutions have raised *theological* difficulties in solving *historical*; and they, the officials, have fastened on the former and ignored the latter.'[113] Neither the historical nor the theological difficulties were solved by *Pascendi*. Theologians like Rahner and Schillebeeckx are continuing to address the questions with which Tyrrell grappled.

Tyrrell's emphasis on Catholicism as a life to be lived permeates contemporary theology and is reflected in catechesis. There is an awareness that dogma, while important, must be seen in relationship to the whole life of a people. To begin with dogma in one's missionary effort (or in catechesis) is akin to teaching a language by beginning with its most theoretical aspect.[114] The new *Rite of Christian Initiation of Adults*, a rite that is being used as a model for catechesis, emphasizes the importance of initiating the catechumen into the life of a Christian community.[115] This life finds expression in worship and apostolic action as well as in a dogmatic tradition. To use Tyrrell's image, dogma is seen as the fruit rather than as the root of Christian living.[116]

Tyrrell demonstrated the possibility of a wider understanding of Catholicism which was open to the modern age. While not tolerated at the time, Tyrrell's belief that this was the spirit which dwelt 'deep down in the nethermost heart of the Catholic community' seems to have been vindicated.[117] His idea of a Catholic religion which would not be the religion of an elite nor of a particular culture, but which would truly be the religion of humanity continues to challenge the Christian Church. In order for this ideal to be realized it may be necessary to let go of aspects which no longer meet the needs of the Church. In this task of discernment Tyrrell's test of life can be helpful.

His love for Catholicism and his hope in its future can still inspire us:

> The very word 'Catholic' is music to my ears, and summons before my eyes the out-stretched all-embracing arms of him who died for the whole *orbis terrarum*. If the Roman Church still holds me it is because, in spite of the narrow sectarian spirit that has so long oppressed her, she cannot deny her fundamental principles; because, as a fact, she stands for the oldest and widest body of corporate Christian experience; for the closest approximation, so far attained, to the still far-distant ideal of a Catholic religion.[118]

6

Tyrrell's Understanding of Authority

No understanding of Catholicism is possible without a consideration of the question of authority. This is particularly true of Catholicism during the modernist period. Tyrrell's understanding of authority flows from and is an essential aspect of his idea of Catholicism. In his life and in his writings he was dramatically involved in a struggle over conflicting interpretations of authority. Maude Petre was convinced that 'if we were to sum up, under one word, the question on which George Tyrrell was eventually at war with ecclesiastical authority, it was that of authority itself'.[1] She saw this as the reason that he was considered by the officials as 'one of the most reprehensible of the leaders' of the 'great liberating movement'.[2]

Tyrrell argued that anyone who accepted the Church as the rule of faith was a Catholic. Protestantism accepts the authority of the Bible, while Catholicism looks to the living Church as its rule of faith. Both are 'religions of authority'. However, Protestantism stresses the principle of individual freedom in the interpretation of the Bible, whereas Catholicism emphasizes obedience to the Church. For Catholics the ultimate authority in religion is the Church.[3] However, the one dogmatic point which a Catholic may dispute without logical suicide is the rule of faith itself. What is its nature, limits and extent?

Tyrrell recognized the need for a conception of ecclesiastical authority which would be true to the nature of the Church, while incorporating the values of the new age. The post-enlightenment world placed a high priority on individual liberty and freedom. It had struggled to throw off absolute forms of government and had set up governments based on democratic principles. Was the Roman Catholic Church an anachronism in such a world? Tyrrell wanted to show that the Catholic principle of authority could be understood in a way that did not contradict the legitimate aspirations of contemporary culture and what he called 'the assured results of criticism'. His hope was for a

> ... rational conception of religious authority which will do no violence either to intelligence or conscience, which will deliver us from the lawlessness of liberal Protestantism on the one side, from the despotism of the Roman theologians on the other, and will realize a true synthesis of law and liberty—no mere juxtaposition of opposites.[4]

Tyrrell did not claim to have reached such a solution to the problem of religious authority. However, he was able to articulate the problem and to offer some fruitful reflections on the subject. One would look in vain for a systematic presentation of Tyrrell's conception of authority. Nevertheless, it is an underlying theme in all that he wrote after 1900. A number of his works are specifically on the question of authority: 'The Mind of the Church', *The Church and the Future*, '*Consensus Fidelium*', 'From Heaven, or Of Men?' and *Medievalism*.[5]

The relationship between what was happening in his life and his theology is particularly evident in his understanding of authority. His personal experiences with ecclesiastical authority stimulated his theological reflection on its nature, limits and extent. It also made him aware of what he considered to be a misunderstanding and an abuse of authority in the Church of his day.[6] His approach to the problem was more theoretical than practical, while he himself appeared more as a prophet than as a reformer.[7]

Tyrrell began by accepting and defending the reality of Catholicism, including the understanding and exercise of authority as he found it in the Roman Catholic Church of his day.[8] However, he pointed out that authority was often misunderstood and exaggerated by persons both within and without the Roman Church. Addressing himself to his English readers, Tyrrell tried to convince them that a true understanding of authority was not opposed to their love of liberty and freedom, although the abuse of authority clearly contradicted the English spirit.[9]

The Protestant-Catholic controversy had led to the popular belief that authority was the very essence of Catholicism. Tyrrell reacted against this misconception. He recognized that the question of authority was at the heart of the Protestant-Catholic controversy, but that Catholicism was more than simply the antithesis of Protestantism. Like de Lubac he refused to consider Catholicism as 'merely Protestantism turned inside out'.[10] The exaggerated emphasis given to authority had created a caricature of both systems. Protestantism was seen as the religion of private judgement, freedom and self-guidance. Catholicism was the religion of authority, obedience and discipline.

> For the outsider, Romanism is authority and nothing else but authority; authority created for its own sake, and as an end in itself, whose sole function is to cramp the intellect and to enslave the soul—a cross, if you like, invented for the torture and death of man's natural reason and will.[11]

Tyrrell tried to dispel this distorted view by insisting that authority in every society is but a means towards achieving the end of the society. It implies a directive, rather than a coercive power. As directive, authority is beneficial; it is repugnant only if it is unjustly coercive. Coercive authority has a secondary place within Catholicism, and the Church desires to minimize the occasions for its use. An external guide to truth is necessary for the unity of the Church. The lack of such a guide leads to disintegration and fragmentation, an effect which is observable among the countless Protestant sects.

Tyrrell began to see the need for 'a change of tactics' in the exercise of authority. The Church in which he found himself was still entrenched in the Counter-Reformation. The way authority is exercised in times of crisis is different from the way it is exercised at other times.

> In the day of battle and in the crisis where collective action is necessary, there is but one judgment and one will—that of the commander; every other will or judgment so far as it is original or different from his is simply in the way. But in the day of calm every opinion is listened to, every hindrance to spontaneity and initiation is removed; all the collective intelligence and spiritual energy of the community which before was pent up and useless, is now let loose and turned to account; and authority emulates the wisdom of a good rider in making the curb felt as little as possible.[12]

Tyrrell hoped that such a change would take place in the way that

102

authority is exercised in the Catholic Church as it moved out of a situation of oppression into an era of greater freedom.

Events in his own life and in the life of the Church soon shattered this hope. At the same time his introduction to historical criticism made him aware of the problematic nature of Catholicism as officially stated and commonly understood. He tried to work out an alternative interpretation which would be no less Catholic, while at the same time more likely to be acceptable to those outside the Roman Church.[13] This interpretation attempted to meet the challenges posed by the scientific study of religion, as well as the legitimate aspirations of the age. It tried to use the 'well-established facts' of historical criticism, not to discredit Catholicism but to support it. At the same time, it attempted to demonstrate that the Catholic principle of authority could be understood in a way that was compatible with such values as individual liberty, freedom and democracy.

Tyrrell's later writings, especially his correspondence, show him more and more disillusioned with the Roman Church and particularly with the way in which authority was interpreted and exercised. This disillusionment led him to reject the official interpretation as a distortion of Catholicism and a 'Vatican heresy'. At the same time, he continued to believe in and to defend what he considered the true Catholic principle of authority.[14]

NATURE OF ECCLESIASTICAL AUTHORITY

Catholicism as the life of a people forms the basis for Tyrrell's views on authority. He recognized the need for authority in humanity's religious search. He believed that this authority resided in the living Church. However, he insisted that it was a spiritual rather than a juridical authority.

Christ had led people, rather than coerced them. Using a number of texts from the gospels, Tyrrell showed that Christ came to serve. Those who follow him should do likewise. In contrast with the religious authorities of his day, Christ did not bind people, but invited them to a new way of life. He came not to impose laws, but to fulfil the law by giving us his spirit. Whereas the official interpretation of the mission of Christ assumed that it was dogmatic,

Tyrrell tried to show that it was prophetic and practical. It was this mission which was carried on by the early Church. In the New Testament, the authority exercised by the Church was spiritual rather than juridical. As a continuation of the spirit of Christ in the world, the Church could claim spiritual authority. Like Christ it could draw humanity into communion. Its authority, like his, should be pastoral and spiritual.

The official Church had misinterpreted the mission of Christ and its own mission. Christ did not come to bring a theological system, but to bring life. We do not see him 'defining theological points "under pain of eternal damnation" '. We see him inspiring others by his spiritual authority, his goodness, his love.[15] The Church, as the continuation of Christ in the world, shares his mission. Juridical authority is necessary if the Church is to be a great international power. However, this is not the mission of the Church. The mission of the Church, like the mission of Christ, is spiritual, and therefore its authority, like his, is spiritual.[16]

Tyrrell urged the separation of spiritual and temporal power, in the same way as he suggested the separation of revelation and theology. As he wrote to Wilfrid Ward, he saw the mixture of revelation and theology and of spiritual and temporal power as two manifestations of the same fallacy:

> I believe in revelation as a man of faith, I believe in theology as a man of reason; I believe each helps and depends on the other, but that the bastard progeny of their mixture is not *a priori* only, but historically the enemy of both, the parent of unbelief and ignorance. So, too, the authority of Church government is lawful and necessary, it is ministerial to spiritual authority—but it is not 'divine' in the same direct sense any more than theological thought is divine in the same sense as revelation.[17]

The confusion which resulted from identifying spiritual with temporal power was as great and as serious as that caused by identifying revelation with theology.

'From Heaven, or of Men?'

All authority comes from God or from Christ. The question for Tyrrell was: 'Where is this God or Christ who is the source of all authority?'

Is He immanent in the whole Church where we can ultimately learn His mind and will; or is He away beyond the stars where we can know nothing of either, save what the episcopate is given to know by some mysterious intuition? By what vehicle does He speak and communicate with us? By voices from the clouds or the gradual evolution of His Mind and Will in the collective spirit of mankind?[18]

Tyrrell argued that all authority comes from the spirit of God working within the spirit of humanity.

Tyrrell admitted that the language of Scripture supported an absolute interpretation of authority. A purely transcendent God is pictured bestowing authority on certain chosen individuals who are responsible to him alone. This interpretation has predominated during most of the history of the Church. However, Tyrrell argued that another interpretation was not only possible, but necessary. The age demanded it; Scripture and the history of the early Church could be used to support it.

Tyrrell maintained that an 'instinctive, unconscious (or sub-conscious) spirit of sane democracy' could be found in the New Testament.[19] Jesus, as a first-century Jew, used the language of transcendence, but his life and teaching implied the truth of divine immanence. He came as one who served and who called his disciples to serve. He taught that we will be judged by God, but by a God who is present in humanity—in the hungry, the thirsty, the naked. His promise was to be with his people, wherever two or three are gathered in his name.

The early Church was aware of the spirit of Christ present in the community, imparting gifts to each person for the good of the whole community. Authority was based on charism. Gradually the Church moved from this charismatic phase to the institutional phase. Charismatic leadership was replaced by an organized hierarchy. The democratic nature of authority within the Christian community was soon forgotten as the Church assimilated the imperial conception of authority current in society. Inspired leaders and prophets were replaced by officers whose authority was determined solely by their position.[20] This process of 'catholicizing' Christianity was necessary for the growth and development of Christianity. However, the Church should not be bound to forms of government which are anachronistic. A democratic interpretation and exercise of authority would enable Catholicism to enter into the new age.

Tyrrell, perhaps somewhat naively, saw democracy as the form of government which belonged to the twentieth century.

> One thing, at least, is certain, that democracy has come to stay; that to the generations of the near future any other conception of authority will be simply unthinkable; that if the authority of Popes, Councils, and Bishops cannot be reinterpreted in that sense, it is as irrevocably doomed as the theologies of man's childhood.[21]

Such a reinterpretation would bring Catholicism out of the Middle Ages and into the twentieth century. The officials of the Church feared a reinterpretation of their authority. This fear seemed to Tyrrell to be at the root of Rome's condemnation of Americanism and its opposition to the Christian-Democrat movement in Italy and to the Worship-Associations in France.[22] However, Tyrrell hoped that eventually the God who is immanent within the entire community would effect a reform based on the reinterpretation of existing institutions. 'So it is that we hope to return to the profoundly Christian and Catholic conception of the democratic character of all authority, whether civil or ecclesiastical, and of "the liberty wherewith Christ has made us free".'[23]

Locus of Authority

The source of authority is God present within the community. The locus of this authority is the whole community. Christ bestowed his spirit on the entire Church. Therefore, authority resides in the whole Christian people. Tyrrell argued that this was the position of the 'liberal' Catholic.

> For him the final authority is Christ as progressively revealed in the life of the Church from first to last; it is the *consensus fidelium*, the spirit of Christianity, as embodied in the present, past, and future multitudes of those who live the life. This however is a purely 'spiritual' and not a 'governmental' authority; it acts by suasion, not by law.[24]

The Church, not just the pope, is the *Vicarius Christi*. Tyrrell claimed that his constant aim was to defend the Catholic principle, *securus judicat orbis terrarum*, against every form of individualism. This included not only Protestantism, but the ultramontane interpretation of Catholicism, which placed all authority in one man rather than in the whole body. Any interpretation which ignored the collective experience of the whole Church destroyed the very essence of Catholicism. Tyrrell believed that Catholicism, properly understood, provided a view of authority which avoided the extremes both of individualism and of ecclesiastical dictatorship. All that he wrote concerning authority was a defence of what he considered the true Catholic principle, and a call for the reinterpretation of the Church's claim to divine authority in the context of the new age.

Historical criticism had challenged the Catholic Church's claim to divine authority. Using the methods and some of the conclusions of criticism, Tyrrell tried to justify the Church's claim, while at the same time revealing the weaknesses of the official Catholic interpretation. Tyrrell summarized the official position:

> Christ and His Apostles are held to have delivered the complete 'Depositum fidei' (i.e. the dogmas, Sacraments and other essential institutions of Catholicism as now existing) to St. Linus and the episcopate united with him; who in turn have transmitted it infallibly to their successors, without substantial increment but only more fully 'explicated', illustrated, systematised.[25]

Such an ahistorical view of the origin and development of the Church and of its authority no longer seemed tenable.

Tyrrell attempted to provide a reinterpretation which would take into account what he considered 'the facts' of history, while remaining faithful to the Catholic principle that divine authority resides in the whole Church. He accepted the eschatological view that Jesus and his apostles expected the imminent coming of the kingdom in glory and therefore would not have made any plans for an on-going institution. He also accepted as a historical fact the 'catholicizing' of early charismatic Christianity into an institutional religion, using the forms which were available at the time this process took place, while trying to show that the acceptance of these 'facts' need not imply a denial of the divine institution of the Church, nor its claim to divine authority.[26]

Tyrrell accepted, and defended, the development of early Chris-

107

tianity into Catholicism, pointing out that all spiritual movements tend to be transformed into permanent institutions. The Catholic or institutional phase of Christianity was the natural issue of the charismatic phase. Only in this way could Christianity be made permanent and universal.

The Protestant attempt to return to pre-Catholic Christianity was doomed to failure, since the conditions of early Christianity no longer existed. By its very nature the charismatic phase was transitory. The way that authority was exercised in those early days of enthusiasm could not be continued in the institutional phase. The same work which previously had been carried on by a few inspired prophets had to be continued by the whole body. 'Provisionally indispensable at first, the charismatic economy led necessarily to dissensions that called for the Catholicising of Christianity—for the storing up in an institution, the vesting in the whole community, of the fruits of that brief period of creative enthusiasm.'[27]

Catholicism had grown in a natural way. Abstracting from any belief in an infallible teaching authority, Tyrrell tried to show how the course of the Church's history was the fulfilment of a divinely ordained scheme, analogous to the natural process of organic growth.[28] Jesus had chosen to entrust his message to the living voice of the apostles. It was to be expected that they in turn would entrust their teaching to the living voice of some corporation which would succeed them. Gradually the Church passed from an inspired prophetic phase to an institutional phase, which claimed to be divinely assisted. The distinction between 'inspiration' and 'divine assistance' was not clear at the time, but the gradual change can be observed. The adequate receptacle for the deposit of faith was not the mind of the individual bishop, or of a local synod of bishops, but the mind of the universal Church, which is discerned, formulated and declared in ecumenical council. Whereas separately they were fallible, joined together they claimed to be infallible. Thus the Church, as a living organism, has grown and developed from a small group of disciples gathered in Jesus' name to a highly-organized institution. Yet even as there is an identity between the baby and the adult, the mind of the infant Church lives in the maturer mind of the present Church. Since this development follows the psychological laws of an individual's spiritual development, it is divine in the way that all natural processes are divine.

When Tyrrell referred to the 'mind of the Church', he did not mean the average opinion of the faithful, but rather a divinely guided consensus that develops slowly within the Church and is finally expressed by an ecumenical council or by the pope, who acts as the voice of the Church. It is the voice of the people, not that of the populace or crowd. It includes the whole Church, priests and laity, as well as pope and bishops.[29]

The development of the mind of the Church takes place as progressive and conservative forces within the Church struggle with one another. Both forces are necessary. Change is effected only when individuals dissent from the official judgement because they see it as no longer adequate. Although at the time these individuals may be condemned, their ideas are gradually adopted. Such a system may repress a great deal of creative thought and effort. It nevertheless has a 'selective' value in eliminating mediocrity. 'Only the strongest, the best, and the most prudent can without disaster force their way through the barriers and barbed wires opposed to every departure from the customary and traditional.'[30]

Divine authority belongs to the *consensus fidelium* as the embodiment of the results of the collective labour of the Church up to the present. It is the rule of faith to which each individual must conform. Even the prophets, when they claim to have assimilated and transcended it, must be judged by this rule. In colourful language, Tyrrell summed up his conviction that authority resides in the whole people:

Authority, then, is not an external influence streaming down from heaven like a sunbeam through a cleft in the clouds and with a finger of light singling out God's arbitrarily chosen delegates from the multitude, over and apart from which they are to stand as His vice-gerents. Authority is something inherent in, and inalienable from, that multitude itself; it is the moral coerciveness of the Divine Spirit of Truth and Righteousness immanent in the whole, dominant over its several parts and members; it is the imperativeness of the collective conscience.[31]

Ecclesiastical Inerrancy and Papal Infallibility

Since the locus of ecclesiastical authority is the whole Church, the question of papal infallibility must be seen in the larger context of ecclesiastical inerrancy. Tyrrell accepted ecclesiastical inerrancy, but insisted on the need for its reinterpretation, which he suggested should be done in the same way as the reinterpretation of the meaning of scriptural inspiration. Tyrrell argued that historical criticism was making it more and more difficult to support a miraculous view of scriptural inspiration. 'God is the author of Sacred Scripture' was not understood in the same way by many Christians at the beginning of the twentieth century as it had been by St Augustine. A development in understanding was taking place. Tyrrell used Coleridge's argument that it was the spirit of the Bible as a whole, rather than detached words and sentences, which was infallible, but he extended this principle to the whole Catholic tradition, of which Scripture is a part. Just as it is possible to present either a miraculous or a non-miraculous conception of scriptural inspiration, so can ecclesiastical inerrancy be considered in either a miraculous or a non-miraculous way. Tyrrell argued for a natural, non-miraculous, divine activity, guiding the Church in all aspects of its tradition. God acts not directly but indirectly, through the spirit present in the whole Church.[32]

Tyrrell suggested that the belief that the pope had a special miraculous teaching authority was really more Protestant than Catholic. Authority based on a special individual charism was opposed to the Catholic principle, *securus judicat orbis terrarum*. It was, like Protestantism, an attempt to go back to pre-Catholic Christianity, when leaders were inspired and possessed charismatic gifts.[33] Tyrrell admitted that the Vatican decrees on papal infallibility were ambiguous. He sympathized with Döllinger and others who questioned the validity of Vatican I. While agreeing that it was neither free, truly representative, nor unanimous, he argued that the same thing could be said about other ecumenical councils. In *Medievalism* he stated that he accepted the validity of the council, but urged a wider interpretation of its decrees than that which had gained acceptance in the Church of his day.[34] He called his interpretation 'amended Gallicanism'.

Tyrrell agreed with Harnack and Sabatier that 1870 was the

logical outcome of the catholicizing process.[35] Papal supremacy was a means towards unity. However, too often unity was confused with uniformity, and spiritual supremacy with juridical supremacy.

Papal infallibility must be viewed within the context of the whole Church. The spirit had been given to the whole Church to preserve her from error. The pope, as the voice of the Church, had an important function within the Church. However, the exaggerated position assigned to him by theologians of the ultramontane school needed to be corrected.

> The Pope as Czar and absolute theocratic Monarch by divine right must, under the logic of the Christian idea, give place to the Pope as really, and not only in name, the 'Servus Servorum Dei', as the greatest, the first-born among many brethren only because he is the most widely and universally serviceable and ministrant.[36]

Tyrrell's writings pointed out some ways in which the exaggerated position of the papacy could be rectified: the recognition of the place of the episcopacy within the universal Church, a more active role for the laity, a clear recognition of the limits of ecclesiastical authority, and the acceptance of criticism and dissent within the Church.

The Role of Officials

If authority resides in the whole body, what is the role of the pope and bishops? Tyrrell saw them as the official guardians of tradition. They are the witnesses and representatives of the collective mind of the Church. It is their task to sift the tradition, to gather up, synthesize and proclaim the *consensus fidelium*.[37] They also have the right and duty to impose it on the individual believer, with an authority that is moral and not purely intellectual. Tyrrell saw this as the difference between his own position and that of Sabatier, who treated church authority as purely intellectual and subject simply to the criteria of collective testimony.[38]

The pope and bishops are representatives of the corporate mind of the Church. They do not represent their own minds and wills, nor are they delegates of their flocks. The use of majority vote, such as was used as Vatican I, seemed to Tyrrell to be the invention of

111

men who had lost the sense of the Church as a single living organism.[39] The pope symbolizes the unity of the local bishops with the universal Church. To be united with Rome is to be united with the whole Church. However, the pope had been separated from the rest of the Church, while the bishops had become mere delegates of the pope. Tyrrell recognized the proper place of the local Church and of the bishop. 'The whole Church lives and speaks in each united part.' [40] There cannot be two Churches, a local and a universal Church, or two voices, the pope's and the bishop's. There is but one Church and one voice. The voice of each bishop, united with Rome, is the voice of Peter.

Tyrrell reacted strongly against any ecclesiology which divided the Church into two components: an active *ecclesia docens* and a passive *ecclesia discens*.[41] In the beginning there had been not a teaching Church and a learning Church, but a teaching Church and a learning world. Every Christian was a teacher and an apostle.[42] While admitting that the distinction between the Church teaching and the Church taught might be useful, Tyrrell pointed out the ways in which the terms were misused. The role of officials must be seen in the context of the whole Church. The Christian people freely submit to the government of officials who have been chosen to carry out certain functions for the good of the whole body. Tyrrell admitted that officials are necessary and supported the episcopal system. However, he also pointed out:

> We must concede, in deference to history, that it was not framed at a stroke by the word of Christ, and that it grew naturally under stress of the conflict between the Church and her environment. Yet as the spontaneous creation of the united Christian people, the episcopal system has an indirectly divine character that must be lacking to systems since elaborated by any separated group of Christians.[43]

While admitting that the claim to apostolic succession, as commonly understood, might be questioned by critics, he was convinced that history supported a continuity within Catholicism from the Apostolic Church to the present.

Although not an exegete himself, Tyrrell was critical of the kind of exegesis used to defend the official interpretation of authority. He argued that what was said to the apostles could not be applied in the same way to the pope and bishops. The former were inspired, while the latter were 'divinely assisted'. Tyrrell also believed that a too literal acceptance of the metaphor which called the Church a kingdom was responsible for a false view of Church, and of the role of church officials.[44]

The Church is greater than the episcopacy or the papacy. The centralization of authority in one person had removed the pope from the rest of the Church. Extreme ultramontanism took away the authority of the bishops and prevented them from fulfilling their proper function as the representatives of the corporate mind of the Church. Tyrrell had strong words to say about this situation, calling it a 'theological heresy and historical ignorance'.[45] He argued that 'the whole constitution of the Church has been turned upside down by this new-fashioned individualistic interpretation of papacy'.[46] The solution which he proposed was to turn 'the pyramid which is now unstably poised on its infallible apex' back onto its base.[47] This position would reflect once more the Catholic principle that authority resides in the whole Church, and that the pope and bishops are the witnesses and the representatives of the collective mind and will of the Church.

Role of the Laity

Even in his early works, Tyrrell argued for the active involvement of the whole Church, laity as well as clergy. He was particularly concerned with the educated laity. What was their role in the Church? Tyrrell refused to assign them a passive role, 'simply paying their fare and sitting idly as so much ballast in the bark of Peter'.[48] They, as well as the clergy, were called to let their light shine, to be the Church present in the world. As leaders, they helped to form public opinion. They had a responsibility for the uncritical multitudes. If Catholicism were to live, there must be an informed Catholic laity who could appropriate the tradition in an intelligent and creative way. Tyrrell insisted that the Church's infallible guidance was not a substitute for one's own judgement, but a rule or instrument for its formation and development. In his *Much-Abused Letter* he encouraged his correspondent to take an interest in religious questions.

Every educated layman, without being a theological expert, ought to be interested in theology, and ought to be competent—more competent perhaps than a pure theologian—to criticise its bearings on knowledge in general, and certainly on any department of knowledge in which he himself happens to be an expert.[49]

The lack of interest in religion on the part of lay Catholics seemed to Tyrrell to be a result of authoritarianism within the Church.

Tyrrell hoped that a change would take place based on a return to the true Catholic principle of authority. Such a change would be faithful to the Catholic tradition, as well as sensitive to the democratic aspirations of the age. Tyrrell did not advocate the laicization of the Church or the subjection of the clergy to the laity. He was opposed to anti-clericalism. He insisted that everyone within the Church—hierarchy, clergy and laity—should be subjected 'to that formless Church, to whose service the hierarchic institution is but instrumental, from which its authority is derived, to which it is responsible, by which it is reformable'.[50]

Tyrrell appreciated the contribution of the individual Christian to the life of the Church. Through the gifts of each person, the Church is enriched. In addition to the official *ecclesia docens* there is also an unofficial *ecclesia docens* made up of persons with personal rather than official authority. These persons, no less than the officials, contribute to the life of the whole body.[51]

For Tyrrell, the laity was not something added on to his ecclesiology; rather it was central to his ecclesiology. The Church is the whole Christian people, some of whom are delegated to perform certain functions for the whole body. These officials represent the entire Church, which acts through them. The Spirit of Christ immanent in the Church bestows his authority on the whole body. 'In her minister, however designated or set apart, it is the Church herself, it is Christ and the Spirit of Christ immanent in the whole body, Who baptises and absolves, and consecrates and anoints, and teaches and rules.'[52] The laity share in the priesthood and in the authority of Christ.

Tyrrell hoped that the laity would be instrumental in effecting a new understanding of authority within the Church. Since their perception of authority was democratic, in time the democratic interpretation of ecclesiastical authority would replace the absolute interpretation which characterized the existing Roman Church.[53]

LIMITS AND EXTENT OF ECCLESIASTICAL AUTHORITY

Ecclesiastical authority had been interpreted in an absolute way which left little room for individual freedom or personal responsibility. Obedience was often considered *the* great virtue. Critics such as Harnack, Sohm and Sabatier illustrated how this situation had developed. They saw this emphasis on obedience as the very essence of Catholicism. Tyrrell considered it the abuse of Catholicism. The Catholic accepted the Church as the rule of faith, but its authority was not unlimited. The limits and extent of ecclesiastical authority needed to be clearly delineated.

Tyrrell was concerned about the relationship between ecclesiastical authority and scientific freedom. Was the scholar free to pursue his studies, or was he hampered by the Church's claim to be the judge of truth? Was the Christian intelligence held captive to the Christian conscience? Was there room for sincere criticism and dissent within the Church? If Catholicism were to be a vibrant force in the contemporary world, these questions had to be considered and answers worked out which would be faithful to the Catholic tradition and responsive to the legitimate aspirations of the age.

Scientific Freedom

The Church recognized the contribution of modern science and taught that there could be no real contradiction between faith and reason. However, the Church proclaimed herself to be the judge of scientific truth.[54] This claim was based on a view of truth as eternal and unchangeable. In the light of a more dynamic view of human knowledge, such a claim was becoming more and more difficult to maintain.

The scientific spirit of the age demanded that each science be allowed to develop freely according to its own method and subject matter. This applied not only to the natural sciences, but also to the scientific study of religion, to scripture studies, historical criticism, the comparative study of religions, and even to theology.

In order to maintain the Church's authority over religious truth, and at the same time respect the rights of science, Tyrrell proposed the recognition of two orders of truth, the prophetic and the scientific. Each has its own proper sphere. Revelation belongs to the prophetic sphere, and as such it is entrusted to the authority of the Church. Science has its own sphere which should be recognized and respected. This distinction between prophetic truth and scientific truth would liberate all sciences, including theology, from ecclesiastical authority. By placing the realms of authority and science on two different planes, collision would no longer be possible.[55]

Tyrrell recognized the Church's role as the divinely assisted guardian of the normative apostolic revelation. '*Depositum custodi* is the substance and the limit of her teaching-office and authority.' [56] In order to protect the *depositum fidei*, the Church had to interpret this revelation for subsequent ages. This interpretation took the form of dogmatic statements using the scientific categories of the particular age which was being addressed. Tyrrell maintained that later generations of Christians need only accept the protective significance of these dogmatic statements, or what he called their 'prophetic truth'. They should not be bound to accept the scientific categories in which this truth found expression. By recognizing and exercising its proper role, as the guardian of revelation, the Church would be faithful to its prophetic mission. By no longer claiming divine authority over the scientific categories used in its dogmatic statements, it would recognize the autonomy of science, as well as the limits of its own authority.

Tyrrell was particularly concerned with theology as a science. He opposed a theology which identified itself with Christian faith and claimed to be infallible. Faith is not theological orthodoxy. A theology which identifies itself with revelation strangles the intellect and forces the believer to accept outmoded forms of thought. Tyrrell called such a theology 'theologism'.

> I will not give the honourable name of theology or science to a hybrid system which, applying logical deduction to the inspired and largely symbolic utterances of prophecy, imposes its conclusions in the name both of revelation and of reason, as binding at once on the conscience and on the understanding; which bullies the mind when it cannot persuade it, and supplements argumentative insufficiency by moral, and even external coercion.[57]

Theology should be free to develop according to its own method, and its subject matter, which is revelation and dogma. Its task is to translate the imaginative language of prophecy into the concep-

116

tual language of contemporary thought. Like any science, it belongs to the jurisdiction of observation and reflection and is a matter not of faith but of understanding. The recognition of the autonomy of theology as a science would free it to develop independently and would reconcile it with the rest of human knowledge.

Tyrrell recognized that his synthesis was incomplete. 'To pretend that this synthesis is complete or wholly satisfactory would be to condemn it as unworthy of serious consideration. There is no final truth in such complex matters; only a truth of tendency and direction.' [58] Loisy had insisted on the separation of history from faith; Tyrrell urged the separation of theology from faith. Both men struggled for scientific freedom. Both wanted the Roman Catholic Church to recognize the limits of its authority and to allow sciences, including theology, to develop freely according to their own methods. A refusal to do so would seriously inhibit the work of Catholic scholars as well as prevent the Roman Catholic Church from assuming its place in the modern world. As with many of the problems of this period, the solutions proposed may not have been adequate, but the questions and concerns articulated by Tyrrell and by Loisy remain with the Church today.

Criticism and Dissent Within the Church

In his insistence upon the limits of ecclesiastical authority, Tyrrell maintained the right of the individual to criticize and even to dissent from the official teaching of the Church. He believed that one could combine a strong loyalty to Catholicism with both criticism and dissent. In fact, loyalty and love for the Church might compel a person to reject its present form. As long as Catholics believed themselves to be in communion with the spirit of the whole Church, they could ignore the views of the officials for a time, a situation that would be comparable to that of the conscientious English pro-Boer during the Chamberlain era.[59]

Tyrrell argued that there was a 'blameless dissent' which was necessary for the development of the *consensus fidelium*. Some persons see more deeply into the mind of the Church.

> Deferential within the limits of conscience and sincerity to the official interpreters of her mind, they must, nevertheless, interpret such interpretations in accordance with the still higher and high-

est canon of Catholic truth; with the mind of Christ. It is He who sends us to them; not they who send us to Him. He is our first and our highest authority. Were they to forbid the appeal, their own dependent authority would be at an end.[60]

Such a view was not accepted by the Church of Tyrrell's time, with its stress on uniformity and obedience. 'The dissident is considered *ipso facto* to be a bad Catholic or none at all.' [61]

Many people, both within and without the Roman Church, questioned Tyrrell's claim to be a Catholic, after his rejection of the encyclical *Pascendi*. To the question 'Can such a person call himself a Catholic?' Tyrrell replied:

> No, if Catholicism is a theory; yes, if it stands for that historical community through whose fortunes and fluctuations and errors and experiences the truth is slowly threshed out. In that view the present crisis is a normal step in that process, an assurance of vitality. Pandemonium may endure for a night—but peace cometh in the morning.[62]

Tyrrell had a strong belief in the primacy of conscience and the importance of inward liberty. He believed that there was room within the Catholic understanding of authority for freedom of conscience. The fact that it was not present within the Roman Church pointed to the abuse of the Catholic principle of authority. In all his writings, there is an effort to reconcile inward liberty with Catholic unity. A reinterpretation of authority which no longer insisted on a rigid uniformity, but which allowed for just criticism and even dissent, would respect personal liberty and Catholic unity. Such a reinterpretation would enable the Church to move forward into the future.

RECOGNITION OF
THE ABUSE OF ECCLESIASTICAL AUTHORITY

Throughout Tyrrell's writings there are numerous references to what he termed the abuses of Catholicism. Such abuses included superstition, traditionalism, dogmatism, collectivism. However, the greatest abuse which he perceived in the Church of his day was the abuse of the Catholic principle of authority. Tyrrell used different words to describe this abuse: ecclesiastical absolutism, ultramontanism, Vaticanism, authoritarianism, sacerdotalism, Jesuitism. Instead of the Catholic principle, *securus judicat orbis terrarum*, authority had become centred in one individual, who as the 'Divine Teacher' ruled over the whole Church. Tyrrell saw this situation as an exaggerated interpretation of the decree *Pastor Aeternus*. In his earlier writings, he suggested an alternative to what had become the official interpretation of authority. Gradually he became convinced that the official interpretation was an abuse and a heresy. He wrote to his friend, Robert Dell, in January 1907: 'I could not stay in the Roman Communion if I had to accept the new Vaticanism as part of the system. I can endure it as a heresy or disease.'[63]

As Tyrrell pointed out, monarchical absolutism had been imported from the civil society into the Church in an age when no other form of government was possible. However, for the Church to continue to hold to such 'medievalism' would cut the Church off from contemporary society. The concentration of authority in one individual not only was opposed to the democratic values of the modern age, but was contrary to the nature of the Church and to the Catholic idea. It confused spiritual and juridical authority, making authority an end in itself, rather than a means of promoting the life of the whole Church. Finally, and most importantly, the spirit of absolutism was completely contrary to the spirit of Christ.

Tyrrell blamed the theologians who supported the extreme view of papal authority. It seemed that the *consensus fidelium* was being replaced by a *consensus theologorum*. These were the men whom the pope consulted, the ones who had the task of 'thinking for the pope'. Tyrrell referred to them as 'Scribes and Rabbis of the New Law'.[64] They had 'fabricated the whole present theology of authority' and imposed it on the whole Church through authorized catechisms and seminary manuals.[65] Tyrrell compared this powerful governing minority within the Church to a dominant political party and tried to distinguish it from the whole Church, although he admitted to von Hügel that the distinction was unreal when the majority clearly supported the officials.[66] As the bureaucracy of the Church, claiming privileges based on their office, they acted as the channel through which the pope communicated with the rest of the Church. 'Popes come and go; but this overgrown bureaucracy that exploits the papacy abides unchanged as to its spirit, its method, its ends.'[67]

Tyrrell recognized that even good people could be involved in a corporate egotism. Just as the Pharisees at the time of Christ prided themselves that they were fulfilling the Law, the Roman officials believed that they were fulfilling God's will.[68]

In describing what he saw as the abuse of the Catholic principle of authority within the Roman Catholic Church of his day, Tyrrell used strong language.[69] He called Pius x a heretic and a schismatic. He suggested that the Pope was leading the Church towards shipwreck and that it was his duty to disobey. 'There are times when a soldier is *bound* to disobey—if he knows his officer is drunk or mad or misinformed. If his venture succeeds he is crowned; if not, he is shot. I shall probably be shot, *"aber ich kann nicht anders"*.'[70]

Tyrrell claimed that he was right, and the official Church, as well as those who followed the official teaching, were wrong. He called for a new understanding of ecclesiastical authority which would be faithful to the Catholic principle, *securus judicat orbis terrarum*. It would recognize the spiritual nature of ecclesiastical authority and acknowledge that this authority belongs to the whole Church. At the same time, it would acknowledge the limits and the extent of this authority.

TYRRELL'S UNDERSTANDING OF AUTHORITY IN THE CONTEXT OF TODAY

Tyrrell boldly tackled many of the difficult questions concerning ecclesiastical authority with which the Roman Catholic Church still wrestles. Some of his insights have been incorporated into Roman Catholic theology and praxis. Although he was responding to a particular situation in the Church, his ideas can be fruitfully reflected upon in the light of the changes which have taken place, not only in the Church but in society, during the past seventy-five years.

The reform that Tyrrell called for involved not the replacement of the existing structures within the Church, but simply the reinterpretation of authority.

There is no need of violent revolution, but only of a quiet, steady re-reading and re-interpretation of existing institutions. For what we have to combat has come about by a like noiseless process of misinterpretation. We need not destroy or even invert the hierarchical pyramid; we need only regard it from above instead of from below.[71]

This reinterpretation of authority would take into account the results of biblical and historical criticism, as well as the democratic sensitivity of the age. Tyrrell argued that 'facts' could not be ignored. To tell lies in order to protect the truth is always wrong. Just as 'facts' were making it necessary to rethink the meaning of the inspiration of the Bible, 'facts' demanded a rethinking of the authority of the Church. It was becoming more and more clear that Christ did not found a hierarchic Church but a small group of followers who subsequently, under the guidance of his Spirit, organized themselves into the Catholic Church. He did not commission some of them to teach and rule over the rest, but all of them to go and teach all nations.[72] A reinterpretation of ecclesiastical authority in the light of such 'facts' of historical criticism and the democratic aspirations of the age would strengthen rather than weaken the Church's claim to divine authority.

Vatican II did regard the 'hierarchical pyramid' from above instead of from below, and in so doing it provides a basis for the reinterpretation of ecclesiastical authority. Instead of beginning with the hierarchical structure of the Church, the *Dogmatic Constitution* began with the mystery of the Church as the people to whom God communicates himself. It is only in the light of the whole people of God that ministry within the Church is considered. All ministers 'who are endowed with sacred power are servants of their brethren, so that all who are of the People of God, and therefore enjoy a true Christian dignity, can work toward a common goal freely and in an orderly way, and arrive at salvation'.[73] Authority is clearly seen in terms of service to the whole Church, not in terms of domination or personal privilege. The emphasis is on the spiritual nature of this authority, which exists 'for the nurturing and constant growth of the People of God'.[74] The *Constitution* then situates the petrine and episcopal ministries within the context of the whole Church. 'The Roman Pontiff, as the successor of Peter, is the perpetual and visible source and foundation of the unity of the bishops and of the multitude of the faithful.'[75] The bishop fulfils the same task in his particular church. At the same time, as a member of the college of bishops, the individual bishops share with the pope supreme authority over the whole Church. Tyrrell, who complained that the pope had been cut off from the rest of the Church and that bishops had become 'purely ornamental', would have rejoiced at the efforts of Vatican II to redress the imbalance which had developed as a result of an over-emphasis on papal authority.

Vatican II considered the relationship between pope and bishops, between universal and local Church. The working out of these relationships is an on-going task. How much centralization and uniformity is necessary or desirable? As Tyrrell insisted: 'The whole Church lives and speaks in each united part.'[76] There cannot be two Churches or two voices.

How is this one voice of the whole Church to be discerned? Do lay Catholics have a part to play in this discernment process, or is their task one of accepting whatever is presented by pope or bishop? Newman in 1859 had referred to the consensus of the laity throughout Christendom as 'the voice of the infallible Church', but his view had been considered dangerous.[77] Vatican II attributed an infallibility of faith to the people of God as a whole. 'The body of the faithful as a whole, anointed as they are by the Holy One, cannot err in matters of belief.'[78] However, as has been pointed out by Rahner, statements such as this made in chapters 2 and 4 of the *Constitution on the Church* were not related with statements on the hierarchical structures presented in chapter 3.[79] Theologians continue to reflect upon the relationship between different segments of the Church in an attempt to overcome the division between an active *ecclesia docens* and a passive *ecclesia discens*. Schillebeeckx describes what may be considered an ideal:

> It is only in the unanimity of the whole community of the Church, guided and accompanied by the world episcopate in its unanimous interpretation of faith, together with the office of Peter as the keystone of the vault of the great *koinōnia* of the same faith, hope and love, that any new theological interpretation is authenticated as a contemporary understanding in faith by the hallmark of the Holy Spirit, the living principle, always present here and now, of *anamnesis*, or calling to mind in faith and faithfulness to the gospel.[80]

How such unanimity is to be achieved is another question.

At least on the level of theory, progress has been made in recognizing the rightful role of the laity within the Church. As Congar insisted in his important work, *Lay People in the Church*, it is not a matter of adding a paragraph or a chapter to one's ecclesiology. 'At bottom there can be only one sound and sufficient theology of laity, and that is a "total ecclesiology".' [81] Vatican II in its *Constitution on the Church* did present such a 'total ecclesiology'. The embodiment of this ecclesiology in the local Church as well as in the universal Church still needs to be effected. Tyrrell's words can be reflected upon with profit in a number of contemporary situations: 'To retain them or to win them back we must restore them to their original active participation in the Church's life of which they have been deprived by the gradual prevalence of the absolutist over the democratic interpretation of priestly authority.' [82]

Tyrrell recognized that at times individuals have an obligation to dissent from a position taken by the Church. He found himself in this difficult situation, when compelled by his love for the Church he had to disagree with its policy. As early as 1901 he wrote to Maude Petre: '. . . indeed it is impossible to unsee what we have once seen.'[83] He saw dissent as the way change is effected: 'History shows us that all substantial advance has been the work not of officials, but of individuals, almost in opposition to officials; not of the system, but of those who have to some extent corrected and modified the system.' [84] A study of the history of the Church in the twentieth century would substantiate this claim. Men such as Teilhard de Chardin, John Courtney Murray, Henri de Lubac and Yves Congar, who had resisted official teaching in the preconciliar period, contributed to the official teaching of Vatican II. Avery Dulles pointed out that by the acceptance of the contribution of these men, Vatican II implicitly taught the legitimacy of dissent.[85]

In the post-conciliar period, the issue which has provoked a great deal of theological reflection on freedom of conscience and the legitimacy of dissent from the official Church position has been the question of contraception. It may be asked whether in this matter the *sensus fidelium* has been taken into account in the formulation of Church teaching.[86]

Closely related to the question of criticism and dissent is that of the relationship between the theologian and the magisterium. Newman complained in the nineteenth century of the control of the Holy See on theology:

This age of the Church is peculiar—in former times, primitive or medieval, there was not the extreme centralization which now is in use. If a private theologian said anything free, another answered him. If the controversy grew, then it went to a Bishop, a theological faculty, or some foreign University. The Holy See was but the court of ultimate appeal . . . . There was a true private judgement in the primitive and medieval schools,—there are no schools now, no private judgement (in the *religious* sense of the phrase), no freedom, that is, of opinion. That is, no exercise of the intellect.[87]

Many theologians after him, including Tyrrell, have uttered the same complaint. Although theologians did play a crucial role in the preparation and carrying out of the Vatican Council, their role in relationship to the magisterium needs further clarification.[88] There is an awareness of the inadequacy of the view which restricts the magisterial function of the Church to the pope and bishops. Theologians do contribute to this function. On the other hand, their task is not one of simply repeating official Church teaching. They need the freedom to ask questions, to explore new ideas, to criticize and even dissent from official positions. This should be carried out within the ecclesial community, a community which recognizes and appreciates their contribution. It is sad that Tyrrell and many other theologians have lacked this support from the Church which they serve.

Tyrrell recognized the need both for institutional, official authority and for authority based on expertise or charism. The relationship between these two authorities can be and often has been a source of tension in the life of the Church. This tension need not be seen as a destructive force, but can contribute to the life of the Church. This view is expressed by Rahner:

Side by side with the official function which is transmitted in a juridical manner, there is and must be the charismatic and the prophetic in the Church which cannot be officially organized right from the start but must, in all patience and humility, be given sufficient room for growth, even though its bearers are sometimes rather 'inconvenient'.[89]

It is important that the Church be open to the gifts which have been given to individuals for the good of the whole body.

No doubt Tyrrell's assessment of the abuses of authority would be shared by many Catholics today. The triumphalism of the past has been replaced by a greater awareness that we are members of a sinful Church. Tyrrell saw the evils that arose from too close an identification of the Church and the kingdom of God.

> The too literal acceptance of the metaphor which calls the Church a kingdom has led insensibly to the debasing of the heavenly reality to the level of its earthly symbol . . . . It is a literalising of His metaphor that has allowed the officialdom of the Church to be viewed, not merely as vested with the same kind of jurisdiction as secular judgments, but as an absolute theocratic monarchy of a type that our civilization has outgrown.[90]

Vatican II's image of a pilgrim people who are on the way to the kingdom and who are called to be a sign of that kingdom is helpful in providing a realistic view of the Church. In spite of both social and individual sin, the Christian believes that God is present with his people. It is this faith which inspires hope for Catholicism as a 'living and lived religion'.[91]

Progress has been made in working out relationships within the Church, but much remains to be done. The way in which authority is understood and exercised is crucial for the life of the Roman Catholic Church and for its relationship to other Christian Churches and to secular powers. Tyrrell's emphasis on the spiritual nature of ecclesiastical authority and on its locus within the whole community, as well as his insistence on the limits of authority and his condemnation of its abuse, can be helpful for the Church today.

7

Tyrrell's Vision, His Limitations and His Influence

Perhaps Tyrrell's greatest contribution was his vision of what Catholicism could be. Vidler describes him as 'a mystic, a prophet, a martyr'.[1] The term 'prophet' seems most appropriate.

Tyrrell considered the question of Catholicism in its historical, theological and pastoral dimensions. He was willing to face the challenges of his age, an age characterized by a new scientific spirit which took the form of historical criticism, and a new conception of authority. While not providing a systematic response to the question of Catholicism, he clarified some of the issues involved and offered suggestions for the direction in which solutions might be found.[2] In his suggestions, Tyrrell urged that Catholicism look into its own tradition, not merely that part of the tradition which had emerged during the post-Reformation, post-Vatican I period. He believed that there were forgotten elements within the Catholic tradition which needed to be reclaimed. He was particularly interested in the mystical element which seemed to have been largely overlooked in the Catholicism of his day. He appreciated the role of religious experience, especially the experience of the saints, as well as the collective experience of believers throughout the ages.

Along with an appreciation for the heritage of the past, Tyrrell maintained a critical stance towards the present. No period in the history of the Church should be absolutized. Tyrrell avoided the error of many nineteenth-century thinkers who naively believed in the inevitability of progress. He insisted that the age, as well as the Church, be criticized. He recognized the sinfulness of the Church and the abuses which marred the beauty of Catholicism. He tried to present an understanding of Catholicism which would be faithful to the tradition and which would take into account the new scientific knowledge and values of the modern age. At the same time, he called for the reform of abuses, especially the abuse of the Catholic principle of authority.

Using the past and the present, Tyrrell was able to suggest a vision of the Church of the future. His resolute refusal to accept a sectarian view of Catholicism, or to limit his understanding of Catholicism to its contemporary neo-scholastic expression, enabled him to widen his conception of Catholicism. He envisioned a Catholicism purged of exclusivism and authoritarianism. In a letter to von Hügel in which he repudiated the 'sectarian conception of Catholicism', he added:

> Whether one can be a Catholic without being exclusive is a question on which I and the secular traditions of the Roman Church differ; and no doubt the presumption is that the Catholic Church knows itself better than I know it. Still it is a presumption that may be rebutted.[3]

The events of the past twenty years suggest that Tyrrell was right. One can be a Catholic without being exclusive.

Tyrrell dreamed of a Catholicism that would be free from an obsolete philosophical system and from an outmoded ecclesiastical structure, a Catholicism free to respond as it had in the past to the legitimate demands of a new age, an age in which historical-mindedness was replacing a static world-view and democracy was overthrowing autocratic forms of government. He hoped that this Catholicism would grow out of the Catholicism of the past and present. Towards the end of his life, he reached the conclusion that this process would be one of transformation and revolution, rather than of evolution. However, even revolutions can be part of the natural course of development.

Like Judaism, Catholicism might have to die in order to enter into this new life.[4] Tyrrell noted the great changes which had occurred in the past. Might not the future hold even greater changes? 'The Church of the Catacombs became the Church of the Vatican; who can tell what the Church of the Vatican may turn into?'[5]

In all of Tyrrell's later writings, he fluctuated between hope in a future Catholicism and despair over the form in which Catholicism seemed imprisoned. He tried to distinguish for himself and others between the Catholicism in which he believed and what he saw as a heretical distortion of the Catholic idea. In January 1908, he wrote to a friend: '. . . I believe in the Roman Church so far as it is Christian and Catholic; I disbelieve in it as far as it is papal.' [6] In spite of condemnation, he considered it his duty to remain within the Roman Catholic Church in order to work for a renewed Catholicism. He had many friends among the Anglican clergy. The thought of settling into a little country rectory was attractive to him. Yet he felt that he had a duty to continue within the Roman Church, attempting to 'wake it up from its medieval dreams'.[7] He realized that he would not succeed but believed that through his failure and that of others renewal would finally come.

Tyrrell admitted that he did not know the form that a renewed Catholicism would assume, nor how nor when it would take place. In language which calls to mind Vatican II, he described his 'foolish dream' to Mercier:

> . . . the Catholic people represented by their bishops and their Pope will assemble, not to decide and impose points of theology, ethics and politics 'under pain of eternal damnation,' but to proclaim the gospel of God's Kingdom upon earth as it was proclaimed by Jesus Christ; to preach 'unity in essentials, liberty in non-essentials, charity in all things.' [8]

Pope John XXIII spoke of 'opening the windows'. Tyrrell had used the same image when he urged Cardinal Mercier to 'boldly throw open the doors and windows of your great medieval cathedral, and let the light of a new day strike into its darkest corners and the fresh wind of Heaven blow through its mouldy cloisters'.[9] Tyrrell referred to his Church of the future as a 'Utopian Church', but insisted that it would be Catholic in form. He saw it as a logical development of the idea of Catholicism. Writing to an Anglican friend he stated: 'I do not think we have yet the data to answer the problem of the religion of the Future; but I feel more and more that it will be a more thoroughly Christian and more thoroughly "Catholic" form of religion than yet realized.' [10] However, this Church of the future would transcend confessional differences. It would include everything that was spiritually fruitful for the Christian life. While everything was not needed by everyone, nothing should be discarded which had proven helpful for the spiritual life. 'The board spread for all must have every sort of fare, so that each may find something, though none can find everything, to his taste and requirement.' [11]

Tyrrell was convinced that there could be only one true religion. However, he saw this as a distant ideal towards which humanity moved, as a 'land to which we ever journey, without hope of reaching it'.[12] The spirit of Christ is already present in all people and in all religions. 'Christianity has but brought the universal principle of salvation to its highest degree of force and explicitness.' [13] However, Christianity had been 'hewn in pieces' by the sword of authority. Tyrrell's Church of the future would bring these pieces together once again. Such a reunion would take the form not of a 'giant sect' but of a truly universal religion. 'Reunited in a sanely interpreted Catholicism, the fragments of shattered Christendom might come together to their mutual reinvigoration, each lending to the others of its particular strength, and all taught by a dear-bought experience.' [14] This 'Church of the Future' would exist not for itself, but for the world. 'The cry of the spiritually starving multitudes, robbed of the bread of life, will at last drown the chatter of idle theologians, and wake the great heart of the Church to the weightier realities of the Gospel.' [15] It would emphasize Christian living more than Christian dogma. As the sacrament of Christ's continuing presence in the world, it would gently lead humanity to the explicit recognition of Christ. The unity to which it would invite all humanity would not be that of uniformity, but that of 'multiform variety in unity'.[16]

Authority in the Church of the future would clearly reside in the community. Officials would perform certain functions as a service to the whole community. They would see themselves as the representatives of the community in which Christ's spirit dwells, rather than the delegates of an 'absentee', transcendent God. The pope would be the *Servus Servorum Dei* in reality, not just in name. The episcopacy would assume its rightful responsibility for the whole Church. The teaching office of the Church would not be limited to the pope and bishops, but would draw upon the resources of the whole community. Priests and laity would recognize their own gifts and use them for the good of the entire body.

Was such a transformation of the Church possible? Tyrrell was aware of the difficulty in effecting change in an institution such as the Roman Catholic Church. In particular, he saw the Roman Curia as a block to reform.[17] Yet he was convinced that the Church of the future would arise out of the existing Roman Church. In the conclusion of his last book, he wrote:

> It is the spirit of Christ that has again and again saved the Church from the hands of her worldly oppressors within and without; for where that spirit is, there is liberty. Deliverance comes from below, from those who are bound, not from those who bind . . . . Are we not hastening to an *impasse*—to one of those extremities which are God's opportunities?[18]

Such, in broad outline, was Tyrrell's vision of what Catholicism could be. For the Church today, it no longer sounds like an impossible dream. We are able to accept the ecumenical perspective and pluralism which Tyrrell suggested. We recognize the evils of authoritarianism within the Church and have adopted the concept of authority as service to the Christian community. We are becoming more conscious of the whole Church as the people of God and recognize the vocation of the lay person within the Church. Much of Tyrrell's vision has been embodied in contemporary Catholicism.

HIS LIMITATIONS

Tyrrell not only had a vision; he also had very obvious limitations. However, his limitations, as well as his vision contribute to an understanding of Catholicism, if only by indicating directions which did not prove fruitful. Fruitfulness was always Tyrrell's own criterion. He hoped that others would use what he had written. In his essay 'From Heaven, or Of Men?' he wrote: 'We often get more instruction and edification from the mistakes than from the successes of our neighbours; and my vain endeavours to struggle out of the labyrinth of my difficulties may possibly suggest the right path to some quieter spectator of my struggles.'[19]

In reference to the modernist period, it has been pointed out that 'the essential need of theology then, more than at most times, was a willingness to face new issues, combined with the utmost caution in accepting new conclusions; the Modernists possessed the former quality in abundance; the latter, it must be admitted, they lacked'.[20] This was true in Tyrrell's case. He courageously faced new issues with all their implications, but he lacked caution in accepting new conclusions. Since he was neither an exegete nor a historian, he had to rely on the conclusions of others. He accepted the results of the biblical and historical criticism of his day as definitive. This may be seen especially in his use of Sohm's distinction between the 'charismatic' and the 'institutional' or 'catholic' phase of Christianity, and in his unqualified acceptance of the eschatological school. Further study has thrown new light on the gospels and the early Church. Tyrrell cannot be criticized for not foreseeing the direction that these studies would take. However, his acceptance of the latest results of criticism as definitive, rather than as a particular stage in historical scholarship, ties his theology to that particular stage. This shortcoming probably would not have upset Tyrrell, who was not writing for ages to come, but for his own age. It does, however, limit the value of his vision for later periods by making it too dependent on a particular stage in historical studies.

Another example of Tyrrell's ready acceptance of the latest results of historical research was his identification of Protestantism with its Liberal Protestant interpretation, especially as it was presented in the writings of Harnack and Sabatier. While refusing to identify Catholicism with its contemporary expression, he too readily equated Protestantism with one of its current expressions. In doing so, he presented an inadequate understanding of Protestantism.[21]

In his attempt to widen the idea of Catholicism from its narrow post-Reformation expression to that of a universal religion for all peoples of all times, Tyrrell's own perspective was limited. His concern was primarily with Western, English-speaking Roman Catholicism. He accepted Harnack's assessment of the Eastern Churches. While admitting that they kept the Christian spirit alive in millions of their adherents, he almost ignored them in his understanding of Catholicism.[22] The struggle within Catholicism, as he experienced it, was between a Roman-dominated Catholicism and a Catholicism adaptable to English-speaking people. Although he referred occasionally to Catholicism in North America or in Ireland, his main focus was Catholicism in England. The principles which he enumerated are applicable to other nationalities, cultures

131

and ages, but his immediate concern was Roman Catholicism in England at the turn of the century.

While stressing that Catholicism was the religion of the 'masses', Tyrrell's ministry was to the educated minority. He may have lost sight of the needs of the larger Church in his concern for Catholics who were disturbed by the results of historical criticism. In spite of his emphasis on the communal aspect, he seems to have been more driven by individual needs, his own and others, than by the pastoral needs of the whole Church. He was aware of this tendency. Referring to the troubled Catholics who came to him for direction, he wrote: '. . . I get a somewhat exaggerated impression of their numerical proportion to the untroubled many, and begin to regard them as representing the rule rather than its exception.' [23] Josephine Ward wrote of him: 'He had become a specialist for those who suffered from difficulties, and his outlook became coloured, as the outlook of any specialist is coloured, by seeing at last nothing but the group of persons who consulted him.' [24] However, he saw the educated minority as having a mission to the multitude. Their difficulties could not be ignored.

Tyrrell wanted Catholicism to enter into the mainstream of contemporary life. In his essay 'From Heaven, or Of Men?' he wrote:

> If a religion is to influence and leaven our civilization and culture it must be recognised as a part of it, as organically one with it; not as a foreign body thrust down from above, but as having grown up with it from the same root in the spirit of humanity.[25]

At times, Tyrrell may have overlooked the need to maintain the distinction between the Church and society, if the Church is to be a prophetic voice within society. In his openness to the legitimate demands of the age, he was not always aware of the ambiguity of these demands. An example of this willingness to embrace contemporary values may be seen in his attitude towards democracy. The experience of the past seventy years has shown the ambiguity associated with democracy.

Tyrrell's emphasis on the symbolic and pragmatic value of dogma resulted in a certain doctrinal relativism. He felt that the Church was moving towards a position in which doctrinal decrees would be 'like the "canonising" of the scriptural books, or even like the canonising of saints—a guarantee that the doctrine, or book, or saint offers food for digestion'.[26] The analogy is an interesting one but does not do justice to the dogmatic tradition. It does, however, emphasize the relationship between dogma and life.

Most of Tyrrell's writings were reactions, rather than carefully worked out positions. He was more a journalist than a theologian. What he had to say was usually thought-provoking and drew attention to what he considered significant at the time. He himself saw his work as tentative and suggestive, rather than definitive. In June 1900 he wrote to a friend:

> My whole life is a continual process of adjusting and readjusting; for the very reason that I am too miserably honest to stick my head in the sand and be comfortable. Still I cannot but feel that the process has been one of growth and development and of a deeper rooting of faith, and I have ceased to anticipate a catastrophe, being too well accustomed to breakers ahead to be scared by them.[27]

Most of his books, especially his later ones, were written to meet particular problems. For Tyrrell, the important thing was that a response should be made to the difficulties which people were experiencing. It did not matter whether this response bore his name as long as it was made. He was willing to have his ideas presented by others and invited others to correct and supplement his efforts.

At times, Tyrrell's tendency to overstate a point detracted from his work.[28] He was aware of this but considered it necessary as a corrective for what he saw as a one-sidedness within contemporary Catholicism. In the Preface to *Oil and Wine*, he admitted a ' "voluntarism" as crude as the "intellectualism" against which it revolts'. [29] In his attempt to emphasize the whole of life, Tyrrell tried to maintain a balance between heart and mind, faith and reason, life and dogma, freedom and authority. At times he deliberately overstressed one side in order to correct what he saw as an imbalance. At other times he seems to have been carried away by his own intense feelings. There was a certain compulsiveness about his writing. In a letter to Father Herbert Thurston he wrote: 'I write all day from morning till night regardless of the price of stationery. It is the only narcotic that is strong enough to make me forget myself and my imaginary woes.' [30] In another letter to the same friend he confided: 'I only write because I must, and sing but as the linnets sing. It is a relief to address an inane sheet of paper which at least if not sympathetic, is silent.' [31]

Tyrrell insisted that all works must be seen within their own historical context and judged according to their literary genre. When this method is applied to Tyrrell's works, one is able to appreciate both his vision and his limitations. His writings should be read in the same questioning spirit with which they were written. Tyrrell described this spirit in his Preface to *Oil and Wine*:

> From first to last, I have written, not from on high, as a teacher, but as an inquirer on the same platform as my readers. . . . [My] end is not to dogmatize, nor to ventilate new opinions, nor to win adherents for them, nor to form a school, nor to prescribe rules of conduct; but simply to suggest, to provoke reflection, to aid it when provoked, to furnish a hodge-podge of materials, good, bad and indifferent, from which real and living minds can freely select such as are fit to be built into their own fabric by their own strenuous labour.[32]

HIS INFLUENCE

It is not easy to assess Tyrrell's influence. As a retreat master, a preacher, a spiritual director, he was very popular. But it was particularly through his writings that he influenced many Christians of his day and that he continues to appeal to both the mind and the heart. Most of his work was done within a short period of ten years. Many of his writings were translated into French, German and Italian. One indication of the popularity of his work is the number of printings of his books. For example, *Hard Sayings*, first published in 1898, was reprinted in 1899, 1900, 1901, 1903, 1904 and 1910. Did this influence continue after *Pascendi*? No doubt many 'orthodox' Catholics were discouraged from further reading of the 'modernists'. Tyrrell's spiritual books were often removed from seminary and convent libraries. Nevertheless, he seems to have had a continuing influence which, in the period of modernist reaction, was not publicly acknowledged.

Maude Petre, Tyrrell's literary executor, having supported him through the last difficult years of his life, continued to devote herself to Tyrrell and his work. She was responsible for publishing *Christianity at the Cross-Roads* towards the end of 1909, the *Autobiography and Life* in 1912, *Essays on Faith and Immortality* in 1914, *Letters* in 1920 and *Von Hügel and Tyrrell: The Story of a Friendship* in 1937. She also kept in touch with persons from many countries. A letter to Miss Petre from Daniel Feuling, a German Benedictine writer, indicates the indirect influence which Tyrrell continued to exert. Feuling wrote in December 1937:

> It is my earnest desire to do something in the way of preserving as much as possible the real values of Father Tyrrell's life-work. Your words to me—the question whether Tyrrell's best thoughts might not, after all, be made fruitful in the Church—are often ringing in my ears.[33]

Maude Petre encouraged scholars to study Tyrrell and his works. Among her papers are letters from Arnold Lunn, J. Lewis May, J. J. Stam and Alec Vidler. At the end of her life she stated in her will:

> I desire to say that I regard it as a privilege to have been able to work for Father Tyrrell's memory; that I would gladly do more than I am doing if I had the required ability; that I think God raised him up, in spite of all or any of his faults, to do a great work for the future of the Church; and that I believe he was a martyr in the cause for which he laboured.[34]

Canon Lilley had predicted that Tyrrell would continue to be read. In his Preface to *Von Hügel and Tyrrell* he wrote:

> So long as men delight in beautiful and sensitive English speech, and so long as they recognize skilled guidance in probing the deepest mysteries of their own being, will the writings of George Tyrrell be read with something of the wonder and delight with which they were hailed in the first years of this century, and certainly not least enthusiastically by men of other communions than his own.[35]

Probably many a searcher for truth has come across Tyrrell's works and found in them nourishment for the mind and heart. Antonia White, in *The Hound and the Falcon: The Story of a Reconversion to the Catholic Faith*, a collection of letters written in 1940–1, refers to a number of Tyrrell's books and to the influence they were having on her as she groped her way back into the Roman Catholic Church. For her Tyrrell was 'an angel of light and his sins only human ones. . . . He was a great spirit but not a saint.' [36] Perhaps it is his very human weaknesses along with his great gifts which have made Tyrrell attractive to many people.

As Lilley pointed out, Tyrrell's influence was not limited to his own communion. It was particularly strong among some High Anglicans. Lilley suggested that Tyrrell helped to correct an over-emphasis on externals among Anglo-Catholics and prepared a number of younger theologians to create an inter-confessional English theology. 'Without him the leading Anglo-Catholic theologians of today would not have been what they are.' [37] Dr Vidler concurs with this judgement and in many ways personifies this influence. In 1934 he wrote of the Church of England:

> The newer type of theology, in which it is now expressing itself, may be held to support the suggestion that what the Roman modernists, in various ways but entirely unsuccessfully, aspired after is likely to be realized, in part at least, in Anglicanism, i.e. a development of the historic Catholic religion whose theology will take account of the progress of human knowledge.[38]

Tyrrell not only had a positive influence on countless individuals, known and unknown, but he also exerted a negative influence. As part of the aftermath of *Pascendi* Tyrrell was presented as a 'horrible example' to young Jesuit novices, or as a proud sceptic. Superiors did not want another George Tyrrell. Yet there remained a certain fascination about this man. Even today his name can evoke a strong positive or negative reaction.

Since Vatican II there has been a renewed interest in Roman Catholic modernism, and more particularly in George Tyrrell. Considerable research has been done in the past fifteen years on Tyrrell and on his writings. He has emerged as a colourful personality who has something to say not only to his comtemporaries, but to those who are interested in religious questions today. He once admitted that he wrote 'for a small circle of readers, those who belong to three generations ahead'.[39] Perhaps he was right.

IMPLICATIONS FOR TODAY

The condemnation of modernism postponed a response to the questions which Tyrrell considered crucial. Many of the questions remain to be answered. Tyrrell's understanding of Catholicism is helpful in promoting authentic renewal within the Roman Catholic Church and in encouraging ecumenical dialogue within the larger Christian Church.

Tyrrell reminded the Church that it existed for the world, that it must be open to the world in order to learn from it and to teach it. He recognized the need to integrate new knowledge and values into Catholicism. This had been done in the past and ought to be done again. He urged the Church to look into its own rich tradition. Only an appreciation of the whole tradition would overcome the tendency to absolutize a particular aspect of that tradition. Tyrrell was well aware of the devastating effects of the Protestant-Catholic controversy on Catholicism. He urged a return to pre-scholastic, pre-Reformation Catholicism in order to discover a richer, fuller Catholicism. His vision of a Catholicism, faithful to the past, open to the present and future and open to the world, can challenge the Roman Catholic Church today in its efforts towards renewal. In many ways it resembles Rahner's vision presented in *The Shape of the Church to Come*.[40]

Tyrrell's indirect method of responding to theological problems is relevant today for many who ask themselves what it means to be a Catholic. His stress on spiritual fruitfulness as the criterion for all developments within the Church is valuable in a changing Church. Tyrrell recognized the value of theology but insisted that it was not revelation; nor should theological orthodoxy be equated with faith. It is a good reminder as the Catholic Church struggles with a plurality of theological expressions of its common faith. As the Church becomes more a world Church and less a Western Church, Tyrrell's conviction that it is not necessary 'to convert a man to Aristotle before converting him to Christ' is important.[41] There is a growing awareness that the Christian proclamation must find expression in each cultural situation, and that this must be done by those who are actually in the particular cultural situation. In doing so the Church becomes truly 'Catholic'.

Tyrrell enables one to situate the post-Vatican I, pre-Vatican II

Church and to recognize the need that existed for a change in the Church's understanding of itself, and of authority within the Church. He provides a perspective from which one can understand the changes which have taken place. He also offers insights into some of the concerns of the post-Vatican II Church: the rôle of the Church in the world, the Church as authoritative teacher, the relationship between the official and the charismatic element within the Church, the place of theology and the theologian, the reinterpretation of dogmatic statements. These, along with many other problems, require further study. It is interesting and helpful to reflect upon the way Tyrrell grappled with these concerns as he struggled to respond to the challenges of his time. He had neither the time, the patience, nor the necessary tools to work out a systematic solution, but he did articulate the questions. In January 1909, he wrote to a friend: 'My own work—which I regard as done—has been to raise a question which I have failed to answer. I am not so conceited as to conclude that it is therefore unanswerable.' [42]

Tyrrell believed passionately in Catholicism, and yet he protested loudly against its abuses. He could see both the good and the bad. Joseph Goetz points out:

> He had enough of a knowledge of ecclesiastical history to know that it was sometimes advisable to wait for the results of the autopsy before assuming that a given tradition or institution was dead. It is perhaps especially this attitude of mind, a kind of devout conservatism linked with a disinterested and somewhat sceptical awareness of the need for radical reform, which is his greatest contribution to the present.[43]

Tyrrell accepted the Church as the principle of authority, but he also championed individual freedom of conscience. It may be argued that he made room for the 'Protestant principle' within the Catholic substance. Both should find a place in a renewed Catholicism.

In addition to the implications for authentic renewal within the Roman Catholic Church, Tyrrell's understanding of Catholicism has important implications for the ecumenical movement. Tyrrell desired a reunion of Christendom based on the convergence of Catholicism and Protestantism. He recognized a complementarity within Catholicism and Protestantism: 'The rights of authority and the rights of personality; the development of the community and

the development of the individual, are not conflicting but complementary ideas.'[44] Ecumenical groups are discovering this complementarity. As a result the religious experience of both Catholics
and Protestants is enriched.

Tyrrell pointed out that Catholics have often overrated what is
distinctive in Catholicism and underrated what is common to all
Christians. 'The practice of defining things briefly by their differences leads to the fallacy of forgetting their other constituents.' [45]
In a letter written in 1908 he remarked:

> Thank God differences of theology, too long identified with dif-
> ferences of faiths, are getting thrust out to their proper level of
> significance, and unity of spirit is fast triumphing over the schis-
> matic results of scholastic discussions. Diversities of manifestation
> will always remain, but they will be estimated at their true pur-
> port and value.[46]

Tyrrell suggested beginning with what was common to all Christians, an approach which has been fruitfully used by a number of
bilateral and multilateral dialogue groups. He also insisted that the
authentic tradition, not its aberrations, should be considered. The
unity he hoped for and worked towards was not based on uniformity
but on mutual respect and the recognition of the riches of both
Catholicism and Protestantism. It is the kind of unity which is the
goal of the ecumenical movement.

Tyrrell's friendship with members of other traditions formed a
basis for his vision of what a future Church might be. In a letter to
Canon Lilley he wrote: 'What strength there is in the consciousness
of being under the force of a spirit that is working, independently,
in so many hearts and centres; the only sort of unity that is an end
in itself and to which confessional union is but a dispensable
means.' [47] It was the spirit of Christ drawing together all the scat-
tered children of God. Tyrrell believed that there was room within
Catholicism for a transcendence of confessional differences.

These are some of the implications for today of Tyrrell's writing,
but what of the man himself? Shortly after Tyrrell's death, von
Hügel wrote to a friend:

> My difficulty in writing about Tyrrell at all, all round and as a
> man, will be that, if to be a saint is to be generous and heroic, to

spend yourself for conscience and for souls, then Tyrrell is a saint; but that, if to be a saint is to be faultless, to be free from resentment, bitterness, and excessive reactions against excesses of your opponents, then Tyrrell is a considerable sinner.[48]

All who come to know Tyrrell probably share von Hügel's difficulty. Was Tyrrell a saint or a sinner? Or was he both? By continuing to question and to probe, by refusing to accept a particular expression of Catholicism as synonymous with the Catholic tradition, by his persistent belief and hope in the future of Catholic Christianity in spite of present difficulties, Tyrrell manifested a certain heroism. He was faithful to his own insights and convictions. He may not have been a saint, but he was a prophet. George Tyrrell and his vision of the Catholic tradition can still inspire us today.

Notes

Notes to Chapter 1

1. Two recent studies on modernism are Thomas M. Loome, *Liberal Catholicism, Reform Catholicism, Modernism: A Contribution to a New Orientation in Modernist Research* (Mainz, Matthias-Grünewald Verlag, 1979) and Gabriel Daly, *Transcendence and Immanence: A Study in Catholic Modernism and Integralism* (Oxford, Clarendon, 1980). For their discussion on the ambiguity associated with the term see Loome, pp. 167–74, and Daly, pp. 2–5.
2. Nicholas Lash, 'Modernism, aggiornamento and the night battle', *Bishops and Writers: Aspects of the Evolution of Modern English Catholicism*, ed. Adrian Hastings (Hertfordshire, Anthony Clarke, 1977), p. 76.
3. Karl Rahner, 'Towards a Fundamental Theological Interpretation of Vatican II', *Theological Studies* 40 (1979), pp. 716–27.
4. *Medievalism: A Reply to Cardinal Mercier* (London, Longmans, 1908), p. 106; hereafter cited as *Med*.
5. *Christianity at the Cross-Roads* (London, Longmans, 1909); reprinted with a Foreword by A. R. Vidler (London, Allen & Unwin, 1963), p. 27. References are to the reprinted edn, hereafter cited as *CC*.
6. *Med*, p. 120.
7. *CC*, p. 29.
8. Cf. Bernard Lonergan, *Doctrinal Pluralism* (Milwaukee, Marquette University Press, 1971), in which he contrasts the classicist mentality with modern historical-mindedness. 'To confine the Catholic Church to a classical mentality is to keep the Catholic Church out of the modern world and to prolong the already too prolonged crisis within the Church' (p. 9).
9. Rahner points out that the doctrinal decrees of Vatican II 'strive for statements that are not entirely conditioned by the linguistic style of a Neo-Scholastic theology'. This is clearer when these texts are compared with the neo-scholastic schemata prepared before the Council. 'Towards a Fundamental Theological Interpretation of Vatican II', *Theological Studies* 40 (1979), p. 719.
10. Langdon Gilkey, *Catholicism Confronts Modernity: A Protestant View* (New York, Seabury, 1975), p. 175.

141

11. Ronald Chapman, 'The Thought of George Tyrrell', *Essays and Poems Presented to Lord David Cecil*, ed. W. W. Robson (London, Constable, 1970), p. 166.

Notes to Chapter 2

1. See Gregory Baum, ed., *Journeys: The Impact of Personal Experience on Religious Thought* (New York, Paulist, 1975). In this work ten Catholic theologians present their reflections on their personal biography and its relation to their theology. Baum believes that as there is a 'sociology of knowledge' relating concepts and truth to the social background in which they emerge and prosper, so there ought to be a 'psychology of knowledge' connecting people's intellectual approach to the significant events of their biography.

2. *Lettres de George Tyrrell à Henri Bremond, présentées, traduites et annotées par Anne Louis-David, Préface de Maurice Nédoncelle* (Paris, Aubier-Montaigne, 1971), p. 42. These letters to a fellow Jesuit provide insight into Tyrrell's character. They were written in English between 1898 and Tyrrell's death in 1909.

3. George Tyrrell, *Through Scylla and Charybdis: Or the Old Theology and the New* (London, Longmans, 1907), pp. 83–4; hereafter cited as *SC*.

4. Chapman, 'The Thought of George Tyrrell', p. 140.

5. *Autobiography of George Tyrrell 1861–1884*. This account by Tyrrell of what he calls '*ma pauvre vie*' forms the first volume of the *Autobiography and Life of George Tyrrell in Two Volumes* (London, Edward Arnold, 1912). Maude Petre arranged and added supplements to the first volume and wrote the second volume, *Life of George Tyrrell from 1884 to 1909*. The first volume will be referred to as *Life* 1, the second as *Life* 2.

6. *Life* 2:2.

7. Lecture delivered in June 1915, 'The Character Study in Autobiography and in Fiction', *Last Lectures* (London, Longmans, 1918; reprint edn: New York, Books for Libraries Press, 1967), p. 203.

8. "Revelation as Experience": An Unpublished Lecture of George Tyrrell', ed. with notes and historical introduction by Thomas Michael Loome, *Heythrop Journal* 12 (1971), pp. 124–6. Even at the time that Maude Petre was working on the *Life* other friends of Tyrrell complained that it was only Petre's perception. Norah Shelley wrote to Katherine Clutton in April 1911 that it seemed 'quite impossible for anyone to write a real "live" history of a man as many-sided as he was, and one of such wide sympathies, if the biographer plainly disdains all impressions but those coming from her own perceptions'. Unpublished letter, Clutton Papers.

9. *Liberal Catholicism, Reform Catholicism, Modernism: A Contribution to a*

New Orientation in Modernist Research, particularly Part II (Specialized Bibliographies) and Part III (Documentation).

10. *Life* 1: especially pp. 66–116.
11. Ibid., p. 98.
12. *Life* 1:82. Dr Newport J. D. White wrote a short memoir after Tyrrell's death which formed a supplement to chapter 5 of *Life* 1. White had been a close friend of Tyrrell's at Rathmines School. They never met nor corresponded after Tyrrell became a Roman Catholic. For White, Tyrrell's change of religion was 'a far greater severance than his death would have been'. In retrospect, he recognized that this change had been necessary for Tyrrell.
13. Ibid., p. 83.
14. Ibid., pp. 111–12.
15. Ibid., pp. 152–3. St Etheldreda's, Ely Place, was the first pre-Reformation shrine restored to Roman Catholic hands in England and Wales. The present church was begun in 1291. There is a tradition that the crypt may have been part of an earlier Roman-British church. One senses in it a rootedness in the past.
16. Ibid., p. 158.
17. Ibid., p. 99.
18. Tyrrell referred to the philosophy and theology taught in Roman Catholic seminaries in the nineteenth century as scholasticism. A more correct term would be neo-scholasticism. The Society of Jesus had been influential in the development of post-Tridentine scholasticism.
19. In a letter to von Hügel, December 1902, Tyrrell wrote:

    I don't think you understand how absolutely and indeed culpably little I have ever cared about my own soul, my present or future peace, except as a condition of helpfulness to others. It is a natural affection that has been left out of my composition for some strong purpose. Like Moses I would rather be damned with the mass of humanity than be saved alone or even with a minority; and so I could not bear to think that there were faith, or moral difficulties pressing on others of which I knew nothing; and that I owed my stability to any sort of ignorance or half-view.

    Life 1:96. Petre referred to Tyrrell's 'strange self-detachment' as the source of his strength and his weakness. Introduction to Tyrrell's *Essays on Faith and Immortality* (London, Edward Arnold, 1914), p. viii; hereafter cited as *EFI*.
20. *Life* 1:139.
21. Ibid., pp. 194–229.
22. Ibid., p. 202.
23. Ibid., pp. 233–52, 269–78; *Life* 2:40–7.
24. *Life* 1:248.
25. Ibid., p. 267.
26. Tyrrell's letters to Henri Bremond, a French Jesuit, provide insight

into Tyrrell's struggle to believe in the Society as a means towards renewal within the Church, and the eventual loss of this faith. See particularly the early letters (July 1898–January 1900), *Lettres*, pp. 39–60. In his Preface and Epilogue to *The Testament of Ignatius Loyola*, tr. E. M. Rix (St Louis, B. Herder, 1900), Tyrrell emphasized the true spirit of Ignatius and suggested that the shortcomings of the Society were due to the abeyance of Ignatius' principles of vitality and flexibility.

27. In 1900 Tyrrell destroyed this work which was almost completed. Petre compiled notes from a retreat preached by Tyrrell in July 1900. With Tyrrell's help these notes, along with other material on the *Exercises*, were edited and published as *The Soul's Orbit* (London, Longmans, 1904). The book is signed by M. D. Petre with Preface by Tyrrell. See Louis-David, *Lettres*, p. 47, n. 3; *Life* 2:80–3.

28. When Mercier suggested that Tyrrell had learned his 'method of immanence' from Protestant thinkers, Tyrrell insisted that he had learned it from Ignatius Loyola. *Med*, pp. 110–12.

29. Tyrrell developed these ideas in 'The Recent Anglo-Roman Pastoral', *Nineteenth Century* 49 (1901), pp. 736–54. The article was published under Lord Halifax's name but was Tyrrell's except for the introduction and conclusion. See Thomas Michael Loome, 'A Bibliography of the Published Works of George Tyrrell (1861–1909)', *Heythrop Journal* 10 (1969), p. 305, for authorship of this article.

30. *Med*, p. 42.

31. *Life* 2:470.

32. In a letter to Reverend L. Martin, General of the Society of Jesus, 11 June 1904, Tyrrell outlined his reasons for choosing the Society and his reasons for rejecting it. This letter forms appendix 3, *Life* 2:458–99.

33. For example, 'The Use of Scholasticism', an essay which first appeared in the *American Catholic Quarterly Review* 23 (1898), pp. 550–61. It was included in *The Faith of the Millions: A Selection of Past Essays*, First Series (London, Longmans, 1901), pp. 205–27; hereafter cited as *FM* 1; the Second Series will be cited as *FM* 2.

34. Letter to von Hügel, 6 December 1897, quoted in *Life* 2:45.

35. *Life* 1:273.

36. The details of Tyrrell's dispute over the teaching of Thomas have been documented by David Schultenover in his study of the Roman Archives of the Society of Jesus. Schultenover quotes a letter addressed to the General in which Tyrrell stated that he felt 'out of place and not wanted in the Society'. 'George Tyrrell: Caught in the Roman Archives of the Society of Jesus', *Proceedings of the Roman Catholic Modernism Working Group of the American Academy of Religion* (Mobile, Spring Hill College Press, 1981), pp. 92–4.

37. Charles Stephen Dessain, ed., *The Letters and Diaries of John Henry*

Newman, 31 vols. (London, Nelson, 1961–77), vol. 13: *Birmingham and London, January 1849 to June 1850* (1963), pp. 333–4.

38. Tyrrell summarized his relationship to Newman in a letter to M. Raoul Gout, 26 May 1906, quoted in *Life* 2:209–10. The nature and extent of Newman's influence on Tyrrell is debated both by Newman scholars and by Tyrrell scholars. See Edmond Darvil Benard, *A Preface to Newman's Theology* (London, B. Herder Book Co. 1945), pp. 128–56; Charles Frederick Harrold, *John Henry Newman* (Connecticut, Archon, 1966), pp. 357–69; Jan Henricus Walgrave, *Newman the Theologian: The Nature of Belief and Doctrine as Exemplified in his Life and Works*, tr. A. V. Littledale (London, Geoffrey Chapman, 1960), pp. 130–7; Nicholas Lash, *Newman on Development: The Search For an Explanation in History* (London, Sheed & Ward, 1975), p. 14; *Life* 2:207–23; Maurice Nédoncelle, Preface to *Lettres de Tyrrell à Bremond*, pp. 13–14. It is an area which requires further study. See Loome, *Liberal Catholicism, Reform Catholicism, Modernism*, p. 17, n. 22.

39. The challenge to Catholicism posed by these Protestant scholars and the efforts of Loisy and Blondel to present a response to that challenge will be developed in chapters 3 and 4. Chapter 5 will show how Tyrrell used ideas from all these writers in developing his own response.

40. Letter to von Hügel, 5 December 1902, quoted in *Life* 2:96. Tyrrell considered that he owed more to von Hügel than to all his other teachers put together. See *Lex Orandi: or Prayer and Creed* (London, Longmans, Green & Co., 1903), p. xxxii; hereafter cited as *LO*.

41. Letter of 4 March 1900 quoted in Maude Petre, *Von Hügel and Tyrrell: The Story of a Friendship* (London, Dent, 1937), p. 123; hereafter cited as *vH & T*.

42. Ibid., especially pp. 118–20; Lawrence Barmann, *Baron Friedrich von Hügel and the Modernist Crisis in England* (Cambridge University Press, 1972), especially pp. 138–82, 222–35. Barmann considers Petre to have been 'less than just to von Hügel'. He defends von Hügel's loyalty and friendship with Tyrrell and suggests that Petre and Bremond were too emotionally involved with Tyrrell to be truly objective. Barmann also points out that Petre's full criticism of the Baron was expressed in print only after von Hügel's death in 1925 (p. 177, n. 2).

43. Tyrrell was almost a co-author of von Hügel's *The Mystical Element of Religion as Studied in Saint Catherine of Genoa and Her Friends*, 2 vols., 2nd edn (London, Dent, 1923; reprint edn, 1927). In the Preface to the 1st edn (1908), von Hügel expressed his indebtedness to 'Rev. G. Tyrrell's *Hard Sayings* 1898 and *Faith of the Millions* 2 vols. 1901, so full of insights into mysticism' (p. xxxi). In his Preface to the 2nd edn (1923), p. vii, he wrote:

> Father Tyrrell has gone, who had been so generously helpful, especially as to the mystical states, as to Aquinas and as to the form of the whole book, for so many years, long before the storms beat

upon him and his own vehemence overclouded, in part, the force and completeness of that born mystic.

44. The relationship of these three elements is worked out by von Hügel in *The Mystical Element*. See vol. 1, *ch. 2*, pp. 50–82.

45. 'A Change of Tactics', *TM* 86 (1896), p. 219. This essay was included in *FM* 1:1–21 as 'A More Excellent Way'.

46. *FM* 1:xvii.

47. *A Much-Abused Letter* (London, Longmans, 1906), p. 30; hereafter cited as *MAL*; written in 1903, it was printed and circulated privately and anonymously in 1904 as 'A Letter to a Friend, a Professor of Anthropology in a Continental University'.

48. Mark Schoof in *A Survey of Catholic Theology 1800–1970* (New York, Paulist Newman, 1970), p. 185, writes of Tyrrell: 'By nature he lacked the patience and caution of the scholar. He was more directly concerned with Christian life itself and with Christian mystical experience and believed that these could no longer be nourished by the dried up formulae of the prevailing theology.'

49. *Nova et Vetera: Informal Meditations for Times of Spiritual Dryness* (London, Longmans, 1897); hereafter cited as *NV*. *Hard Sayings: A Selection of Meditations and Studies* (London, Longmans, 1898); hereafter cited as *HS*. *Oil and Wine* (London, Priory, 1906); hereafter cited as *OW*; written in 1901, printed and privately circulated in 1902. Problems with censors delayed its publication. *Lex Credendi: A Sequel to Lex Orandi* (London, Longmans, 1906); hereafter cited as *LC*.

50. See John D. Root, 'George Tyrrell and the Synthetic Society', *Downside Review* 98 (1980), pp. 42–59.

51. It was included in *EFI*, pp. 158–71. For Petre's account of Tyrrell's difficulties over this article see *Life* 2:112–30.

52. Tyrrell wrote a Preface to *XVI Revelations of Divine Love Shewed to Mother Juliana of Norwich 1373* (London, Kegan Paul, Trench, Trubner, 1902). This edn was based on the earliest printed edn 1670.

53. Letter to von Hügel, March 1900, quoted in *Life* 2:119–20. Schultenover's study of the Roman Archives of the Society of Jesus documents this profound difference between the English and the Roman authorities. *Proceedings of the Roman Catholic Modernism Working Group of the American Academy of Religion* (1981), pp. 94–101.

54. The details of this struggle with his superiors are recounted in *Life* 2:224–81; Barmann, *von Hügel and the Modernist Crisis*, pp. 161–82; *Lettres*, pp. 82–208; *vH&T*, pp. 121–56.

55. Letter to Cardinal Vaughan, Christmas Day 1901, preserved in the Archives of the Archdiocese of Westminster, London.

56. *Life* 2:138.

57. Ibid., pp. 140–1.

58. Ibid., p. 238.

59. Ibid., p. 245. Tyrrell was not sure whether he had been 'expelled' or 'released' from the Society. David Schultenover discusses this issue in

George Tyrrell: In Search of Catholicism, pp. 327–35. See particularly n.41, pp. 426–7. Further light is thrown on the relationship between the ecclesiastical authorities and the Society by Schultenover's study of the Roman Archives. He quotes a letter written 15 May 1906 by Meyer, the General's assistant for the English-speaking provinces, to Sykes, the English provincial: '. . . Fr. Tyrrell was dismissed from the Society — *by command of the Supreme Pontiff himself* — because of his false, dangerous and scandalous ideas.' *Proceedings of the Roman Catholic Modernism Working Group of the American Academy of Religion* (1981), p. 113.

60. *Lettres*, p. 206. Louis-David notes that what seems a possible solution today was not one in 1906. See p. 207, n. 8.

61. Letter to Robert Dell, August 1906; quoted in *Life* 2:306. For a careful study of the relationship between Tyrrell and Mercier, see R. Boudens, 'George Tyrrell and Cardinal Mercier: A Contribution to the History of Modernism', *Eglise et Théologie* 1 (1970), pp. 313–51.

62. In an unsigned article, 'The Abbé Loisy: Criticism and Catholicism', *Church Quarterly Review* 58 (1904), pp. 180–95, Tyrrell praised the efforts of Loisy:

> It is precisely as the incarnation of a spirit which is stirring among the dry bones; as the representative of a universal cause; as the advocate of a small but rapidly increasing school of thought that Abbé Loisy stands out distinct from the number of those whose names are added to the Index year by year without exciting more than a passing murmur of discontent from a small circle of the victims' friends and adherents (p. 181).

63. Tyrrell's theory of authority will be presented in chapter 6.

64. A similar struggle has taken place within the Roman Catholic Church during the years following Vatican II.

65. John Henry Newman, *A Letter Addressed to His Grace the Duke of Norfolk on the Occasion of Mr. Gladstone's Recent Exposition* (London, B. M. Pickering, 1875); reprinted in *Newman and Gladstone: The Vatican Decrees* (Notre Dame, Ind., University Press, 1962), pp. 75–228.

66. One of the most enthusiastic supporters of extreme ultramontanism had been W. G. Ward. In a review of Wilfrid Ward's 2-vol. work on his father, *William George Ward and the Oxford Movement* and *William George Ward and the Catholic Revival* (London, Macmillan, 1889, 1890), Tyrrell presented the extreme ultramontane interpretation as well as the more moderate position which he believed to be the true Catholic view. This was the first article in which Tyrrell expressed his ideas on the collective mind of the Church, an insight which would receive greater clarification and emphasis in his later writings. See 'The Oxford School and Modern Religious Thought', *TM* 79 (December 1893), pp. 560–8; *TM* 80 (January 1894), pp. 59–68.

67. For the text of the pastoral, see 'The Church and Liberal Catholicism: Joint Pastoral Letter by the Cardinal Archbishop and the Bishops of

the Province of Westminster', *Tablet* 97 (5 January 1901), pp. 8–12. In its news commentary the *Tablet* referred to it as 'the voice of the Catholic Church in this country' (p. 5). It was endorsed by Leo XIII. The pope's letter of congratulations to the bishops was printed in full in the *Tablet* 97 (23 March 1901), p. 441. William J. Schoenl describes the problems which evoked the pastoral, as well as the crisis which followed its publication and Tyrrell's reaction to it in 'George Tyrrell and the English Liberal Catholic Crisis, 1900–01', *Downside Review* 92 (July 1974), pp. 171–84. Maisie Ward, *Insurrection Versus Resurrection* (London, Sheed & Ward, 1938) devotes a chapter to the joint pastoral and its effects on her father and other leading English Catholics. In discussing Tyrrell's reaction she writes: 'Many years later Wilfrid Ward said that he thought it had had almost a determining influence in driving Tyrrell to the extreme left' (p. 134). David Schultenover, *George Tyrrell: In Search of Catholicism* (Shepherdstown, Patmos, 1981) points out that before the joint pastoral Tyrrell's apologetic was primarily pastoral, whereas after it his apologetic became polemical and bitter. See *Life* 2:146–61 for Petre's account of the joint pastoral controversy.

68. Quoted in *Life* 2:111.
69. 'The Church and Liberal Catholicism', p. 8.
70. Letter to Rooke Ley, 5 January 1901, quoted in *Life* 2:152.
71. Letter to Bremond, 22 January 1901, *George Tyrrell's Letters*, sel. and ed. M. D. Petre (London, T. Fisher Unwin, 1920), p. 69.
72. 'The Recent Anglo-Roman Pastoral', *Nineteenth Century* 49 (1901), pp. 736–54.
73. Ibid., p. 740.
74. Newman made the same distinction in his *Letter to Norfolk*, p. 188. 'Hence the infallibility of the Apostles was of a far more positive and wide character than that needed by and granted to the Church. We call it, in the case of the Apostles, inspiration; in the case of the Church *assistentia*.'
75. Ward accused Halifax of not recognizing that the pastoral was not an exhaustive theological treatise, but a document which presupposed for its interpretation the authorized theology of the Church. Maisie Ward quoted her father's response to the Halifax article in *Insurrection Versus Resurrection*, pp. 137–41.
76. *The Church and the Future* was reprinted under Tyrrell's name with an Introduction by M. D. Petre in 1910; hereafter cited as *CF*.
77. An English translation of *Lamentabili Sane* and of *Pascendi Dominici Gregis* is included in *All Things in Christ: Encyclicals and Selected Documents of Saint Pius X*, ed. Vincent A. Yzermans (Westminster, Newman, 1954), pp. 223–8, 89–132. Schoof in *A Survey of Catholic Theology 1800–1970*, p. 186, comments on the encyclical: 'All that it in fact did was to cut off a new road, insisting that the old road was still quite good

enough and had been—so it would seem by implication—mapped out often enough.'

78. Loome, *Liberal Catholicism, Reform Catholicism, Modernism*, p. 167.

79. *Transcendence and Immanence: A Study in Catholic Modernism and Integralism*, p. 3.

80. Tyrrell's response appeared in the *Giornale*, 25 September 1907, and in *The Times*, 30 September and 1 October 1907.

81. 'The Pope and Modernism', *The Times*, 1 October 1907, p. 5.

82. The Encyclical: A Criticism in the Times', *Tablet* 110 (12 October 1907), pp. 561–3. Jean Rivière referred to the debate over the infallibility of *Pascendi* in *Dictionnaire de théologie catholique*, vol. 10, pt 2, col. 2034 (Paris, Letouzey et Ané, 1928). While insisting on the importance of the encyclical as a direct act of the supreme pontifical authority, Rivière supported the position that the encyclical was part of the ordinary teaching of the Church.

83. 'The Pope and Modernism', *The Times*, 30 September 1907, p. 4.

84. Quoted in *Life* 2:341–2.

85. Letter to Augustin Leger, 24 December 1907, quoted in *Life* 2: 340.

86. '*Beati Excommunicati*' was never published in English. It was published in French with the title '*L'excommunication salutaire*', *Grande Revue* 44 (1907), pp. 661–72. The original MS is in the Petre Papers, British Library, Add. MSS 52369. Daniel Kilfoyle included a copy of the original work in his dissertation, 'The Conception of Doctrinal Authority in the Writings of George Tyrrell (1861–1909)', appendix, pp. 217–29. The quotation from Augustine is in *De vera religione* 6. Tyrrell notes that this was written about three years after Augustine's conversion and that it was not retracted. See also *SC*, p. 81 and *CF*, p. 146, for Tyrrell's view on excommunication.

87. 'The Pope and Modernism', *The Times*, 1 October 1907, p. 5.

88. Tyrrell was not excommunicated by name as was Loisy. In his *Mémoires pour servir à l'histoire religieuse de notre temps*, vol. 2 (Paris, Emile Nourry, 1931), pp. 583–4, Loisy commented on Tyrrell's excommunication:

> On n'a pas osé excommunier Tyrrell publiquement et nommément; on l'a fait discrètement avertir qu'il était privé des sacrements, c'est-à-dire que l'Eglise le tenait pour retranché de sa communion; il était donc ex-communié. L'évêque de Southwark fit néanmoins passer dans les journaux, à la fin d'octobre, une information où il déclarait que Tyrrell n'était 'pas excommunié, comme on l'avait dit, mais privé des sacrements.' Distinction toute verbale, et pour l'usage du public anglais.

Loisy himself was publically excommunicated by name 7 March 1908. Ibid., p. 643.

89. 'The Condemnation of Newman', *Guardian*, 20 November 1907.

90. *Med*, p. 9.

91. Mercier's unpublished response to Tyrrell's *Medievalism* forms an ap-

pendix to Boudens' article, 'George Tyrrell and Cardinal Mercier', pp. 340–51. The quotation is from p. 343.

92. *Med*, p. 187. *Med* was Tyrrell's most polemic work. Gabriel Daly in 'Tyrrell's "Medievalism" ', *TM* 228 (1969), p. 20, comments: 'Tyrrell always had reservations about it and did not wish it to be remembered; yet it is a faithful reflection of his most typical attitudes, convictions, strengths and weaknesses.'

93. Maude Petre in *Life* 2 gave the impression that Tyrrell made his permanent residence in Storrington. Loome in his notes on 'Revelation as Experience' corrects this, showing that Tyrrell actually spent more months with the Shelley family than with Petre. *Heythrop Journal* 12 (1971), pp. 125–6.

94. Letter to Rev. J. M. Lloyd-Thomas quoted in *Life* 2:409. Petre discussed Tyrrell's attraction to Anglicanism and his Old Catholic sympathies in *Life 2*: 366–87. Louis-David points out that Tyrrell spoke only to his Catholic friends about returning to Anglicanism. *Lettres*, p. 274, n. 9.

95. This point is emphasized by Loome, who stresses that Tyrrell understood 'his own intellectual position as a development of a Roman Catholic ecclesiastical tradition in which he stood in substantial continuity'. *Liberal Catholicism, Reform Catholicism, Modernism*, pp. 45–8.

96. Letter to Bishop Herzog, quoted in *Life* 2:383–4.

97. Alban Goodier, in his review of J. Lewis May's *Father Tyrrell and the Modernist Movement, Dublin Review* 383 (1932), p. 288, referred to Tyrrell as 'a victim of an insidious disease'. Thurston, in his review of the same work, *TM* 160 (1932), p. 81, wrote of 'a mind insensibly disordered by the approaches of disease'. Maisie Ward in *Insurrection Versus Resurrection*, p. 189, wrote:

> Depression, irritability, a certain lack of mental stability are the well-known results of Bright's disease from which Tyrrell suffered. I cannot but feel that, somewhat out of his depths in the subjects into which he had been urged, his utterances were sometimes rather the issue of bodily anguish and mental distress than deliberately adopted conclusions.

Louis-David, in her notes on Tyrrell's letters to Bremond, referred a number of times to the effect of illness on Tyrrell; e.g. *Lettres*, pp. 21, 192, 250, 262. Crehan attempted to trace the course of Tyrrell's illness and to link this to events in his life. 'What Influenced and Finally Killed George Tyrrell?' *Catholic Medical Quarterly* 26 (1974), pp. 75–85.

98. Quoted in Petre's Introduction, *CC*, p. 15.

99. For the events surrounding Tyrrell's death, see *Life* 2: 420–46; Barmann, *von Hügel and the Modernist Crisis*, pp. 222–33. Katherine Clutton presents her recollection of the events in 'The Death of George Tyrrell', *The Modern Churchman* 22 (1933), pp. 678–86.

100. Petre Papers in British Library, Add. MSS 52368, p. 129.

101. *Life* 2:434.

102. The text of Bremond's address is given in *Life* 2:443–6 and in *Lettres*, pp. 303–7.
103. Five scrapbooks of press cuttings 1906–14 relating to George Tyrrell and the modernist movement in the Roman Catholic Church were presented to the Cambridge University Library by Maude Petre in December 1937.
104. The article from the *Guardian* which quoted Tyrrell's letter to Bishop Herzog as well as the *Tablet* article, 30 October 1909, which also printed the letter in order to prove that Tyrrell had ceased to be a Catholic, are included in vol. 3 of the press cuttings. The letter to Herzog is also quoted in *Life* 2:383–4.
105. 'Recent Literature', *London Quarterly Review*, January 1910, pp. 134–6. Quote is from p. 136.
106. An early work in which Tyrrell pointed out the abuses of Catholicism was *External Religion: Its Use and Abuse* (London, Sands, 1899). This work, hereafter cited as *ER*, was a collection of Lenten conferences delivered to Oxford undergraduates in 1899. The same theme is developed in many of his later works.

Notes to Chapter 3

1. For a description of Roman theology at the end of the nineteenth century see Daly, *Transcendence and Immanence*, pp. 7–25. Avery Dulles, *A History of Apologetics* (London, Hutchinson, 1971), pp. 182–3, describes the influence of Giovanni Perrone, s.j., on seminary manuals.
2. *Documents of Vatican I, 1869–1870*, tr. John F. Broderick (Collegeville, Liturgical Press, 1971), pp. 44–5 (DS 3012).
3. *Alfred Loisy: His Religious Significance* (Cambridge University Press, 1944), p. 41.
4. For the significance of Baur and Harnack, see G. Wayne Glick, *The Reality of Christianity: A Study of Adolf von Harnack as Historian and Theologian* (New York, Harper & Row, 1967); Peter C. Hodgson, *The Formation of Historical Theology: A Study of Ferdinand Christian Baur* (New York, Harper & Row, 1966); Wilhelm Pauck, *Harnack and Troeltsch: Two Historical Theologians* (New York, Oxford University Press, 1968), especially appendix 1, 'Adolf von Harnack and Ferdinand Christian von Baur: Troeltsch's Contribution to a *Festschrift* Dedicated to Harnack on the Occasion of His Seventieth Birthday', pp. 97–115; Jaroslav Pelikan, *Historical Theology: Continuity and Change in Christian Doctrine* (New York, Corpus, 1971; London, Hutchinson, 1971).
5. Adolf Harnack, *Reden und Aufsätze* 2 (Giessen, Topelmann, 1904), p. 220. Harnack's lecture, delivered to a theological conference in Giessen, was translated into English by Joseph King and appeared in the *Contemporary Review* (August 1886), pp. 221–38.

6. Ibid., p. 230.
7. Harnack was a prolific writer. References in this study will be principally to his classical work, *Dogmengeschichte*, and to his more popular work, *Das Wesen des Christentums*. The first edn of *Dogmengeschichte* appeared in 1885–9. The third edn was translated into English by Neil Buchanan and published as *History of Dogma*, 7 vols. (London, Williams, *circa* 1900). It was republished in 4 vols. (New York, Dover, 1961). References are to the Dover edn, hereafter cited as *HD*. *Das Wesen des Christentums* was delivered as a lecture series in the University of Berlin, 1899–1900. The work was translated by Thomas Bailey Saunders and published as *What is Christianity?* (New York, Putnam, 1901); reprint edn with Introduction by Rudolph Bultmann (New York, Harper & Row, 1957); references are to the reprint edn, hereafter cited as *WC*.
8. *HD* 1:13, Harnack developed his conception of the gospel in his 'Presuppositions to the History of Dogma', *HD* 1:58–75. In response to the criticism that he judged the development of dogma by the gospel but did not clearly state his conception of the gospel, Harnack summarized his view in the Preface to the 3rd edn of vol. 3 of the original German text, *HD* 5:vii. See also *WC*, especially pp. 49–77. Clearly operative in Harnack's conception of the gospel are his Liberal Protestant theological assumptions. Harnack was reacting as a man of his time, although he did not seem to realize how historically conditioned his view of the gospel really was. Glick refers to Harnack's 'axiology' and his 'covert norms'. *Reality of Christianity*, pp. 3–15, 321–49.
9. *HD* 2:4. For a summary of Harnack's interpretation of the development of Catholicism see *WC*, pp. 190–217.
10. *HD* 2:2, n. 1.
11. Harnack included a special excursus on the relationship between 'Roman' and 'Catholic'. Ibid., pp. 149–68.
12. *HD* 7:84.
13. Ibid., pp. 112–13.
14. Harnack's attitude towards the Roman Catholic Church is exemplified in an address given to some students in 1891: '*Was wir von der römischen Kirche lernen und nicht lernen sollen*', *Reden und Aufsätze* 2, pp. 248–64. For others' assessment of Harnack's attitude towards the Roman Church, see Gottfried Maron, '*Harnack und der römische Katholizismus*', *Zeitschrift für Kirchengeschichte* 80 (1969), pp. 176–93; J. de Ghellinck, '*La carrière scientifique de Harnack*', *Revue de l'Histoire Ecclésiastique* 26 (1930), p. 963.
15. *WC*, p. 263. Harnack judged the Greek Catholic Church to be totally secular, with the exception of monasticism.
16. Hatch's most important contribution to historical criticism was his Hibbert lectures, 'Greek Influence on Christianity', delivered in 1888 and published after his death as *The Influence of Greek Ideas and Usages Upon the Christian Church* (London, Williams & Norgate, 1890); reprint edn, *The Influence of Greek Ideas on Christianity*, with a Foreword by

Frederick C. Grant (New York, Harper & Brothers, 1957). References in this study are to the reprint edn. Tyrrell recommended this work to Maude Petre, 15 August 1900: 'Far better than Harnack . . . would be Hatch's Hibbert Lectures.' Letters from George Tyrrell to Maude Petre, 1898–1908 (London, British Library, Add. MSS 52367).

17. Hatch, *The Influence of Greek Ideas*, pp. 351–2.
18. Ibid., p. 138.
19. Ibid., p. 282.
20. Sohm stated in *Kirchenrecht 1: Die geschichtlichen Grundlagen* (Munich, Duncker & Humblot, 1892), p. 700: '*Das Wesen der Kirche ist geistlich, das Wesen des Rechtes ist weltlich. Das Wesen des Kirchenrechtes steht mit dem Wesen der Kirche in Widerspruch.*' When Tyrrell read this work he was convinced that it necessitated a radical reconstruction of Catholicism. Letter to von Hügel, 28 February 1903. Correspondence between George Tyrrell and Friedrich von Hügel, 1897–1909 (London, British Library, Add. MSS 44928).
21. Sohm, *Outlines of Church History*, tr. May Sinclair (London, Macmillan, 1909), p. 35.
22. Harnack, *The Constitution and Law of the Church in the First Two Centuries*, ed. H. D. A. Major, tr. F. L. Pogson (London, Williams & Norgate, 1910), p. ix.
23. Ibid., p. 5.
24. In the aftermath of the war of 1870, the Protestant theological college of Strasbourg emigrated to Paris. The results of German historical criticism thus stimulated French Protestant thought. Sabatier's work had a profound effect on Liberal Protestantism and on Roman Catholic modernism. His most important works are: *Equisse d'une philosophie de la religion d'après la psychologie et l'histoire* (Paris, 1897) and *Les religions d'autorité et la religion de l'esprit* (Paris, 1903). Both works were translated into English: *Outlines of a Philosophy of Religion Based on Psychology and History*, tr. T. A. Seed (New York, George H. Doran, n.d.; reprint edn, New York, Harper & Brothers, 1957); references in this study are to the reprint edn; *Religions of Authority and the Religion of the Spirit*, tr. Louise Seymour Houghton (New York, George H. Doran, 1904).
25. Sabatier, *Outlines of a Philosophy of Religion*, p. 176.
26. Sabatier, *Religions of Authority*, p. 281.
27. Sabatier, *Outlines of a Philosophy of Religion*, p. 177.
28. Johannes Weiss, *Die Predigt Jesu vom Reiche Gottes* (Göttingen, Vandenhoeck & Ruprecht, 1892). This work was translated and edited by Richard Hyde Hiers and David Larrimore Holland as *Jesus' Proclamation of the Kingdom of God* (Philadelphia, Fortress, 1971). I have used this edn. Weiss published a second, much enlarged edn of his work in 1900.

Albert Schweitzer, *Das Messianitäts- und Leidensgeheimnis. Eine Skizze des Lebens Jesu* (Tübingen, Mohr, 1901). This work, the second part of a treatise entitled *Das Abendmahl*, was translated by W. Lowrie as *The Mystery of the Kingdom of God: The Secret of Jesus' Messiahship and Passion*

(London, A. & C. Black, 1914; reprint edn, 1950). Schweitzer's ideas on eschatology are reiterated and developed in subsequent works, particularly *Von Reimarus zu Wrede* (Tübingen, Mohr, 1906). This work was translated by W. Montgomery and published as *The Quest of the Historical Jesus: A Critical Study of Its Progress from Reimarus to Wrede* (London, A. & C. Black, 1910; 3rd edn, with a new Introduction, 1954).

29. Weiss applied his conclusions primarily to the preaching of Jesus. Schweitzer, who had not read Weiss when he wrote *Das Abendmahl*, went further in what he called '*konsequente Eschatologie*', applying these conclusions not only to the preaching of Jesus, but also to his ministry, and especially to his passion and death. In his Introduction to *The Quest of the Historical Jesus*, 3rd edn, Schweitzer wrote: 'Johannes Weiss shows the thoroughly eschatological character of Jesus' preaching about the Kingdom of God. My contribution is to find the eschatological clue, not only to his preaching but also to his life and work' (p. viii). Hiers and Holland, in their Introduction to *Jesus' Proclamation of the Kingdom of God*, pp. 30–4, point out that Schweitzer may have exaggerated the difference between Weiss and himself. Weiss applied eschatological ideas not only to the preaching of Jesus, but also to his struggle against Satan. Weiss, as well as Schweitzer, connected Jesus' decision to die in Jerusalem with his eschatological beliefs, but Weiss did not work out this theory as precisely as did Schweitzer.

30. Walter Lowrie in his Introduction to *The Mystery of the Kingdom of God: The Secret of Jesus' Messiahship and Passion* remarked that this work of Schweitzer received 'scant attention' in Germany when it was first published in 1901. See pp. 17–18. W. G. Kümmel in ' "*L'Eschatologie consequente*" *d'Albert Schweitzer jugée par ses contemporains*', *Revue d'Histoire et de Philosophie Religieuse* 37 (1957), pp. 58–70, commented that Schweitzer was not well received by either liberals or conservatives. His interpretation is more appreciated today than it was by his contemporaries.

31. Schweitzer, *The Quest of the Historical Jesus*, p. 396.

32. Schweitzer, *The Mystery of the Kingdom*, p. 251.

33. Frederick C. Grant remarked in his Foreword to Hatch's *The Influence of Greek Ideas on Christianity*, pp. x-xi: 'It is clearly evident that since 1900 the whole outlook and perspective of research into the origins of Christianity have been altered, chiefly by rereading the New Testament in the light of contemporary ancient Jewish and pagan eschatological hopes and ideas.'

34. Loisy's and Tyrrell's use of the eschatological view, as opposed to the Liberal Protestant view, in their defence of Catholicism, will be considered later.

35. For example, James George Frazer, *The Golden Bough: A Study in Magic and Religion*, 2 vols. (London, Macmillan, 1890; 2nd edn rev. in 3 vols., 1900). Additional vols. were written between 1900 and 1915. Frazer

used the comparative method to throw light on the origin of current beliefs and practices.

36. Ernst Troeltsch, *The Absoluteness of Christianity and the History of Religions*, tr. David Reid with an Introduction by James Luther Adams (Richmond, Va., John Knox, 1971). This work was based on a lecture given by Troeltsch in 1901.
37. Ibid., p. 122.
38. *CC*, p. 44.
39. Matthew Arnold, *Literature and Dogma: An Essay Toward the Better Apprehension of the Bible* (London, Smith, Elder, 1873); edited, abridged and with an Introduction by James C. Livingston (New York, Frederick Ungar, 1970).
40. For Sabatier's interpretation of dogma, see *The Vitality of Christian Dogmas and their Power of Evolution*, tr. Mrs Emmanuel Christen (London, A. & C. Black, 1898); *Outlines of a Philosophy of Religion*, pp. 223–337; *Religions of Authority*, pp. 342–79.
41. Sabatier, *Outlines of a Philosophy of Religion*, pp. 223–4.
42. Ibid., p. 336.
43. *Dei Filius*, p. 48 (DS 3020).
44. Ibid., p. 43 (DS 3008).

Notes to Chapter 4

1. A. Firmin, '*Le développement chrétien d'après le Cardinal Newman*', *Revue du Clergé Français* 17 (1899), pp. 5–20. This article by Loisy was one of six published in the *Revue* under the name A. Firmin. They were taken from an unpublished treatise on apologetics. Tyrrell discussed the difference between Newman's questions and those facing the 'modernists' in *Christianity at the Cross-Roads*.
2. Lash, *Newman on Development*, p. 147. Benard, in *A Preface to Newman's Theology*, p. 120, insisted that the resemblance between Loisy and Newman was 'only verbal'. See also Jan Henricus Walgrave, *Newman the Theologian: The Nature of Belief and Doctrine Exemplified in His Life and Works*, tr. A. V. Littledale (London, Geoffrey Chapman, 1960), pp. 293–5.
3. *L'Evangile et l'Eglise* (Paris, Picard, 1902) was written in response to Harnack's *Das Wesen des Christentums*. It was translated by Christopher Home as *The Gospel and the Church* (New York, Scribner, 1904); hereafter cited as *GC*. *Autour d'un petit livre*, 2nd edn (Paris, Picard, 1903), provided a further explanation of Loisy's method and the material dealt with in *L'Evangile*. It was written in the form of letters to various persons.
4. *GC*, pp. 2–3; *Autour*, pp. 11–20. He insisted: '*On n'écrit pas l'histoire à genoux, les yeux fermés devant le mystère divin*' (*Autour*, p. 11).
5. *GC*, p. 4.

6. Ibid., pp. 115–16.
7. Ibid., p. 150.
8. Ibid., p. 166.
9. Ibid., p. 181.
10. Ibid., pp. 210–11.
11. Ibid., p. 217.
12. Ibid., p. 224.
13. *Autour*, p. 205.
14. Glick, *The Reality of Christianity*, pp. 334–5.
15. Emile Poulat, '*Critique historique et théologie dans la crise moderniste*', *Recherches de Science Religieuse* 58 (1970), p. 538.
16. *CC*, p. 49.
17. Loisy told his story in *Choses passées* (Paris, Emile Nourry, 1913), tr. Richard Wilson Boynton and published as *My Duel With the Vatican: The Autobiography of a Catholic Modernist* (New York, Greenwood, 1968), and in *Mémoires pour servir à l'histoire religieuse de notre temps*, 3 vols. (Paris, Emile Nourry, 1930–1). Quotation from *My Duel With the Vatican*, p. 224.
18. See *My Duel with the Vatican*, pp. 165–73, and *Mémoires* 1, pp. 361–5, for Loisy's account of his work at Neuilly.
19. Vidler discussed 'the enigma of Loisy' in *A Variety of Catholic Modernists* (Cambridge University Press, 1970). He concluded that Loisy was sincere. He also published 'Last Conversation With Alfred Loisy', *Journal of Theological Studies*, n.s. 28 (1977), pp. 84–9, in which he quoted Loisy as saying 'that if he had not been chased out of the Church he would have been able to accommodate himself inside until his dying day' (p. 87). Others have been less positive in their judgement of Loisy. Loome, in *Liberal Catholicism, Reform Catholicism, Modernism*, p. 169, writes: 'It may even have been the case that Loisy, from the very beginning, had not really held the position articulated in *L'Evangile et l'Eglise* and that the book was more an intellectual exercise than a sincerely held *apologia* for Catholicism.' Daly sums up the various views on Loisy in *Transcendence and Immanence*, pp. 51–3. See also Valentine Moran, 'Loisy's Theological Development', *Theological Studies* 40 (1979), pp. 411–52. Recent studies, with the exception of Loome's, confirm Vidler's conviction concerning Loisy's sincerity.
20. See René Marlé, *Au coeur de la crise moderniste: Le Dossier inédit d'une controverse* (Paris, Aubier, 1960), pp. 48–113; Emile Poulat, *Histoire, dogme et critique dans la crise moderniste* (Paris, Casterman, 1962), pp. 514–33; Poulat, '*Critique historique et théologie dans la crise moderniste*', *Recherches de Science Religieuse* 58 (1970), pp. 535–50. Daly devotes a chapter to the debate between Loisy and Blondel in *Transcendence and Immanence*, pp. 69–90.
21. Introduction to *Total Commitment: Blondel's L'Action* (Washington, Corpus Books, 1968), p. 29.

22. Loisy's response to Blondel, 22 February 1903, quoted by Marlé, *Au Coeur de la crise moderniste,* p. 96.
23. This work first appeared in *La Quinzaine* (January-February 1904). It was translated along with Blondel's '*Lettre sur les exigences de la pensée contemporaine en matière d'apologétique et sur la méthode de la philosophie dans l'étude du problème religieux*', by Alexander Dru and Illtyd Trethowan in *The Letter on Apologetics and History and Dogma* (New York, Holt, Rinehart & Winston, 1964).
24. Ibid., p. 247. Von Hügel entered into the discussion with his '*Du Christ éternel et de nos christologies successives*', *La Quinzaine* 58 (June 1904), pp. 285–312.
25. Blondel, *History and Dogma*, p. 252.
26. Ibid., pp. 248–52.
27. *The Letter on Apologetics*, p. 184. '*Lettre sur les exigences de la pensée contemporaine en matière d'apologétique et sur la méthode de la philosophie dans l'étude du problème religieux*' appeared in *Annales de Philosophie Chrétienne* (January to July 1896) as a series of articles to correct misunderstandings concerning *L'Action: Essai d'une critique de la vie et d'une science de la pratique* (Paris, Alcan, 1893; reprint edn, Paris, Presses Universitaires de France, 1950), Blondel's famous doctoral thesis. *The Letter* was also misunderstood. See Prefatory Note by I. Trethowan, pp. 119–24.
28. Ibid., p. 169.
29. Ibid., p. 206.
30. Jean Lacroix, *Maurice Blondel: An Introduction to the Man and His Philosophy*, tr. John C. Guiness (New York, Sheed & Ward, 1968), p. 90.
31. Blondel describes his struggle to discern his vocation in *Carnets intimes 1883–1894* (Paris, Cerf, 1961), pp. 545–58.
32. *Letter on Apologetics*, pp. 146–7. The same concern may be found in many of Newman's writings, especially *Grammar of Assent* and *Apologia Pro Vita Sua*. Newman recognized the importance of the subjective element in religious inquiry. He was aware of the psychological processes by which he had come to recognize the Catholic Church as the true Church. He did not try to give proof, but simply described his own experience.

Notes to Chapter 5

1. *FM* 1:80.
2. Ibid., p. 17.
3. *OW*, p. 11.
4. *FM* 1:36.
5. Ibid., p. 21.
6. Ibid., pp. 8–9.
7. Henri Bremond in 'Father Tyrrell As an Apologist', *New York Review* 1 (1905–6), pp. 762–70, pointed out the need for the apologist to

mediate between contemporary thought and ecclesiastical tradition, as well as the need to be familiar with both worlds. Bremond considered Tyrrell well qualified to fulfil this task.

8. Tyrrell often referred to the abuse of scholasticism and the evils of rationalism. See especially 'The Use of Scholasticism', *FM* 1:205–27; 'Rationalism in Religion', *FM* 1:85–114; 'Adaptability As a Proof of Religion', *FM* 2: 277–347.

9. *Med*, p. 108.

10. 'Tyrrell's "Medievalism" ', *TM* 228 (1969), p. 19.

11. *LO*, p. xxxii.

12. Tyrrell provided few direct references to his sources. From his correspondence it is possible to ascertain the books he was reading at a particular time. David Schultenover did a parallel study of Tyrrell's works and his correspondence up to 1903. See 'Foundations and Genesis of Tyrrell's Philosophy of Religion and Apologetic' (Ph.D. dissertation, University of St Louis, 1975) and *George Tyrrell: In Search of Catholicism*.

13. *CC*, p. 19.

14. *Letters*, p. 89.

15. Letter to Fawkes, 3 June 1909, quoted in *Life* 2:400.

16. Quoted in *Life* 2:91–2.

17. Wilfred Lawrence Knox and Alec R. Vidler, *The Development of Modern Catholicism* (London, Philip Allan, 1933), p.171.

18. *SC*, pp. 360–1.

19. *CC*, p. 59.

20. *HS*, p. xvii.

21. This conception of Catholicism as a natural religion occurs in many of Tyrrell's writings, e.g., 'The Making of Religion', *FM*2:215–76; 'Adaptability As a Proof of Religion', *FM*2:277–347; 'Reflections on Catholicism', *SC*, pp. 20–84. The same arguments are used in *Med* and in *CC*.

22. *FM* 2:271; also *LC*, p. 97.

23. *SC*, p. 23.

24. Ibid., pp. 45–6.

25. Letter to Maude Petre, 28 August 1905, quoted in *Life* 2:206.

26. *LC*, pp. 131–2; cf. Sabatier, p. 43 above.

27. *SC*, p. 47; also *MAL*, pp. 77–8; *ER*, p. 69. An early reference to the way in which Catholicism has transformed paganism may be found in *NV*, p. 239, where Tyrrell refers to Mary as 'the great all-Mother of humanity, a conception dimly shadowed in the dark gropings of the pagan mind'.

28. *CC*, p. 167. Tyrrell considered that in some sense the science of religion would be a science of Catholicism. *CC*, p. 181.

29. Ibid., pp. 181–2.

30. *EFI*, p. 106.

31. *OW*, p. 151.

32. Ibid., p. 72.
33. *SC*, p. 75.
34. *Life* 1:119.
35. *HS*, p. 413. Tyrrell rejected 'false individualism' as antagonistic to true personal liberty as well as to altruism, but recognized a true individualism. See 'The New Sociology', *TM* 84 (1895), pp. 502–22.
36. *HS*, p. 406, from 'The Mystical Body', *HS*, pp. 397–448; see also 'The Communion of Saints', *OW*, pp. 321–7.
37. *ER*, p. 70.
38. *OW*, p. x.
39. *MAL*, p. 64.
40. *SC*, p. 77. See also *SC*, pp. 50–5; *CF*, p. 79; *MAL*, pp. 61–2 for Tyrrell's view on schism.
41. *CF*, p. 144.
42. *SC*, p. 77.
43. Ibid., p. 78.
44. *CC*, p. 25. The importance of tradition and the need for it to be criticized are constant themes in Tyrrell's writings. See *SC*, pp. 72, 307; *MAL*, p. 79.
45. 'Mercier's Lenten Pastoral', *Med*, p. 6. Tyrrell's response to Mercier's statement on tradition is on pp. 55–6.
46. *SC*, p. 81.
47. *OW*, p. ix.
48. *SC*, p. 4.
49. Studies have been made of Tyrrell's writings from the point of view of his understanding of revelation and dogma: Daniel Kilfoyle, 'The Conception of Doctrinal Authority in the Writings of George Tyrrell' (Th. D. dissertation, New York Union Theological Seminary, 1970); James Laubacher, *Dogma and the Development of Dogma in the Writings of George Tyrrell* (Baltimore, Watkins Printing Co., 1939); Francis O'Connor, 'George Tyrrell and Dogma', *Downside Review* 85 (1967), pp. 16–34, 160–82; O'Connor, 'Tyrrell: The Nature of Revelation', *Continuum* 3 (1965), pp. 168–77.
50. Tyrrell, 'Sabatier on the Vitality of Dogmas', *TM* 91 (1898), pp. 592–602; republished in *FM* 1:115–35. For Sabatier's understanding of dogma, see pp. 50–1 above. Other articles which reflect Tyrrell's early understanding of dogma are: 'Ecclesiastical Development', *TM* 90 (1897), pp. 380–90; 'Authority and Evolution, the Life of Catholic Dogma', *TM* 93 (1899), pp. 493–504.
51. *FM* 1:124.
52. Ibid., pp. 124–5.
53. Ibid., pp. 130–1.
54. *LO*, p. 39. This idea was also expressed in Tyrrell's allegory, *The Civilizing of the Matafanus*.
55. *CF*, p. 157. Tyrrell's understanding of dogma at this stage is expressed in *CF*, appendix 2, pp. 156–60, and in *LO*.

56. Tyrrell presented the differences between the old and the new theology as strongly as possible in '*Semper Eadem 1*', *TM* 103 (1904), pp. 1–17; republished in *SC*, pp. 106–32. This article caused considerable controversy. See *Life* 2:210–12.

57. *TM* refused to publish this article. It appeared as 'The Limits of the Theory of Development', *Catholic World* 81 (1905), pp. 730–44; republished in *SC*, pp. 133–54.

58. Tyrrell considered that Newman understood 'idea' in the same way that he did, i.e., as a spiritual force or impulse. *CC*, p. 43. Newman scholars disagree with Tyrrell. Walgrave emphasized that Newman's 'idea' is from the beginning genuine knowledge, though it may be unconscious or implicit. *Newman the Theologian*, pp. 293–5. See also Benard, *A Preface to Newman's Theology*, pp. 128–56.

59. *SC*, p. 143.

60. Ibid., p. 147. In *CC*, p. 41, Tyrrell again referred to the *University Sermon* as giving Newman's own conception, while the *Essay* was 'undoubtedly written with one eye fixed on his scholastic critics, and with a view to dissemble the difference between their conception and his own as much as possible'.

61. *CC*, pp. 44–5.

62. *SC*, p. 154.

63. *CC*, p. 21.

64. Ibid.

65. Tyrrell's understanding of revelation and its relationship to theology is developed in *SC*, especially in '*Lex Orandi, Lex Credendi*', pp. 85–105; 'The Rights and Limits of Theology', pp. 200–41; 'Revelation', pp. 264–307; ' "Theologism"—A Reply', pp. 308–54.

66. *SC*, p. 275.

67. Ibid., p. 276. Note the influence of Blondel.

68. *LC*, p. xv.

69. *Letters*, pp. 56–61. This letter, dated 10 April 1907, was a response to a question concerning the Virgin Birth. In this last phase, note the similarities between Tyrrell and Sabatier. See pp. 50–1 above.

70. *Letters*, p. 57.

71. Ibid., p. 59.

72. Ibid., p. 60.

73. Ibid.

74. This unpublished lecture has been edited with notes and historical introduction by Thomas Michael Loome, *Heythrop Journal* 12 (1971), pp. 117–49. The original manuscript is preserved in the British Library, Add. MSS 52369.

75. Ibid., pp. 145–6.

76. *CC*, p. 142.

77. *LO*, p. 161.

78. Ibid., p. 2.

79. *MAL*, p. 82.

80. *LO*, p. 28.
81. *HS*, p. 431.
82. Ibid., p. 434.
83. *EFI*, p. 117.
84. *CF*, p. 115. For an earlier consideration of this problem, see 'The Mystical Body', *HS*, pp. 397–448, especially pp. 422–30.
85. *CF*, p. 115.
86. Ibid., pp. 16–17.
87. For Tyrrell's assessment of Protestantism, see *CF*, pp. 117–24. In this section the influence of Harnack, Sohm and Sabatier is evident.
88. Ibid., pp. 124–5.
89. Ibid., p. 137. Tyrrell here adopts Troeltsch's thesis.
90. *CC*, p. 177.
91. Ibid., p. 178.
92. Ibid., p. 179.
93. *SC*, p. 36.
94. *CC*, p. 47.
95. Ibid., p. 60.
96. Ibid., pp. 60–77.
97. 'Towards a Fundamental Theological Interpretation of Vatican II', *Theological Studies* 40 (1979), pp. 716–27.
98. *The Spirit of Catholicism*, rev. edn, tr. Dom Justin McCann (London, Sheed & Ward, 1937), p. 260.
99. Rahner, 'Reflections on Methodology', *Theological Investigations* 11, tr. David Bourke (London, Darton, Longman & Todd, 1974; New York, Seabury, 1974), pp. 68–114.
100. *Foundations of Christian Faith: An Introduction to the Idea of Christianity*, tr. William V. Dych (London, Darton, Longman & Todd, 1978), p. 346.
101. In 'Tracts For the Millions', *FM* 2:136–57, Tyrrell noted that Catholicism supported those too weak to stand alone. However, this support provided by Catholic surroundings was disappearing. Rahner discusses the same phenomenon in *The Shape of the Church to Come*, tr. Edward Quinn (New York, Seabury, 1974).
102. *Catholicism: A Study of Dogma in Relation to the Corporate Destiny of Mankind*, tr. from the 4th French edn by Lancelot C. Sheppard (London, Burns & Oates, 1950), p. 153.
103. *CF*, p. 136.
104. *Lumen Gentium*, 13; quotation from *The Documents of Vatican II*, ed. Walter Abbott (New York, Guild, 1966; London, Geoffrey Chapman, 1966), p. 32.
105. *CC*, p. 177. See 'Declaration on the Relationship of the Church to Non-Christians', *Documents of Vatican II*, pp. 660–8.
106. *CC*, p. 177.
107. *Documents of Vatican II*, p. 715.
108. 'Decree on Ecumenism', 11, *Documents of Vatican II*, p. 354.
109. *MAL*, p. 86.

110. *Change in Focus: A Study of Doctrinal Change and Continuity* (London, Sheed & Ward, 1973), p. ix.
111. *CC*, pp. 21–2.
112. *Change in Focus*, p. 62.
113. Quoted in *Life* 2:349.
114. *CF*, pp. 137–8.
115. The Latin text was promulgated in January 1972, the approved English text in 1976. In the Introduction it states that the initiation of catechumens takes place step by step in the midst of the community of the faithful. The catechumens become familiar with living the Christian way of life.
116. *CF*, p. 138.
117. *OW*, p. xiii.
118. *Med*, p. 185.

Notes to Chapter 6

1. *Life*, 2:448.
2. Ibid., p. 320.
3. *CF*, pp. 13–14. Note the influence of Sabatier. See pp. 41–4 above.
4. 'The Abbé Loisy: Criticism and Catholicism', *Church Quarterly Review* 58 (1904), p. 195.
5. 'The Mind of the Church', *TM* 96 (1900), pp. 125–42, 233–40; republished in *FM* 1:158–204. '*Consensus Fidelium*', *New York Review* 1 (1905), pp. 133–8; republished as 'The Corporate Mind', *SC*, pp. 254–63. 'From Heaven, or Of Men?' *Il Rinnovamento* 1 (1907), pp. 394–414; republished in *SC*, pp. 355–86. References are to the republished versions.
6. See pp. 19–29 above for Tyrrell's personal struggles with authority as well as the struggles which were taking place in the Roman Catholic Church at the time.
7. This observation was made by B. M. Reardon, 'George Tyrrell, 1861–1961', *Modern Churchman*, n.s. 4 (1961), p. 163.
8. 'Ecclesiastical Developments', *TM* 90 (1897), pp. 380–90, is an example of Tyrrell's support for an authoritarian Church.
9. 'A More Excellent Way', *FM* 1:1–21, especially pp. 13–15.
10. De Lubac, *Catholicism*, p. 168; *FM* 1:15.
11. *FM* 1:14.
12. *ER*, p. 135.
13. *CF*, p. 129. Tyrrell confided to von Hügel that he wrote this book to convince himself that his position as a Catholic was an honest one. London, British Library, Add. MSS 44928.
14. *Med* represents this final stage in Tyrrell's understanding of authority.
15. Ibid., p. 63.
16. Tyrrell's arguments for the spiritual nature of ecclesiastical authority

are developed in *CF*, appendix 1, 'On Church Government', pp. 147–56.

17. Letters, p. 101.
18. *SC*, p. 381.
19. Ibid., p. 365.
20. Tyrrell accepted Sohm's thesis on Catholicism as the institutionalization of Christianity. Cf. pp. 40–1 above.
21. *SC*, pp. 381–2.
22. Ibid., p. 382.
23. Ibid., p. 386.
24. *CF*, p. 142.
25. Ibid., p. 29.
26. *CF*, pp. 54–64. Harnack considered this process inevitable, but reacted against the Catholic claim that the institutions which developed were of divine origin. See pp. 37–40 above. Sohm was more negative in his criticism of the catholicizing of Christianity, a development which he considered incompatible with the true nature of Christianity. See pp. 40–1 above. The influence of both these critics on Tyrrell is obvious, even as he argued against them. Note also the influence of Sabatier (pp. 41–4 above) and of Loisy (pp. 53–60 above).
27. *CF*, p. 121.
28. See 'The Mind of the Church', *FM*1:158–204, and 'Reflections on Catholicism', *SC*, especially pp. 58–64. In 'The Mind of the Church', Tyrrell made use of the ideas of William Hurrell Mallock in *Doctrine and Doctrinal Disruption: Being an Examination of the Intellectual Position of the Church of England* (London, A. & C. Black, 1900) as a response to Harnack. Mallock, a rationalist, regarded the Roman system as a phenomenon whose form and growth could be explained by natural laws.
29. *SC*, p. 59; see also 'The Corporate Mind', *SC*, pp. 254–63.
30. Ibid., p. 63.
31. Ibid., pp. 369–70.
32. *SC*, pp. 66–71; *Med*, p. 79; 'Prophetic and Scriptural Inspirations', *CF*, appendix 3, pp. 161–70; *CF*, pp. 140–1.
33. *CF*, p. 99.
34. *Med*, pp. 79–87. See p. 23 above for interpretations of Vatican I. In a letter to Bishop Herzog, Old Catholic bishop, Tyrrell denied 'the ecumenical authority of the exclusively Western Councils of Trent and the Vatican'. This letter was published in the *Guardian*, 20 October 1909. It is quoted in *Life* 2:383–4.
35. Tyrrell's description of the development of papal supremacy resembles that of Harnack, Sohm and Sabatier. See chapter 3 above. Tyrrell traced the growth of the conception of papal supremacy in *Med*, pp. 67–77.
36. *CF*, p. 103.

37. This is emphasized in many of Tyrrell's writings, e.g., *SC*, pp. 65, 262; *OW*, p. xi; *CF*, p. 156.
38. *Letters*, pp. 89–90.
39. *Med*, pp. 131–2.
40. *SC*, p. 358.
41. See Tyrrell's reactions to the joint pastoral of the English hierarchy, pp. 23–6 above.
42. *Med*, pp. 53, 62–3.
43. *CF*, p. 133.
44. Ibid., p. 160.
45. *Med*, p. 100.
46. Ibid., p. 57.
47. *Letters*, p. 103, addressed to Hon. Wm Gibson, 7 December 1906.
48. *ER*, pp. 129–30. This collection of conferences to Catholic undergraduates, delivered at Oxford in 1899, stressed the role of the educated lay person in the Church.
49. *MAL*, p. 92.
50. *SC*, p. 384.
51. *CF*, pp. 131–2.
52. *SC*, p. 386.
53. Tyrrell expressed this hope to Gibson, 7 December 1906; *Letters*, p. 103.
54. See *Dei Filius*, especially chapter 4, 'Faith and Reason', pp. 46–8, 51 (DS 3015–20, 3041–3).
55. *SC*, p. 335. This distinction between two generically different orders of truth was very important in Tyrrell's thought. It was the basis for a number of essays in *SC*: '*Lex Orandi, Lex Credendi*', pp. 461–73; 'The Rights and Limits of Theology', pp. 200–41; 'Prophetic History', pp. 242–53, in which he distinguished between the 'prophetic' reading of history and the scientific reading of the same; 'Revelation', pp. 264–307; and ' "Theologism"—A Reply', pp. 308–54. It also provided the basis for his response in *MAL*.
56. *SC*, p. 327.
57. Ibid., pp. 350–1. Note the influence of Sabatier on Tyrrell's idea of a scientific theology. See p. 50 above.
58. *SC*, p. 335.
59. *CF*, p. 143. Tyrrell developed his ideas on the place of criticism in the Church in 'The Ethics of Conformity', *CF*, appendix 3, pp. 139–46; also in *MAL*.
60. *SC*, p. 19; see also pp. 60–4, 368–9.
61. *CF*, p. 107.
62. Letter written in February 1906, quoted in *Life* 2:406.
63. *Letters*, p. 106.
64. *CF*, pp. 34–5.
65. *MAL*, p. 87.
66. *vH&T*, p. 151.
67. *Med*, p. 165.

68. *LC*, pp. 149–50.
69. This was emphasized by David Wells in 'The Pope as Antichrist: The Substance of George Tyrrell's Polemic', *Harvard Theological Review* 65 (1972), pp. 271–83. Wells pointed out that many of Tyrrell's positions were quietly adopted at Vatican II and added, 'though, of course, his intemperance can never be pardoned' (p. 283).
70. Letter to the Old Catholic Bishop, Vernon Herford, April 1907; *Letters*, p. 113.
71. *SC*, p. 385.
72. *Med*, pp. 138–9.
73. *Lumen Gentium*, 18, *Documents of Vatican II*, p. 37.
74. Ibid.
75. Ibid., 23, p. 44.
76. *SC*, p. 358.
77. Newman, *On Consulting the Faithful in Matters of Doctrine*, ed. with Introduction by John Coulson (London, Geoffrey Chapman, 1961), p. 63. This work first appeared in the *Rambler*, July 1859; reprinted 1871 as an appendix to the 3rd edn of *The Arians of the Fourth Century*. Coulson refers to its publication as 'political suicide' for Newman (p. 1).
78. *Lumen Gentium*, 12, *Documents of Vatican II*, p. 29.
79. 'The Teaching Office of the Church in the Present-Day Crisis of Authority', *TI* 12, tr. David Bourke (New York, Seabury, 1974; London, Darton, Longman & Todd, 1974), p. 5, n. 4.
80. *God the Future of Man*, tr. N. D. Smith (New York, Sheed & Ward, 1968), p. 44.
81. *Lay People in the Church: A Study for a Theology of Laity*, tr. Donald Attwater (London, Bloomsbury Publishing, 1957), p. xxvii.
82. *SC*, p. 383.
83. *Life* 2:145.
84. *OW*, p. 180. A similar attitude towards dissent has been expressed by Adrian Hastings, *In Filial Disobedience* (Essex, Mayhew-McCrimmon, 1978).
85. 'The Theologian and the Magisterium', *Catholic Theological Society of America Proceedings* 31 (1976), pp. 240–1.
86. Richard McCormick in his 'Notes on Moral Theology: 1978', *TS* 40 (1979), pp. 80–97, does a review of works dealing with *Humanae Vitae* and the Magisterium on the occasion of the tenth anniversary of the encyclical.
87. *Letters and Diaries of John Henry Newman*, ed. Charles Stephen Dessain, vol. 20, p. 447. From a letter to Emily Bowles, 19 May 1863.
88. For a survey of recent studies on the relationship between the theologian and the teaching office of the Church, see Richard McCormick, 'Notes on Moral Theology: 1976', *TS* 38 (1977), pp. 84–100; 'Notes on Moral Theology: 1979', *TS* 41 (1980), pp. 98–123. Also Rahner, 'Theology and the Church's Teaching Authority After the Council', *TI* 9, tr. Graham Harrison (New York, Herder & Herder, 1972; London, Dar-

ton, Longman & Todd, 1972), pp. 83–100; 'Freedom in the Church', *TI* 2, tr. Karl-H. Kruger (Baltimore, Helicon Press, 1963; London, Darton, Longman & Todd, 1963), pp. 97–114; 'The Teaching Office of the Church in the Present-Day Crisis of Authority', *TI* 12, tr. David Bourke (New York, Seabury, 1974; London, Darton, Longman & Todd, 1974), pp. 3–30.

89. 'Freedom in the Church', *TI* 2:107.
90. *CF*, p. 160.
91. *CC*, p. 181.

Notes to Chapter 7

1. Alec R. Vidler, *The Modernist Movement in the Roman Catholic Church: Its Origins and Outcome* (Cambridge University Press, 1934), p. 142.
2. *CC* is the closest that Tyrrell came to a systematic response, but it is more a sketch than a complete treatise.
3. *vH&T*, p. 175, quotation from a letter written in June 1908.
4. *MAL*, p. 89; also letter to Bremond, January 1902, *Lettres*, p. 106.
5. *MAL*, p. 100.
6. Quoted in *Life* 2:413.
7. Letter to Rev. T. MacClelland, November 1907, quoted in *Life* 2:373.
8. *Med*, p. 187.
9. Ibid., p. 183.
10. Letter to Rev. R. Abbott, August 1904; quoted in *Life* 2:407.
11. *SC*, p. 56.
12. *CF*, p. 113.
13. *CC*, p. 177.
14. *CF*, pp. 135–6.
15. Ibid., p. 136.
16. Ibid., p. 137.
17. *Letters*, pp. 135–6.
18. *CC*, p. 182. The same hope is expressed in *CF*, p. 136, and *SC*, pp. 384–5.
19. *SC*, p. 361.
20. Knox and Vidler, *The Development of Modern Catholicism*, p. 142.
21. See *CF*, pp. 117–24, as an example of Tyrrell's presentation of Protestantism.
22. Harnack did not deal with the Greek Church after the third century because he considered that there had been no further development of dogma. *HD* 1:5. Tyrrell accepted Harnack's position. *CF*, p. 116.
23. *MAL*, p. 38.
24. 'Josephine Ward on Maude Petre's Modernism', *Insurrection versus Resurrection*, appendix A, p. 554.
25. *SC*, p. 383.

26. Letter to Lilley, 7 March 1904. Lilley Papers, University of St Andrews, MSS 30776.

27. *Letters*, p. 159.

28. In his Preface to *Lettres*, Maurice Nédoncelle used three words to describe Tyrrell's work: '*mobilité*, overstatement, *fidelité*' (p. 17).

29. *OW*, p. ix.

30. Joseph Crehan, 'More Tyrrell Letters—I', *TM* 226 (1968), p. 179.

31. Crehan, 'Tyrrell in His Workshop', *TM* 231 (1971), p. 114.

32. *OW*, pp. vi-vii, written in January 1907.

33. Petre Papers, British Library, Add. MSS 45744, pp. 204–5.

34. James A. Walker, 'Maude Petre (1863–1942). A Memorial Tribute', *Hibbert Journal* 41 (1942–3), p. 341.

35. *vH&T*, pp. x-xi.

36. Antonia White, *The Hound and the Falcon: The Story of a Reconversion to the Catholic Faith* (London, Longmans, 1965), p. 93.

37. *vH&T*, p. xi.

38. Alec R. Vidler, *The Modernist Movement in the Roman Catholic Church: Its Origins and Outcome*, p. 266. Vidler discussed at some length the influence of Roman Catholic modernism on the Church of England. See pp. 241–68.

39. On a card to Waller, 9 June 1903, British Library, Add. MSS 43680.

40. In this work Rahner describes the Church of the future as an open Church, an ecumenical Church, a Church from the roots, a democratized Church, a socio-critical Church. See pp. 93–132.

41. *FM* 2:279–80.

42. *Letters*, p. 119.

43. 'Father Tyrrell and the Catholic Crisis', *New Blackfriars* 50 (1969), p. 597.

44. *Med*, p. 101.

45. *OW*, p. 11.

46. *Letters*, p. 165.

47. Letter to A. L. Lilley, 22 November 1906, Lilley Papers, St Andrews University Library, MSS 30812.

48. To Rev. Canon Newsom, 7 September 1909, *Selected Letters 1896–1924*, ed. with a Memoir by Bernard Holland (London, Dent, 1927), pp. 167–8.

Selected Bibliography

THE WRITINGS OF GEORGE TYRRELL

The following bibliography includes only those writings of George Tyrrell which pertain to this study. For a more complete bibliography of Tyrrell's writings, see Thomas Michael Loome, 'A Bibliography of the Published Works of George Tyrrell (1861–1909)', *Heythrop Journal* 10 (1969), pp. 280–314, and 'A Bibliography of the Printed Works of George Tyrrell: Supplement', *Heythrop Journal* 11(1970), pp. 161–9. Entries are listed chronologically, by date of publication.

Books

Nova et Vetera: Informal Meditations for Times of Spiritual Dryness. London, Longmans, 1897, 1898[2], 1900[3], 1905[4], 1913[5].

Hard Sayings: A Selection of Meditations and Studies. London, Longmans, 1898, 1899[2], 1900[3], 1901[4], 1903[5], 1904[6], 1910[7].

External Religion: Its Use and Abuse. London, Sands, 1899. Longmans, 1900[2], 1903[3], 1906[4], 1914[5].

The Faith of the Millions: A Selection of Past Essays. Two series. London, Longmans, 1901, 1902[2], 1904[3].

Oil and Wine. Printed and privately circulated in 1902. London, Longmans, 1907, 1907[2], 1911[3].

The Church and the Future. Privately printed in 1903 and signed Hilaire Bourdon. Reprinted under Tyrrell's name with an Introduction by M. D. Petre. London, Priory Press, 1910, 1910[2].

Lex Orandi: or Prayer and Creed. London, Longmans, 1903, 1904[2], 1907[3].

A Much-Abused Letter. Printed and circulated privately and anonymously in 1904 as 'A Letter To a Friend, a Professor of Anthropology in a Continental University'. Reprinted under Tyrrell's name with an Introduction and an Epilogue. London, 1906, 1907[2], 1910[3].

The Soul's Orbit: or Man's Journey to God. Compiled with additions by M. D. Petre. London, Longmans, 1904.

Lex Credendi: A Sequel to Lex Orandi. London, Longmans, 1906, 1907[2].

Through Scylla and Charybdis: or The Old Theology and the New. London, Longmans, 1907.

Medievalism: A Reply to Cardinal Mercier. London, Longmans, 1908, 1908[2], 1909[3], 1909[4].

Christianity at the Cross-Roads. London, Longmans, 1909, 1910[2], 1910[3], 1913[4]. Reprint edn with a Foreword by A. R. Vidler. London, George Allen & Unwin, 1963.

Autobiography and Life of George Tyrrell. 2 vols. Vol. 1: *Autobiography of George Tyrrell 1861–1884*, arranged with supplements by M. D. Petre. Vol. 2: *Life of George Tyrrell from 1884 to 1909*, by M. D. Petre. London, Edward Arnold, 1912.

Essays on Faith and Immortality, arranged by M. D. Petre. London, Edward Arnold, 1914.

Articles

Only those articles pertinent to this study and not included in the above collections of essays are listed here.

'The Oxford School and Modern Religious Thought.' *The Month* 79 (December 1893), pp. 560–8. *The Month* 80 (January 1894), pp. 59–68.

'Who Made the Sacraments?' *The Month* 83 (January 1895), pp. 120–30.

'The New Sociology.' *The Month* 84 (August 1895), pp. 502–22.

'Socialism and Catholicism.' *The Month* 89 (March 1897), pp. 280–8.

'Ecclesiastical Development.' *The Month* 90 (October 1897), pp. 380–90.

'Sacerdotalism in the Catholic Church.' *American Ecclesiastical Review* 18 (April 1898), pp. 350–64.

'Authority and Evolution, the Life of Catholic Dogma.' *The Month* 93 (May 1899), pp. 493–504.

'Dogma and Dogmatism.' *The Catholic World* 72 (January 1901), pp. 468–77. Published under the pseudonym 'E.F.G.'.

'The Recent Anglo-Roman Pastoral.' *The Nineteenth Century* 49 (May 1901), pp. 736–54. Although published under Lord Halifax's signature, the article was by Tyrrell except for the introduction and conclusion.

'The Limitations of Newman.' *The Monthly Register* 1 (October 1902), pp. 264–5.

'Religion and Ethics.' *The Month* 101 (February 1903), pp. 130–45.

'The Abbé Loisy: Criticism and Catholicism.' *Church Quarterly Review* 58 (April 1904), pp. 180–95.

'The Pope and Modernism.' *The Times*, 30 September 1907, p. 4; 1 October 1907, p. 5.

'L'Excommunication salutaire.' *La Grande Revue* 44 (10 October 1907), pp. 661–72.

'The Prospects of Modernism.' *Hibbert Journal* 6 (January 1908), pp. 241–55.

'Mediaevalism and Modernism.' *Harvard Theological Review* 1 (July 1908), pp. 304–24.

'The Point at Issue.' In *Jesus or Christ? Hibbert Journal Supplement for 1909*, pp. 5–16. London, Williams & Norgate, 1909.

' "Revelation As Experience": An Unpublished Lecture of George Tyrrell.' Ed. with notes and historical introduction by Thomas Michael Loome. *Heythrop Journal* 12 (April 1971), pp. 117–49. Originally composed as a lecture, it was delivered by Tyrrell before an audience of professors and students of King's College, London, 26 March 1909.

Correspondence

Correspondence between George Tyrrell and Friedrich von Hügel, 1897–1909. London, British Library, Add. MSS 44927–31.

George Tyrrell's Letters. Sel. and ed. M. D. Petre. London, T. Fisher Unwin, 1920.

Letters from George Tyrrell to Maude Petre, 1898–1908. London, British Library, Add. MSS 52367.

Lettres de George Tyrrell à Henri Bremond. Présentées, traduites et annotées par Anne Louis-David. Préface de Maurice Nédoncelle. Paris, Aubier-Montaigne, 1971.

Letters from George Tyrrell to Alfred Lilley. St Andrews University Library, MSS 30764–882.

SELECTED SECONDARY SOURCES

Abbot, Walter, general ed., and Gallagher, Joseph, tr. ed. *The Documents of Vatican II*. New York, Guild, 1966; London, Geoffrey Chapman, 1966.

Adam, Karl. *The Spirit of Catholicism*. Rev. edn tr. Dom Justin McCann. London, Sheed & Ward, 1937.

Adolfs, Robert. *The Grave of God: Has the Church a Future?* Tr. N. D. Smith. New York, Harper & Row, 1966. London, Burns & Oates, 1967.

Arnold, Matthew. *Literature and Dogma: An Essay Toward the Better Apprehension of the Bible.* London, Smith, Elder, 1873. Ed., abridged and with an Introduction by James C. Livingston. New York, Frederick Ungar, 1970.

Aubert, Roger. 'Modernism.' In *Sacramentum Mundi* 4:99–104. Ed. Karl Rahner et al. Montreal, Palm, 1969; London, Burns & Oates, 1968.

'Recent Literature on the Modernist Movement.' In *Historical Investigations. Concilium* 17, pp. 91–108. Ed. Roger Aubert. New York, Paulist, 1966.

Augustine, Aurelius, Saint. *De vera religione.* In *Augustine: Earlier Writings.* Tr. with introductions by John Burleigh. *Library of Christian Classics* vol. 6. Philadelphia, Westminster, 1953.

Ballard, Richard. 'George Tyrrell and the Apocalyptic Vision of Christ.' *Theology* 78 (1975), pp. 459–67.

Barmann, Lawrence F. *Baron Friedrich von Hügel and the Modernist Crisis in England.* Cambridge University Press, 1972.

Barth, Karl. *From Rousseau to Ritschl.* Tr. Brian Cozens from eleven chapters of *Die Protestantische Theologie im 19. Jahrhundert.* London, SCM, 1959.

Protestant Theology in the Nineteenth Century: Its Background and History. Tr. Brian Cozens and John Bowden. London, SCM, 1972.

Baum, Gregory. *The Credibility of the Church Today: A Reply to Charles Davis.* New York, Herder & Herder, 1968.

(ed.) *Journeys: The Impact of Personal Experience on Religious Thought.* New York, Paulist, 1975.

Baur, Ferdinand Christian. *The Church History of the First Three Centuries.* 2 vols. Tr. A. Menzies. 3rd edn. London, Williams & Norgate, 1878–9.

Bedoyère, Michael de la. *The Life of Baron von Hügel.* London, Dent, 1951.

Belfield, John. 'The "Theological" Method of George Tyrrell: A Study of the Modernist Crisis in the Light of George Tyrrell's Thought.' S.T.D. dissertation, Catholic University of America, 1964.

Benard, Edmond Darvil. *A Preface to Newman's Theology.* London, B. Herder Book Co., 1945.

Berthelot, René. *Un romantisme utilitaire: étude sur le mouvement prag-*

matiste. 3 vols. Vol. 3: *Le pragmatisme religieux chez William James et chez les catholiques modernistes*. Paris, F. Alcan, 1922.

Blondel, Maurice. *L'Action: Essai d'une critique de la vie et d'une science de la pratique*. Paris, Alcan, 1893; reprint edn, Paris, Presses Universitaires de France, 1950.

— *Carnets intimes 1883–1894*. Paris, Cerf, 1961.

— *The Letter on Apologetics and History and Dogma*. Tr. with an Introduction by Alexander Dru and Illtyd Trethowan. New York, Holt, Rinehart & Winston, 1964. London, Harrill, 1964.

— *Lettres philosophiques*. Paris, Aubier-Montaigne, 1961.

— *Le Problème de la philosophie catholique*. Paris, Bloud et Gay, 1932.

Bokenkotter, Thomas S. *Cardinal Newman as Historian*. Louvain, Publications Universitaires, 1959.

Bonsirven, Joseph. *Le Règne de Dieu*. Paris, Aubier-Montaigne, 1957.

Boudens, R. 'George Tyrrell and Cardinal Mercier: A Contribution to the History of Modernism.' *Eglise et Théologie* 1 (1970), pp. 313–51.

Bouillard, Henri. *Blondel and Christianity*. Tr. James M. Somerville. Washington, Corpus Books, 1969.

Bremond, Henri. 'Father Tyrrell As an Apologist.' *New York Review* 1 (1905–6), pp. 762–70.

— *The Mystery of Newman*. Tr. H. C. Corrance. Introduction by George Tyrrell. London, Williams & Norgate, 1907.

Bremond, Henri, et Blondel, Maurice. *Correspondance: Les Commencements d'une amitié (1897–1904). Etablie, présentée et annotée par André Blanchet*. Paris, Aubier-Montaigne, 1970.

Briggs, Charles A. 'The Encyclical Against Modernism.' *North American Review* 187 (1908), pp. 199–212.

Broderick, John F., ed. and tr. *Documents of Vatican I, 1869–1870*. Collegeville, Liturgical Press, 1971.

Bruce, Alexander Balmain. *Apologetics: or Christianity Defensively Stated*. New York, Charles Scribner's Sons, 1892.

[Buonaiuti, Ernesto.] *The Programme of Modernism: A Reply to the Encyclical of Pius x, Pascendi Dominici Gregis*. Tr. from the Italian with an Introduction by A. Leslie Lilley. London, J. Fisher Unwin, 1908.

Burke, Ronald, and Gilmore, George, eds. *Three Discussions: Biblical Exegesis, George Tyrrell, Jesuit Archives*. Proceedings of the Roman Catholic Modernism Working Group of the American Academy of Religion. Mobile, Spring Hill College Press, 1981.

— *Current Research in Roman Catholic Modernism*. Proceedings of the

Roman Catholic Modernism Working Group of the American Academy of Religion. Mobile, Spring Hill College Press, 1980.

Proceedings of the Roman Catholic Modernism Group of the American Academy of Religion. Mobile, Spring Hill College Press, 1979.

Burke, Thomas F. 'The Errors Condemned.' *Catholic World* 86 (January 1908), pp. 524–31.

Carlen, Sr M. Claudia. *A Guide to the Encyclicals of the Roman Pontiffs from Leo XIII to the Present Day (1878–1937).* New York, H. W. Wilson, 1939.

Catechism of the Council of Trent for Parish Priests Issued by Order of Pope Pius V. Tr. John A. McHugh and Charles J. Callan. Rev. 2nd edn. New York, Joseph F. Wagner, 1934.

Chadwick, Owen. *From Bossuet to Newman: The Idea of Doctrinal Development.* Cambridge University Press, 1957.

Chapman, Ronald. 'The Thought of George Tyrrell.' In *Essays and Poems Presented to Lord David Cecil*, pp. 140–68. Ed. W. W. Robson. London, Constable, 1970.

Chenu, M.-D. *Toward Understanding Saint Thomas.* Tr. A. M. Landy and D. Hughes. Chicago, Regnery, 1964.

'The Church and Liberal Catholicism: Joint Pastoral Letter by the Cardinal Archbishop and the Bishops of Westminster.' *Tablet* 97 (5 January 1901), pp. 8–12; (12 January 1901), pp. 50–2.

Congar, Yves. *A History of Theology.* Tr. and ed. Hunter Guthrie. New York, Doubleday, 1968.

Lay People in the Church: A Study for a Theology of Laity. Tr. Donald Attwater. London, Bloomsbury Publishing, 1957.

'*R. Sohm nous interroge encore.*' *Revue des Sciences Philosophiques et Théologiques* 57 (1973), pp. 263–94.

Sainte Eglise: Etudes et approches ecclésiologiques. Paris, Cerf, 1963.

Corrance, Henry C. Review of the *Autobiography and Life of George Tyrrell*, arranged with supplements by M. D. Petre. *Hibbert Journal* 11 (1913), pp. 441–5.

Coulson, John, and Allchin, A. M., eds. *The Rediscovery of Newman: An Oxford Symposium.* London, Sheed & Ward, 1967.

Crehan, Joseph. 'More Tyrrell Letters—1.' *The Month* 226 (1968), pp. 178–85.

'Tyrrell in His Workshop.' *The Month* 231 (1971), pp. 111–15, 119.

'What Influenced and Finally Killed George Tyrrell?' *Catholic Medical Quarterly* 26 (1974), pp. 75–85.

Cross, F. L. 'Newman and the Doctrine of Development.' *Church Quarterly Review* 115 (1933), pp. 245–57.

(ed.) *Oxford Dictionary of the Christian Church*. 2nd edn. London, Oxford University Press, 1974.

Currier, Charles W. 'Modernism in the Past Year: A Review.' *Ecclesiastical Review* 39 (1908), pp. 465–72, 618–27.

Daly, Gabriel. 'Some Reflections on the Character of George Tyrrell.' *Heythrop Journal* 10 (1969), pp. 256–74.
Transcendence and Immanence: A Study in Catholic Modernism and Integralism. Oxford, Clarendon, 1980.
'Tyrrell's "Medievalism".' *The Month* 228 (1969), pp. 15–22.

Dell, Robert Edward. 'A Liberal Catholic View of the Case of Dr. Mivart.' *Nineteenth Century* 47 (1900), pp. 669–84.

Donovan, Daniel. 'The Lesson of Alfred Loisy.' *Ecumenist* 15 (1976), pp. 5–11.

Dru, Alec. 'Modernism and the Present Position of the Church.' *Downside Review* 82 (1964), pp. 103–10.

Duffy, Eamon. 'George Tyrrell and Liberal Protestantism: An Essay in Development.' *King's Theological Review* 2 (1979), pp. 13–21.

Dulles, Avery. *A History of Apologetics*. London, Hutchinson, 1971.
Revelation Theology: A History. New York, Herder & Herder, 1969. London, Burns & Oates, 1970.
'The Theologian and the Magisterium.' *Catholic Theological Society of America Proceedings* 31 (1976), pp. 235–46.

Elliot, John H. 'A Catholic Gospel: Reflections on "Early Catholicism" in the New Testament.' *The Catholic Biblical Quarterly* 31 (1969), pp. 213–23.

'The Encyclical: A Criticism in *The Times*.' *Tablet* 110 (12 October 1907), pp. 561–3.

'The Encyclical on the Teachings of Modernists in Our Seminaries.' *Ecclesiastical Review* 37 (1907), pp. 504–11.

'The Encyclical *Pascendi*.' *Dublin Review* 142 (1908), pp. 1–10.

Fawkes, Alfred. *Studies in Modernism*. London, Smith, Elder, 1913.

Fesquet, Henri. *Catholicism: Religion of Tomorrow?* Tr. Irene Uribe. New York, Holt, Rinehart & Winston, 1964.

Feuillet, A. '*Le Règne de Dieu et la personne de Jésus d'après les évangiles synoptiques*.' In *Introduction à la Bible: Nouveau Testament*, pp. 771–818. Eds. A. Robert and A. Feuillet. Tournai, Desclée, 1959.

Fitzer, Joseph. 'Tyrrell and Le Roy: Their Case Reopened.' *Communio Viatorum* 18 (1975), pp. 201–24.

Fransen, Peter. 'The Authority of the Councils.' In *Problems of Authority*, pp. 43–78. Ed. J. M. Todd. Baltimore, Helicon, 1962.

Frazer, James George. *The Golden Bough: A Study in Magic and*

Religion. 2 vols., 1890. 2nd rev. edn in 3 vols. London, Macmillan, 1900.

Gerard, John. 'The Papal Encyclical: From a Catholic's Point of View.' *Hibbert Journal* 6 (1908), pp. 256–63.

Ghellinck, J. de. '*La carrière scientifique de Harnack*.' *Revue de l'Histoire Ecclésiastique* 26 (1930), pp. 962–91.

Gibson, William. 'An Outburst of Activity in the Roman Congregations.' *Nineteenth Century* 45 (1899), pp. 785–94.

Gilkey, Langdon. *Catholicism Confronts Modernity: A Protestant View*. New York, Seabury, 1975.

Glick, G. Wayne. *The Reality of Christianity: A Study of Adolf von Harnack as Historian and Theologian*. New York, Harper & Row, 1967.

Goetz, Joseph. 'Analogy and Symbol: A Study in the Theology of George Tyrrell.' Ph.D. dissertation, University of Cambridge, 1969.

'Coleridge, Newman and Tyrrell: A Note.' *Heythrop Journal* 14 (1973), pp. 431–6.

'Father Tyrrell and the Catholic Crisis.' *New Blackfriars* 50 (1969), pp. 589–98.

Gooch, George Peabody. *History and Historians in the Nineteenth Century*. Rev. 2nd edn. Toronto, Longmans, 1967.

Goodier, Alban. 'Father Tyrrell and the Modernist Movement.' Review of book by J. Lewis May. *Dublin Review* 383 (1932), pp. 288–93.

Groot, Jan. 'The Church As Sacrament of the World.' Tr. Theodore Westow. In *The Sacraments in General: A New Perspective. Concilium* 31, pp. 51–66. New York, Paulist, 1967.

Guibert, Joseph de. *The Jesuits: Their Spirituality, Doctrine and Practice*. Tr. William Young. Chicago, Loyola University Press, 1964.

Haight, Roger D. 'Mission: The Symbol for Understanding the Church Today.' *Theological Studies* 37 (1976), pp. 620–49.

Hamilton, Robert. 'Faith and Knowledge: The Autobiography of Maude Petre.' *Downside Review* 85 (1967), pp. 148–59.

Hanbury, Michael. 'Von Hügel and Tyrrell.' *The Month* 218 (1964), pp. 323–6.

Harnack, Adolf. *Christianity and History*. Tr. T. B. Saunders with an Introductory Note. London, A. & C. Black, 1898.

The Constitution and Law of the Church in the First Two Centuries. Ed. H. D. A. Major. Tr. F. L. Pogson. London, Williams & Norgate, 1910.

Entstehung und Entwicklung der Kirchenverfassung und des Kirchenrechts in den zwei ersten Jahrhunderten, nebst einer Kritik der Abhandlung R. Sohm's 'Wesen und Ursprung des Katholizismus.' Leipzig, J. C. Hinrichs, 1910.

History of Dogma. Tr. from the 3rd German edn by Neil Buchanan. 7 vols. in 4. New York, Dover, 1961.

The Mission and Expansion of Christianity in the First Three Centuries. 2 vols. Tr. and ed. James Moffat. 2nd rev.edn. New York, Harper, 1962.

Outlines of the History of Dogma. Tr. Edwin Knox Mitchell. London, Hodder & Stoughton, 1893.

Reden und Aufsätze. 2 vols. Giessen, Töpelmann, 1904.

What Is Christianity? Tr. Thomas Bailey Saunders. Rev. 2nd edn. New York, Putnam, 1901. London, Williams & Norgate, 1901. Reprint edn with Introduction by Rudolf Bultmann. New York, Harper & Row, 1957.

Harrold, Charles Frederick. *John Henry Newman.* Hamden, Conn., Archon, 1966.

Hartnett, Thomas P. 'A Modernist Ecclesiology: The Relationship of Church and Doctrine in the Writings of George Tyrrell.' *Dunwoodie Review* 11 (1971), pp. 125–69.

Harvey, Van Austin. *The Historian and the Believer: The Morality of Historical Knowledge and Christian Belief.* New York, Macmillan, 1966.

Hastings, Adrian. *In Filial Disobedience.* Essex, Mayhew-McCrimmon, 1978.

Hatch, Edwin. *The Growth of Church Institutions.* London, Hodder & Stoughton, 1887.

The Influence of Greek Ideas and Usages Upon the Christian Church. London, Williams & Norgate, 1890; reprint edn, *The Influence of Greek Ideas on Christianity.* Foreword by Frederick C. Grant. New York, Harper & Row, 1957.

Memorials of Edwin Hatch. Ed. Samuel C. Hatch. London, Hodder & Stoughton, 1890.

The Organization of the Early Christian Churches. New York, Burt Franklin, 1881; reprint edn, 1972.

Healey, C. J. 'Aspects of Tyrrell's Spirituality.' *Downside Review* 95 (1977), pp. 133–48.

'M. Petre: Her Life and Significance.' *Recusant History* 15 (1979), pp. 23–42.

'Tyrrell On the Church.' *Downside Review* 91 (1973), pp. 35–50.

Heaney, John J. *The Modernist Crisis: von Hügel.* London, Geoffrey Chapman, 1969.

Hodgson, Peter C. *The Formation of Historical Theology: A Study of Ferdinand Christian Baur*. New York, Harper & Row, 1966.

Holmes, Edward. 'Tyrrell On the Church.' *Hibbert Journal* 24 (1926), pp. 322–33.

Hügel, Friedrich von. '*Du Christ éternel et de nos christologies successives*.' *La Quinzaine* 58 (1904), pp. 285–312.

Essays and Addresses on the Philosophy of Religion. London, Dent, 1921.

Essays and Addresses on the Philosophy of Religion. Second Series. London, Dent, 1926.

'Father Tyrrell: Some Memorials of the Last Twelve Years of His Life.' *Hibbert Journal* 8 (1910), pp. 233–52.

The Mystical Element of Religion As Studied in Saint Catherine of Genoa and Her Friends. 2 vols. 2nd edn. London, Dent, 1923; reprint edn, 1927.

Selected Letters 1896–1924. Ed. with a Memoir by Bernard Holland. London, Dent, 1927.

Hurley, Michael. 'George Tyrrell: Some Post-Vatican II Impressions.' *Heythrop Journal* 10 (1969), pp. 243–55.

Inge, W. R. 'The Meaning of Modernism.' *The Quarterly Review* 210 (1909), pp. 571–603.

Review of *Christianity at the Cross-Roads*, by George Tyrrell. *Hibbert Journal* 8 (1910), pp. 434–8.

James, William. *The Varieties of Religious Experience: A Study in Human Nature*. Introduction by Reinhold Niebuhr. London, Longmans, 1935.

Jenkins, R. G. F. 'Tyrrell's Dublin Days.' *The Month* 228 (1969), pp. 8–15.

'The Joint Pastoral' [news commentary]. *Tablet* 97 (5 January 1901), pp. 5–6.

Joly, Henri. *St. Ignatius of Loyola*. Tr. Mildred Partridge. Preface by George Tyrrell. London, Duckworth, 1899.

Kavanaugh, James J. *The Struggle of the Unbeliever*. New York, Trident, 1968.

Kilfoyle, Daniel. 'The Conception of Doctrinal Authority in the Writings of George Tyrrell.' Th.D. dissertation, New York Union Theological Seminary, 1970.

Knox, Wilfred Lawrence, and Vidler, Alec R. *The Development of Modern Catholicism*. London, Philip Allan, 1933.

Kümmel, Werner Georg. ' "*L'Eschatologie conséquente*" *d'Albert Schweitzer jugée par ses contemporains*.' *Traduit de l'allemand par H.*

Mehl. *Revue d'Histoire et de Philosophie Religieuse* 37 (1957), pp. 58–70.

Promise and Fulfilment: The Eschatological Message of Jesus. 2nd edn. Tr. Dorothea Barton. London, SCM, 1961.

Küng, Hans. 'Early Catholicism in the New Testament As a Problem in Controversial Theology.' In *The Living Church: Reflections On the Second Vatican Council*, pp. 234–93. Tr. Cecily Hastings and N. D. Smith. London, Sheed & Ward, 1963.

The Church. Tr. Ray and Rosaleen Ockenden. New York, Sheed & Ward, 1967. London, Burns & Oates, 1967.

Laberthonnière, Lucien. *Le Réalisme chrétien et l'idéalisme grec.* Paris, P. Lethielleux, 1904.

Lacroix, Jean. *Maurice Blondel: An Introduction To the Man and His Philosophy.* Tr. John C. Guiness. New York, Sheed & Ward, 1968.

Lapati, Americo D. *John Henry Newman.* New York, Twayne, 1972.

Lash, Nicholas. *Change in Focus: A Study of Doctrinal Change and Continuity.* London, Sheed & Ward, 1973.

'Modernism, Aggiornamento and the Night Battle.' In *Bishops and Writers: Aspects of the Evolution of Modern English Catholicism.* Ed. Adrian Hastings. Hertfordshire, Anthony Clarke, 1977.

Newman On Development: The Search For an Explanation in History. London, Sheed & Ward, 1975.

'The Modernist Minefield.' *The Month,* n.s. 13 (1980), pp. 16–19.

'The Notions of "Implicit" and "Explicit" Reason in Newman's University Sermons: A Difficulty.' *Heythrop Journal* 11 (1970), pp. 48–54.

Latourelle, René. *Theology of Revelation.* New York, Alba House, 1966.

Laubacher, James. *Dogma and the Development of Dogma in the Writings of George Tyrrell (1861–1909).* Baltimore, Watkins Printing, 1939.

Lease, Gary. *Witness To the Faith: Cardinal Newman On the Teaching Authority of the Church.* Shannon, Irish University Press, 1971.

Lebreton, Jules. 'Catholicisme: Réponse à M. Tyrrell.' *Revue Pratique d'Apologétique* 4 (1907), pp. 527–48.

L'Encyclique et la théologie moderniste. Paris, Beauchesne, 1908.

'La foi et la théologie d'après M. Tyrrell.' *Revue Pratique d'Apologétique* 3 (1907), pp. 542–50.

Lemius, J. B. *Catéchisme sur le modernisme d'après l'encyclique Pascendi Dominici Gregis de S. S. Pie x.* Paris, Librairie Saint-Paul, 1907.

Le Roy, Edouard. 'Qu-est-ce qu'un dogme?' In *Dogme et critique*, pp. 1–34. Paris, Bloud, 1907.

Lilley, A. Leslie. 'A Real Catholicism.' *The Interpreter* 6 (1910), pp. 264–77.

Modernism: A Record and Review. London, Pitman, 1908.

Loisy, Alfred. *Autour d'un petit livre*. 2nd edn. Paris, Alphonse Picard et fils, 1903.

[Firmin, A.] '*Le développement chrétien d'après le Cardinal Newman*.' *Revue du Clergé Français* 17 (1899), pp. 5–20.

George Tyrrell et Henri Bremond. Paris, Emile Nourry, 1936.

The Gospel and the Church. Tr. Christopher Home. New York, Scribner, 1904. London, Pitman, 1904.

Mémoires pour servir à l'histoire religieuse de notre temps. 3 vols. Paris, Emile Nourry, 1930–1.

My Duel With the Vatican: the Autobiography of a Catholic Modernist. Tr. Richard Wilson Boynton. With a new Introduction by E. Harold Smith. New York, Greenwood, 1968.

Revue de 'Jean Adam Möhler et l'école catholique de Tubingue' par M. Vermeil. Revue d'Histoire et de Littérature Religieuses, n.s. 4 (1913), pp. 569–71.

Revue de 'De Charybde à Scylla' et 'Le christianisme à la croisée des chemins' par G. Tyrrell. Revue Critique d'Histoire et de Littérature, n.s. 72 (1911), pp. 17–19.

Lonergan, Bernard. *Doctrinal Pluralism*. Milwaukee, Marquette University Press, 1971.

Method in Theology. New York, Herder & Herder, 1972. London, Darton, Longman & Todd, 1972.

Loome, Thomas M. 'The Enigma of Baron Friedrich von Hügel as Modernist.' *Downside Review* 91 (1973), pp. 13–34, 123–40, 204–30.

Liberal Catholicism, Reform Catholicism, Modernism: A Contribution To a New Orientation in Modernist Research. Mainz, Matthias-Grünewald, 1979.

'Tyrrell's Letters to André Raffalovich.' *The Month* 229 (1970), pp. 95–101, 138–49.

Louis-David, Anne. 'Friends and Modernists.' Review of *A Variety of Catholic Modernists* by Alec Vidler. *Heythrop Journal* 12 (1971), pp. 54–61.

Loyola, Ignacio de, Saint. *The Spiritual Exercises of St. Ignatius: Based On Studies in the Language of the Autograph*. Ed. Louis Puhl. Chicago, Loyola University Press, 1951.

The Testament of Ignatius Loyola. Tr. E. M. Rix. Preface and Epilogue by George Tyrrell. St Louis, B. Herder, 1900. London, Sands, 1900.

Lubac, Henri de. *Catholicism: A Study of Dogma in Relation to the Corporate Destiny of Mankind*. Tr. from the 4th Fr. edn by Lancelot C. Sheppard. London, Burns & Oates, 1950.

Lundström, Gösta. *The Kingdom of God in the Teaching of Jesus: A History of Interpretation From the Last Decades of the Nineteenth Century to the Present Day*. Tr. Joan Bulman. Edinburgh, Oliver & Boyd, 1963.

Lunn, Arnold. *Roman Converts*. London, Chapman & Hall, 1924; reprint edn. New York, Books for Libraries Press, 1966.

McBrien, Richard P. *Do We Need the Church?* New York, Harper & Row, 1969. London, Collins, 1969.

MacCaffrey, James. 'The Papal Encyclical On Modernism.' *Irish Ecclesiastical Record* 22 (1907), pp. 561–75.

McCormick, Richard. 'Notes on Moral Theology: 1976.' *Theological Studies* 38 (1977), pp. 84–100.

'Notes on Moral Theology: 1979.' *Theological Studies* 41 (1980), pp. 98–123.

McGiffert, Arthur C. 'Modernism and Catholicism.' *Harvard Theological Review* 3 (1910), pp. 24–46.

Macpherson, Duncan. 'Von Hügel on George Tyrrell.' *The Month* 232 (1971), pp. 178–80.

Macquarrie, John. *Principles of Christian Theology*. New York, Scribner, 1966. London, SCM, 1967.

Twentieth-Century Religious Thought: The Frontiers of Philosophy and Theology, 1900–1960. New York, Harper & Row, 1963. London, SCM, 1966.

Mallock, William Hurrell. *Doctrine and Doctrinal Disruption: Being an Examination of the Intellectual Position of the Church of England*. London, A. & C. Black, 1900.

Marchini, Antonio. *Summula theologiae dogmaticae*. N.p., Mortariae-Viglebani, 1898.

Marlé, René. *Au coeur de la crise moderniste: Le dossier inédit d'une controverse*. Paris, Aubier, 1960.

Maron, Gottfried. '*Harnack und der römische Katholizismus*.' *Zeitschrift für Kirchengeschichte* 80 (1969), pp. 176–93.

May, J. Lewis. *Father Tyrrell and the Modernist Movement*. London, Eyre & Spottiswoode, 1932.

Mehok, Charles. 'The Ecclesiology of George Tyrrell.' S.T.D. dissertation, Catholic University of America, 1970.

'Hans Küng and George Tyrrell on the Church.' *Homiletic and Pastoral Review* 72 (1972), pp. 57–66.

Ménégoz, Eugene. 'The Theology of Auguste Sabatier of Paris.' *Expository Times* 15 (1903–4), pp. 30–4.

Mercier, Désiré Joseph, Cardinal. *Modernism*. Tr. Marian Lindsay. London, Burns & Oates, 1910.

Misner, Paul. 'Newman's Concept of Revelation and the Development of Doctrine.' *Heythrop Journal* 11 (1970), pp. 32–47.

Moran, Valentine. 'Loisy's Theological Development.' *Theological Studies* 40 (1979), pp. 411–52.

Murphy, John T. 'The Pope's Encyclical On Modernism.' *American Catholic Quarterly Review* 33 (1908), pp. 130–7.

Neuner, Josef. 'The Idea of Catholicity—Concept and History.' In *The Church: Readings in Theology*, pp. 61–92. New York, P. J. Kenedy, 1963.

Newman, John Henry. *Apologia Pro Vita Sua*. Introduction by Philip Hughes. New York, Doubleday, 1956.

An Essay in Aid of a Grammar of Assent. Introduction by Etienne Gilson. New York, Doubleday, 1955.

An Essay On the Development of Christian Doctrine. Edn of 1845. Ed. with an Introduction by J. M. Cameron. London, Penguin, 1974.

An Essay On the Development of Christian Doctrine [Edn. of 1878]. Foreword by Gustave Weigel. New York. Doubleday, 1960.

A Letter Addressed to His Grace the Duke of Norfolk on the Occasion of Mr. Gladstone's Recent Exposition. London, B. M. Pickering, 1875; reprinted in *Newman and Gladstone: The Vatican Decrees*. Introduction by Alvan S. Ryan. Notre Dame, Ind., University Press, 1962.

The Letters and Diaries of John Henry Newman. Ed. Charles Stephen Dessain. 31 vols. London, Thomas Nelson & Sons, 1961–77. Vols. 13 and 20.

On Consulting the Faithful in Matters of Doctrine. Ed. with Introduction by John Coulson. London, Geoffrey Chapman, 1961.

'The Theory of Developments in Religious Doctrine.' *Newman's University Sermons: Fifteen Sermons Preached before the University of Oxford 1826–43*. Introductory Essays by D. M. MacKinnon and J. D. Holmes. London, SPCK, 1970.

Nilson, Jon. 'Was Loisy a Modernist?' *The Irish Theological Quarterly* 46 (1979), pp. 73–87.

O'Connor, Francis. 'George Tyrrell and Dogma.' *Downside Review* 85 (1967), pp. 16–34, 160–82.

'Tyrrell's Crossroads'. *Heythrop Journal* 5 (1964), pp. 188–91.

'Tyrrell: The Nature of Revelation.' *Continuum* 3 (1965), pp. 168–77.

O'Grady, John T. 'Did Modernism Die?' *The Month* 225 (1968), pp. 265–73.

Ong, Walter J. 'Newman's Essay On Development in Its Intellectual Milieu.' *Theological Studies* 7 (1946), pp. 3–45.

Osborne, Charles E. 'George Tyrrell, a Friend's Impressions.' *Hibbert Journal* 8 (1910), pp. 253–63.

Padberg, John William. 'The Modernist Crisis Half a Century Later.' *Catholic Theological Society of America Proceedings* 20 (1965), pp. 51–66.

Pauck, Wilhelm. *Harnack and Troeltsch: Two Historical Theologians*. New York, Oxford University Press, 1968.
'The Significance of Adolf von Harnack's Interpretation of Church History.' *Union Seminary Quarterly Review*, Special Issue (1954), pp. 13–24.

Pègues, T. M. '*Autour de l'encyclique*.' *Revue Thomiste* 15 (1907), pp. 663–74.

Pelikan, Jaroslav. *The Christian Tradition: A History of The Development of Doctrine*. 5 vols. Vol. 1: *The Emergence of the Catholic Tradition (100–600)*. Chicago, University of Chicago Press, 1971.
Development of Christian Doctrine: Some Historical Prolegomena. New Haven, Yale University Press, 1969.
Historical Theology: Continuity and Change in Christian Doctrine. New York, Corpus, 1971. London, Hutchinson, 1971.
The Riddle of Roman Catholicism. New York, Abingdon, 1959.

Perrin, Norman. *The Kingdom of God In the Teaching of Jesus*. London, SCM, 1963.

Petre, M. D. *Alfred Loisy: His Religious Significance*, Cambridge University Press, 1944.
'George Tyrrell and Friedrich von Hügel in Their Relation to Catholic Modernism.' *Modern Churchman* 17 (1927), pp. 143–54.
Modernism: Its Failure and Its Fruits. London, T. C. & E. C. Jack, 1918.
My Way of Faith. London, Dent, 1937.
Von Hügel and Tyrrell: The Story of a Friendship. Preface by A. L. Lilley. London, Dent, 1937.

Phelan, Gerald. *St. Thomas and Analogy*. Milwaukee, Marquette University Press, 1948.

'The Pope and Liberal Catholicism: Letter to the English Bishops' [from Leo XIII]. *Tablet* 97 (23 March 1901), p. 441.

Poulat, Emile. '*Critique historique de théologie dans la crise moderniste*.' *Recherches de Science Religieuse* 58 (1970), pp. 535–50.

Histoire, dogme et critique dans la crise moderniste. Paris, Casterman, 1962.

'*Le Modernisme, d'hier à aujourd'hui.*' *Recherches de Science Religieuse* 59 (1971), pp. 161–78.

Principe, W. 'The Hermeneutic of Roman Catholic Dogmatic Statements.' *Studies in Religion* 2 (1972), pp. 157–75.

Quinn, Richard. *The Recognition of the True Church According to John Henry Newman.* Washington, Catholic University of America Press, 1954.

Rahner, Hugo. *Ignatius the Theologian.* Tr. Michael Barry. London, Geoffrey Chapman, 1968.

The Spirituality of St. Ignatius Loyola: An Account of Its Historical Development. Tr. Francis John Smith. Chicago, Loyola University Press, 1953.

Rahner, Karl. 'Christology Within an Evolutionary View of the World.' *Theological Investigations* 5, pp. 157–92. Tr. Karl-H. Kruger. Baltimore, Helicon, 1966. London, Darton, Longman & Todd, 1966.

'The Concept of Mystery in Catholic Theology.' *Theological Investigations* 4, pp. 36–73. Tr. Kevin Smyth. Baltimore, Helicon, 1966. London, Darton, Longman & Todd, 1966.

'Current Problems in Christology.' *Theological Investigations* 1, pp. 149–200. Tr. Cornelius Ernst. Baltimore, Helicon, 1961. London, Darton, Longman & Todd, 1961.

'Democracy In the Church?' *The Month*, n.s. 226 (1968), pp. 103–19.

'Dogmatic Notes on "Ecclesiological Piety".' *Theological Investigations* 5, pp. 336–65. Tr. Karl-H. Kruger. Baltimore, Helicon, 1966. London, Darton, Longman & Todd, 1966.

'Dogmatic Reflections On the Knowledge and Self-Consciousness of Christ.' *Theological Investigations* 5, pp. 193–215. Tr. Karl-H. Kruger. Baltimore, Helicon, 1966. London, Darton, Longman & Todd, 1966.

The Dynamic Element In the Church. Tr. W. J. O'Hara. London, Burns & Oates, 1964. New York, Herder & Herder, 1964.

'Exegesis and Dogmatic Theology.' *Theological Investigations* 5, pp. 67–93. Tr. Karl-H. Kruger. Baltimore, Helicon, 1966. London, Darton, Longman & Todd, 1966.

Foundations of Christian Faith: An Introduction to the Idea of Christianity. Tr. William V. Dych. London, Darton, Longman & Todd, 1978. New York, Seabury, 1978.

'Freedom In the Church.' *Theological Investigations* 2, pp. 89–107.

Tr. Karl-H. Kruger. Baltimore, Helicon, 1963. London, Darton, Longman & Todd, 1963.

Hearers of the Word. Tr. Michael Richards. New York, Herder & Herder, 1969.

'The Historicity of Theology.' *Theological Investigations* 9, pp. 64–82. Tr. Graham Harrison. New York, Herder & Herder, 1972. London, Darton, Longman & Todd, 1972.

'History of the World and Salvation-History.' *Theological Investigations* 5, pp. 97–114. Tr. Karl-H. Kruger. Baltimore, Helicon, 1966. London, Darton, Longman & Todd, 1966.

'The New Claims Which Pastoral Theology Makes Upon Theology As a Whole.' *Theological Investigations* 11, pp. 115–36. Tr. David Bourke. New York, Seabury, 1974. London, Darton, Longman & Todd, 1974.

'On the Theology of the Incarnation.' *Theological Investigations* 4, pp. 105–20. Tr. Kevin Smyth. Baltimore, Helicon, 1966. London, Darton, Longman & Todd, 1966.

'Pluralism in Theology and the Unity of the Creed in the Church.' *Theological Investigations* 11, pp. 3–23. Tr. David Bourke. New York, Seabury, 1974. London, Darton, Longman & Todd, 1974.

'The Position of Christology in the Church Between Exegesis and Dogmatics.' *Theological Investigations* 11, pp. 185–214. Tr. David Bourke. New York, Seabury, 1974. London, Darton, Longman & Todd, 1974.

'Reflection on Methodology in Theology.' *Theological Investigations* 11, pp. 68–114. Tr. David Bourke. New York, Seabury, 1974. London, Darton, Longman & Todd, 1974.

'Reflections on the Problems Involved in Devising a Short Formula of the Faith.' *Theological Investigations* 11, pp. 230–44. Tr. David Bourke. New York, Seabury, 1974. London, Darton, Longman and Todd, 1974.

The Shape of the Church to Come. Tr. Edward Quinn. New York, Seabury, 1974. London, SPCK, 1974.

'The Teaching Office of the Church in the Present-Day Crisis of Authority.' *Theological Investigations* 12, pp. 3–30. Tr. David Bourke. New York, Seabury, 1974. London, Darton, Longman & Todd, 1974.

'Theology and Anthropology.' *Theological Investigations* 9, pp. 28–45. Tr. Graham Harrison. New York, Herder & Herder, 1972. London, Darton, Longman & Todd, 1972.

'Theology and the Church's Teaching Authority After the Council.' *Theological Investigations* 9, pp. 83–100. Tr. Graham Harrison.

New York, Herder & Herder, 1972. London, Darton, Longman & Todd, 1972.

'Thoughts on the Possibility of Belief Today.' *Theological Investigations* 5, pp. 3–22. Tr. Karl-H. Kruger. Baltimore, Helicon, 1966. London, Darton, Longman & Todd, 1966.

'Toward a Fundamental Theological Interpretation of Vatican II.' *Theological Studies* 40 (1979), pp. 716–27.

'What Is a Dogmatic Statement?' *Theological Investigations* 5, pp. 42–66. Tr. Karl-H. Kruger. Baltimore, Helicon, 1966. London, Darton, Longman & Todd, 1966.

Rahner, Karl and Ratzinger, Joseph. *Revelation and Tradition.* Tr. W. J. O'Hara. Montreal, Palm, 1966.

Ranchetti, Michele. *The Catholic Modernists: A Study of the Religious Reform Movement, 1864–1907.* Tr. Isabel Quigley. London, Oxford University Press, 1969.

Ratté, John. *Three Modernists: Alfred Loisy, George Tyrrell, William L. Sullivan.* London, Sheed & Ward, 1968.

'Transcendence in the Modernist Crisis.' *Catholic Theological Society of America Proceedings* 22 (1968), pp. 221–44.

'When Does Renewal Become Heresy? The Specter of Modernism.' *Commonweal*, 23 July 1965, pp. 530–3.

Ratzinger, Joseph. *Introduction to Christianity.* Tr. J. R. Foster. New York, Seabury, 1969. London, Burns & Oates, 1969.

Reardon, B. M. 'George Tyrrell, 1861–1961.' *Modern Churchman*, n.s. 4 (1961), pp. 160–7.

'Liberal Protestantism and Roman Catholic Modernism.' *Modern Churchman*, n.s. 13 (1969), pp. 72–86.

(ed.). *Roman Catholic Modernism.* London, A. & C. Black, 1970.

Rexroth, Kenneth. 'Loisy, Tyrrell and Sullivan.' Review of *Three Modernists* by John Ratté. *Commonweal*, 22 March 1968, pp. 12–14.

Rigaux, Béda. '*La seconde venue de Jésus.*' In *La Venue du Messie: Messianisme et eschatologie*, pp. 173–216. Ed. Edouard Massaux. Louvain, Desclée de Brouwer, 1962.

Rivière, Jean. *Le modernisme dans l'église: Etude d'histoire religieuse contemporaine.* Paris, Letouzey et Ané, 1929.

'Modernisme.' *Dictionnaire de théologie catholique.* Vol. 10, pt. 2, cols. 2009–47. Paris, Letouzey et Ané, 1928.

Robinson, J. A. T. *Jesus and His Coming: The Emergence of a Doctrine.* London, SCM, 1957.

Root, John. 'English Catholic Modernism and Science.' *Heythrop Journal* 18 (1977), pp. 271–88.

'George Tyrrell and the Synthetic Society.' *Downside Review* 98 (1980), pp. 42–59.

Sabatier, Auguste. *Outlines of a Philosophy of Religion Based on Psychology and History.* Tr. T. A. Seed. New York, George H. Doran Co., n.d. London, Hodder & Stoughton, 1902; reprint edn, New York, Harper & Brothers, 1957.

Religions of Authority and the Religion of the Spirit. Tr. Louise Seymour Houghton. New York, George H. Doran, 1904.

The Vitality of Christian Dogmas and Their Power of Evolution: A Study in Religious Philosophy. Tr. Mrs Emmanuel Christen. Preface by W. H. Fremantle. London, A. & C. Black, 1898.

Sagovsky, Nicholas. 'The Christology of George Tyrrell.' *King's Theological Review* 2 (1979), pp. 23–31.

Saint–Jean, Raymond. *L'Apologétique philosophique: Blondel 1893–1913.* Paris, Aubier, 1966.

Schillebeeckx, Edward. *God the Future of Man.* Tr. N. D. Smith. New York, Sheed & Ward, 1968.

Schnackenburg, Rudolf. *God's Rule and Kingdom.* Tr. John Murray. Montreal, Palm, 1963. London, Nelson, 1963.

Schoenl, William J. 'George Tyrrell and the English Liberal Catholic Crisis 1900–01.' *Downside Review* 92 (1974), pp. 171–84.

'The Reappearance of English Liberal Catholicism in the Early 1890's.' *Clergy Review* 62 (1977), pp. 92–105.

Schoof, Mark. *A Survey of Catholic Theology 1800–1970.* Tr. N. D. Smith. New York, Paulist Newman, 1970.

Schultenover, David. 'The Foundations and Genesis of George Tyrrell's Philosophy of Religion and Apologetic.' Ph.D. dissertation, University of St Louis, 1975.

George Tyrrell: In Search of Catholicism. Shepherdstown, Patmos, 1981.

'George Tyrrell: Caught in the Roman Archives of the Society of Jesus.' *Proceedings of the Roman Catholic Modernism Working Group of the American Academy of Religion,* pp. 85–114. Eds. Ronald Burke and George Gilmore. Mobile, Spring Hill College Press, 1981.

Schutz, Roger, and Thurian, Max. *Revelation: A Protestant View.* New York, Newman, 1968.

Schweitzer, Albert. *The Kingdom of God and Primitive Christianity.* Tr. L. A. Garrard. London, A. & C. Black, 1968.

My Life and Thought: An Autobiography. Tr. C. T. Campion. London, Allen & Unwin, 1933.

The Mystery of the Kingdom of God: The Secret of Jesus' Messiahship and Passion. Tr. with an Introduction by Walter Lowrie. London, A. & C. Black, 1914; reprint edn, 1950.

The Quest of the Historical Jesus: A Critical Study of Its Progress from Reimarus to Wrede. Tr. W. Montgomery. 3rd edn. London, A. & C. Black, 1954.

Scott, W. 'The Notion of Tradition in Maurice Blondel.' *Theological Studies* 27 (1966), pp. 384–400.

Smith, S. F. 'The Encyclical "Pascendi Gregis".' *The Month* 110 (1907), pp. 449–68.

Snope, H. S. 'Two Jesuits and Their Church, Teilhard and Tyrrell.' *Modern Churchman*, n.s. 5 (1962), pp. 255–60.

Sohm, Rudolf. *Kirchenrecht*. 2 vols. Vol. 1: *Die geschichtlichen Grundlagen*. Munich, Duncker & Humblot, 1892.

Outlines of Church History. Tr. May Sinclair from the 8th German edn. London, Macmillan, 1909.

Wesen und Ursprung des Katholizismus. Leipzig, B. G. Teubner, 1912.

Somerville, James M. *Total Commitment: Blondel's L'Action*. Washington, Corpus Books, 1968.

Stevens, George. 'Auguste Sabatier and the Paris School of Theology.' *Hibbert Journal* 1 (1903), pp. 553–68.

Thomas Aquinas, Saint. *Summa Theologiae*. Latin text and English tr., notes, appendices, glossaries. Blackfriars. New York, McGraw-Hill, 1964.

Thurston, Herbert. 'Old Unhappy Far-off Things.' Review of *Father Tyrrell and the Modernist Movement* by J. Lewis May. *The Month* 160 (1932), pp. 80–2.

Trevor, Meriol. *Prophets and Guardians: Renewal and Tradition in the Church*. London, Hollis & Carter, 1969.

'Who Were the Modernists?' *New Blackfriars* 49 (1968), pp. 600–8.

Troeltsch, Ernst. *The Absoluteness of Christianity and the History of Religions*. Tr. David Reid. Introduction by James Luther Adams. Richmond, Va., John Knox Press, 1971.

Vidler, Alec R. 'Last Conversations With Alfred Loisy.' *Journal of Theological Studies*, n.s. 28 (1977), pp.84–9.

The Modernist Movement in the Roman Catholic Church: Its Origins and Outcome. Cambridge University Press, 1934.

Twentieth-Century Defenders of the Faith. London, SCM, 1965.

A Variety of Catholic Modernists. Cambridge University Press, 1970.

Vieban, A. 'Who Are the Modernists of the Encyclical?' *Ecclesiastical Review* 38 (1908), pp. 489–508.

Vorgrimler, Herbert, gen. ed. *Commentary on the Documents of Vatican II*. 5 vols. London, Herder & Herder, 1967–9.

Walgrave, Jan Henricus. *Newman the Theologian: The Nature of Belief and Doctrine As Exemplified in His Life and Works*. Tr. A. V. Little-dale. London, Geoffrey Chapman, 1960.

Walker, James A. 'Maude Petre (1863–1942). A Memorial Tribute.' *Hibbert Journal* 41 (1942–3), pp. 340–6.

Ward, Maisie. *The Wilfrid Wards and the Transition*. 2 vols. Vol. 2: *Insurrection Versus Resurrection*. London, Sheed & Ward, 1938.

Ward, Wilfrid. 'Catholic Apologetics—A Reply.' *Nineteenth Century* 45 (1899), pp. 955–61.

'The Character Study in Autobiography and in Fiction.' In *Last Lectures*, pp. 198–220. London, Longmans, 1918; reprint edn, New York, Books for Libraries Press, 1967.

Weaver, Mary Jo. 'Wilfrid Ward, George Tyrrell, and the Meaning of Modernism.' *Downside Review* 96 (1978), pp. 21–34.

Weiss, Johannes. *Christ: The Beginning of Dogma*. Tr. V. D. Davis. London, Philip Green, 1911.

Jesus' Proclamation of the Kingdom of God. Tr., ed. and with Intro-duction by Richard Hyde Hiers and David Larrimore Holland. Philadelphia, Fortress, 1971.

Wells, David F. 'George Tyrrell: Precursor of Process Theology.' *Scottish Journal of Theology* 26 (1973), pp. 71–84.

'The Pope As Antichrist: The Substance of George Tyrrell's Po-lemic.' *Harvard Theological Review* 65 (1972), pp. 271–83.

The Prophetic Theology of George Tyrrell. Chico, Ca., Scholars Press, 1981.

Whelan, Joseph P. *The Spirituality of Friedrich von Hügel*. Foreword by B. C. Butler. London, Collins, 1971.

White, Antonia. *The Hound and the Falcon: The Story of a Reconversion to the Catholic Faith*. London, Longmans, 1965.

Yzermans, Vincent, ed. *All Things In Christ: Encyclicals and Selected Documents of Saint Pius x*. Westminster, Newman, 1954.

Index